The Burden of Responsibility

The Burden of Responsibility

BLUM

CAMUS

ARON

AND THE

FRENCH

TWENTIETH

CENTURY

Tony Judt

THE UNIVERSITY OF CHICAGO PRESS

CHICAGO AND LONDON

The University of Chicago Press, Chicago 60637
The University of Chicago Press, Ltd., London
© 1998 by The University of Chicago
All rights reserved. Published 1998
Paperback edition 2007
Printed and bound by CPI Group (UK) Ltd,
Croydon, CR0 4YY

17 16 15 14 13 12 11   3 4 5 6 7

ISBN-13: 978-0-226-41418-8 (cloth)
ISBN-13: 978-0-226-41419-5 (paper)
ISBN-10: 0-226-41418-3 (cloth)
ISBN-10: 0-226-41419-1 (paper)

Library of Congress Cataloging-in-Publication Data

Judt, Tony.
    The burden of responsibility : Blum, Camus, Aron,
and the French twentieth century / Tony Judt.
        p.   cm.
    Includes bibliographical references and indexes.
    ISBN 0-226-41418-3 (alk. paper)
    1. France—Intellectual life—20th century—
Political aspects. 2. Blum, Léon, 1872–1950—
Contributions in ethics. 3. Camus, Albert,
1913–1960—Contributions in ethics. 4. Aron,
Raymond, 1905–1983—Contributions in ethics.
5. Intellectuals—France—Political activity—
History—20th century. I. Title.
DC33.7.J83   1998
944.08′092′2—dc21   98-22269
                                      CIP

CONTENTS

$\mathcal{T}$hese essays were originally conceived for the Bradley Lectures at the University of Chicago, and I am grateful to the Bradley Foundation and to Professor Robert Pippin, chair of the Committee on Social Thought at the University of Chicago, for the opportunity they afforded me to develop some of my thoughts on France and French intellectuals.

New York University generously gave me leave to work on this and other projects, and some of that leave was spent in 1995 as the guest of the Institut für die Wissenschaften vom Menschen (IWM) in Vienna, where my stay was supported in part by a grant from the Volkswagen Foundation. I am grateful to these institutions for their support, and to the director of the IWM, Professor Kryzstof Michalski, for his unfailing hospitality. My editor at the University of Chicago Press, T. David Brent, has been tolerant and supportive despite having had to wait rather longer for this book than originally anticipated.

Versions of the essays on Albert Camus and Raymond Aron were presented at Northwestern University, Michigan State University, McGill University, and the University of Vienna, as well as at the University of Chicago itself, in public lectures and in seminars. Audiences and participants at these events, and my own students at the Institute of French Studies at New York University, offered many criticisms and suggestions, and this is a better book for their contribution. Its idiosyncrasies and errors are of course my own.

In quoting from the work of my three subjects I have taken the liberty of translating them anew in almost every case, rather than using existing English-language versions. Where this is not the case, I have indicated as much in the notes. Full reference to the original source, and some suggestions for further reading, can be found in the notes and in a short bibliographical note, "Further Reading," at the end.

This book is dedicated to the memory of François Furet. It was at his invitation that I initially agreed to prepare these lectures, and with his enthusiastic encouragement that I devoted them to Blum, Camus, and Aron. Furet was an admirer of all three men, though his links, intellectual and personal, were of course closest to Raymond Aron. He directed the institute in Paris named after Aron, and when he died he was at work on a study of Alexis de Tocqueville, perhaps Aron's favorite French thinker. But Furet was in some measure the natural heir of Blum and Camus no less than Aron. His scholarly work on the history of the French Revolution, rejecting first the Marxist interpretation and then the newly conventional "cultural history," assured him academic opposition on both sides of the Atlantic. His courageous condemnation of the political cant of his age, whether "anti-anti-Communist" or "multicultural," made him political enemies in France and abroad. And his growing influence upon public understanding of the French past aroused his opponents to paroxysms of resentment, notably on the occasion of the bicentenary of the Revolution, when attacks on Furet and his "school" took on a markedly personal and ad hominem character.

All this would have been very familiar to the men to whom these essays are devoted. Like them, François Furet was a public intellectual whose qualities as an "insider" did not prevent him being treated at various times and in various circles as an outsider and even a renegade. Like them, he went against the grain, in Furet's case twice over: first by undermining and recasting the history of the Revolution, France's national "foundation myth," and then by publishing, late in life, an enormously influential essay on Communism, the myth (or illusion, in Furet's words) of the twentieth century. Like them, he was at times better appreciated abroad than at home. And like them, his influence and ideas have triumphed over his critics and will surely outlast them. It has been widely observed that there was not and is not a Furet school of French history. But then there is no Aron school of French social thought, no Camus school of French moralists, no Blum school of French social democracy. These men did not stand for some contending version of French intellectual or political engagement; they stood, in the end, only for themselves and what they believed. And that is why, in time, they have come to stand for much of what is best in France.

The Burden of Responsibility

"Le romantisme français," dit Goethe, "est né de
la Révolution et de l'Empire: Gloire et Liberté!
Du mouvement socialiste nous verrons naître
un nouveau lyrisme: Justice et Bonheur!"

LÉON BLUM

S'il existait un parti de ceux qui ne sont pas
sûrs d'avoir raison, j'en serais.

ALBERT CAMUS

Ce n'est jamais la lutte entre le bien et le mal,
c'est le préférable contre le détestable.

RAYMOND ARON

The Misjudgment of Paris

~

*H*istory is not written as it was experienced, nor should it be. The inhabitants of the past know better than we do what it was like to live there, but they were not well placed, most of them, to understand what was happening to them and why. Whatever imperfect explanation that we can offer for what took place before our time depends upon the advantages of hindsight, even though that same hindsight is itself an insuperable impediment to complete empathy with the history we are trying to understand. The shape of past events depends upon a perspective taken in place and in time; all such shapes are partial truths, though some acquire a more lasting credibility.

We know this intuitively because it best describes the protean profile of our own lives. But the moment we recognize that it is also true for others, and that *their* version of *our* life is also partly plausible, we are forced to concede that there may be an infinity of possible explanations of multiply intersecting and overlapping individual pasts. For social and psychological convenience we live with a recognized common version of the trajectory of individual lives—our own and those of our friends, colleagues, and acquaintances. But this lowest common denominator of identity works in large measure because we do not, most of the time, have good reason to interrogate the narrative we have assigned to ourself or to others. Except at moments of unusual crisis we don't engage in intrusive experimental questioning of our present relationship to the person we once were; and for most of us such efforts to unpack the nature and meaning of our pasts take up a very small share of our waking hours. It is easier, and safer, to proceed as though these matters were settled. And even if we did choose to wonder, incessantly and unhealthily, who we were and are and how we came to be that way and what we should do in the light of the conclusions we reach from such self-investigation, nothing very much would change in our relationship to most other people, whose own worlds would continue largely unaffected by such narcissistic musings on our part.

But what is true of individuals is not true of nations. The meaning to be assigned to a common history, its implications for relations within and between states in the present, the moral and ideological standing of alternative and mutually exclusive accounts of collective behavior and decisions in the distant or recent past, are the most contested of all national terrains; and it is the past that is almost always at issue, even when the present or future is ostensibly under discussion. In many places the nation itself exists in large measure just by virtue of such quarrels; there is no one agreed or conceded version of the collective past that can come out of such efforts to instrumentalize it, because it is the very disagreements themselves that constitute the fundamental identity of the community.

This is a distinctively modern affair. In empires, states, and communities of the more distant past there were not, under normal circumstances, competing sources of political authority, nor were there incommensurable accounts of who might exercise power and why. History, as a source of present legitimacy, was unitary—and thus, in the sense that we now experience it, was not history at all. Most people who have at one time lived on this planet had no autonomous access to their history. Their version of how they came to be what they were was parochial and functional, and was inseparable from the larger story as told by those who ruled over them—a story of which they were in any case only vaguely aware. So long as power and authority remained the monopoly of a family, a caste, an estate, or a theocratic elite, the dissatisfactions of the present and even the expectations for the future remained in thrall to a version of the common past that might sometimes be resented but faced no subversive competition.

All of this changed with the revolutionary upheavals that gave rise to politics as we now know it. In order to render credible and legitimate the claims and promises of a postrevolutionary order, it was necessary to establish that, just like the men and the order that they had displaced, the newcomers had a story to tell about the history of the society and state they wanted to rule. And since that story had above all to justify the uniquely disruptive course of events that had brought about this change, it needed not only to assert its own claim but to disqualify utterly that of the old order. Modern political power thus rested upon a particular assertion about history; as a result, history became political.

This development is usually and rightly associated with the era of the French Revolution, and more precisely with that Revolution itself. For not only did the French revolutionaries themselves understand quite well the fundamentally disjunctive nature of their undertakings; their heirs and opponents respected that intuition by treating the Revolution itself as the proper and primary terrain for historical dispute. Whoever "controlled" the understanding of the French Revolution controlled France, or at any rate was in a position to set the terms of disputes over political legitimacy in post-Revolutionary France. The meaning of French history in the decade that followed the "seizure" of the Bastille in 1789 provided the essential coordinates of political theory and practice not just for Marx and his successors but for Tocqueville and the liberal descent as well as for Joseph de Maistre and his counterrevolutionary heirs. And not only in France—the "proper" interpretation of the French Revolution set the ideological agenda for radical and reactionary speculation throughout the world for much of the two centuries that followed.

But it was in France that the Revolution happened, and it is not altogether a matter of chance that the most enduring and divisive effects upon the practice of politics and public life have been felt in the Revolution's place of birth. France is the oldest unitary nation-state in Europe. The revolutionaries of the late eighteenth century thus already had a lot of history to claim. Since then, the events of the Revolution and their domestic consequences have provided a uniquely rich loam from which to harvest dissent, disagreement, and division, all made more contentious and conflicted for being fought out on a territory and over a population whose geographical, institutional, and linguistic identity was long since confirmed and fixed.

The contrast with France's European neighbors is quite striking. The divisions and enmities within Germany or Italy that led to civil conflicts and political disasters either predated the coming of a nation-state or were pathologies of early statehood. To be sure, there are German and Italian disputes about the status and interpretation of the common past, and some of these resemble French disagreements. But they frequently concern not intra-German or intra-Italian pasts but diverging understandings of local or regional pasts that only quite recently became part of a single national German or Italian history (to considerable regret, in some instances). Further east and southeast the national past before 1939, or 1919, or 1878 often had and has only a "virtual" existence, and historical disputes are fought out over terrain that is not so much political as mythical, though none the less bloody for that.

France, then, is distinctive. It is symptomatic that it should be the only country that has seen the appearance of a major series of scholarly publications devoted to its own *lieux de mémoire*—those "sites of memory" that collectively represent the national understanding of its own heritage. Of even greater symbolic interest is the fact that whereas *La République* and *La Nation* are dealt with in four medium-sized volumes, the editor felt constrained to devote three huge tomes to *Les France*, with the largest section being given over to "Conflicts and Divisions." It would be hard to conceive of a similar scholarly monument to the common historical memory of any other European nation-state, difficult to see why it would require six thousand pages to achieve its purpose, and highly unlikely that quite so much of that space would have to be devoted to explaining the pasts that divide its citizens.[1] It is the tension between the intuitive obviousness of French unity and the depth and endurance of the quarrels that have divided France in modern times that is most characteristic of the country and its past.

In the twentieth century the three most widely remarked-upon symptoms of France's disunited condition have been the enduring quarrels within and between the families of the political Left and Right; the regime of Vichy and its polluting impact upon the national moral environment for decades to come; and the chronic instability of political institutions, reproducing that of the previous century just as the latter in its turn had echoed and played out the political and constitutional struggles of the revolutionary decade itself. In the forty years from the end of World War One through the Algerian war, France experienced four different constitutional regimes, running the gamut from parliamentary republic to authoritarian gerontocracy; in the third of these regimes, the Fourth Republic, there was on average one government for every six months of its brief, fourteen-year life.

All three of these symptoms of what observers and historians took to calling the "French disease" derived directly from contested understandings of the past in general and the French Revolutionary legacy in particular. *Left* and *Right* were terms whose use and application dated from the ideolog-

<hr>

1. See Pierre Nora, ed., *Les Lieux de mémoire*, 7 vols. (Paris: Gallimard, 1984–92)

ical topography of the revolutionary assemblies; divisions within these two families orbited around variant interpretations of the lessons to be learnt from that Revolution and the degree of one's fervor for it or against it. Typically, the dispute between Socialists and Communists in France hinged on mutually exclusive claims to the inheritance and mantle of the "unfinished" business of the bourgeois Revolution; and it was appropriate that one of the few themes on which the denizens of Pétain's "National Revolution" could initially agree was their wish to unmake the Revolution and its heritage. As for French inability to construct a stable and broadly acceptable system of parliamentary or presidential rule, it had very little to do with the nature of French society, which for much of the period was distinguished by its self-sufficient, conservative stability. What was unstable was the consensus on how to govern this society, a result of the serial discrediting of alternative constitutional models and forms of political power between 1789 and the advent of the Third Republic a century later.

The quarrels of Left and Right and the related problem of political instability seemed to many observers during the first two-thirds of the twentieth century to be the most important and urgent of France's difficulties, just because their roots lay so deep in competing political memories and versions of the "true" French path. To participants themselves, of course, it was not the instability or the conflicts that caused trouble, but rather the intractable refusal of their political opponents to see the world their way. As for ideological quarrels, these seemed to their protagonists to be so obviously of the first importance that attention to other concerns was at best casual and fleeting. Today this appears odd, a curiosity of a time long past. But just a few decades ago, French public life was occupied and preoccupied with doctrinal language and quarreling to the occasional near-exclusion of anything else. This was true of the ideological Right until its discredit in the abyss of Vichy, and would remain true of the Left well into the 1970s.

There are, though, other ways of thinking about France's recent history, less dependent upon the lens and language of the revolutionary past. The conventional institutional chronology, with its turning points in 1940, 1944–46 and 1958, is vulnerable to the charge that it underestimates the direction and timing of social and economic transformation. An alternative narrative would emphasize remarkable social continuity—and accompanying economic stagnation—from the mid-nineteenth century into the early 1950s. France remained—above all in the self-perception of its inhabitants—a rural, agricultural society, with an uncommonly low rate of population growth and a marked preference for continuity over the sorts of changes that were transforming its neighbors in the same era.

From one perspective this propensity for preserving the past in the face of a threatening present—reinforced by the experience of World War I, which propelled the nation into two decades of nostalgic denial—served the country well. France survived the interwar depression without the economic collapse and accompanying political paroxysms experienced by other continental states. But from a different angle the national inclination to blinkered archaism, the distaste for modernization and reform, contributed to the coming of Vichy, whose promise of a return to premodern values and institutions echoed all too reassuringly the instincts of the political class and the electorate alike. And it was not the postwar Fourth Republic per se but rather new international realities and opportunities, recognized by a younger generation of bureaucrats and administrators in spite of the ignorance of their political masters, that propelled France after the mid-fifties into an unprecedented onrush of economic, demographic, and social change.

Another version of the years 1930–70 has France caught in a three-way struggle between a timid and unadventurous society, an incompetent and divided political class, and a small core of civil servants, scholars, and businessmen, frustrated at the country's stagnation and decline. In this perspective the Popular Front of 1936, whatever its ideological patina, was above all a first, faltering step toward the overhaul of the country's economic institutions and system of government. Doomed to misfire in the supercharged political atmosphere of the thirties, the drive for change was paradoxically picked up again by some junior participants in the Vichy "experiment." Under the cover of the National Revolution and the abolition of parliamentary constraint upon administrative initiative, they overhauled parts of the local and national governing apparatus—their efforts bearing unacknowledged fruit in the achievements of the modernizing ministries of the next decade. Only after 1958 with the Fifth Republic—and even then occasionally against the wishes of its founder—did social change, administrative renewal, and political institutions come into line, with the result that France was able to overcome its "disease" and experience "normal" economic and political life.

What most strikes the historian of today is how little the *contemporary* sense of France's dilemmas and choices in the first two-thirds of our century was affected by any of these alternative narratives. The contrast between archaism and modernity, a theme in scholarly (and especially foreign) analyses of France from the late forties on, was rarely mentioned by French politicians or public commentators. And when it was invoked, it was often in order to praise the country and its people for having avoided the disruptions that had brought such sorrow to France's neighbors, and whose ultimate risks and outcome could be seen with frightening clarity across the Atlantic.

Similarly, it occurred to very few French public figures to speculate on alternatives to the conventional Left/Right, republican/authoritarian disposition of the French past and present. This was partly through a lack of imagination, but mostly because persons who entertained such thoughts had tended to end badly. Even the most imaginative and critical republicans of the late nineteenth century were not disposed to think kindly of constitutional revision, despite the manifest shortcomings of the Third Republican system of politics and government, for fear of association with the praetorian goals of Marshal MacMahon, General Boulanger, and (still a fresh memory) Louis-Napoléon Bonaparte. Their trepidation was confirmed after 1918: many of the most intelligent (and politically frustrated) interwar critics of doctrinal and political rigidity in France—as elsewhere—notoriously ended up in the fascist or neofascist camp.

Right-wing thinkers and politicians, in a roughly parallel process of reasoning, regarded almost any concession to the representatives of the radical Republican tradition as a harbinger of compromise with extreme Jacobinism and thus a betrayal of their own past loyalties—an illusion encouraged both by moderate socialists who chose to present themselves as true revolutionaries, and by Communists whose legitimacy depended upon their aggressive claim to have inherited all that was most extreme in the language and ambitions of the Revolutionary tradition. Even after the Occupation of 1940–44, and the discrediting of a large part of the conservative political inheritance, the political Left was no better placed to exorcise its demons. Once Pétain and Vichy had refreshed people's memories of the dangers of unrestricted presidential authority, especially when exercised by former general officers, it took another generation before most French politicians and political analysts could think clearly about the advantages of efficient executive authority, and learn to distinguish it in principle from a permanent coup d'état.

In twentieth-century France, then, history and memory conspired to exclude any sustained attention to what now appear to have been the country's true dilemmas—one of them being precisely the intolerable burden of competing pasts. The contribution of intellectuals was significant in this respect. It is not necessary here to describe once again the prominence of intellectuals in the public life of twentieth-century France; the point has been made well and often enough by intellectuals themselves, who in recent years have been the most assiduous and enthusiastic narrators of their own contribution to the national story. But it is not by chance that most histories of intellectual life and writings in France cleave quite closely to the conventional narrative of political history: for it was intellectuals who contributed more than most to the self-understanding of modern France in just those conventional terms.

One reason for this is that the history of intellectual participation in public life was circumscribed by just those occasions when it seemed incumbent on writers, teachers, and thinkers to choose sides, to align themselves with one or other side in the great national conflicts. To be for or against Dreyfus; to be an international socialist or an integral nationalist in the years before World War I; to be Fascist or anti-Fascist in the thirties; to stand with Resistance or Collaboration during the Occupation years; to choose between Communism and "capitalism," East and West, in the Cold War; to favor decolonization or the defense of empire; to advocate radical antiauthoritarian politics (at home and abroad) or firm presidential government; and always and everywhere to be Left or Right: these were the terms in which intellectuals defined themselves and thus contributed to defining and confirming French public debate for most of the past century. The very idea of an *intellectual* who did not think in these terms, or chose to transgress them, or to disengage from such public identifications altogether seemed a contradiction in terms.

Even the best-known critique of intellectual engagement, Julien Benda's 1927 essay *La Trahison des clercs*, trails its coat in this respect. Benda's principal target was the nationalist writers and publicists associated with Charles Maurras's *Action française*. We tend to forget today how prominent this school of thinkers was, from the early twentieth century through 1940, and how much it thus seemed to Benda that an attack on intellectuals for betraying their proper role of detached seekers after truth must begin with the leading thinkers of the *Right*. But Benda did not wish to suggest that public engagement itself was wrong, simply that it should be the outcome of independent reasoning in good faith.

What was wrong with Maurras and his followers was that they began with the hypothesis that France and the Fren..h nation came first and must always be put first, a premise that (in Benda's view) vitiated any effort at dispassionate individual reflection and moral choice. With the experience and example of the Dreyfus affair always in mind, Benda argued that the task of the intellectual is to seek justice and truth, to protect the rights of individuals—and then to proceed accordingly when it came to aligning oneself with one side or another in the great choices of the age.

But once *justice, truth*, and *rights* themselves fell victim to ideological definition in the course of the thirties, Benda's distinction lost its meaning and lacked any detached point of reference—as we may see from Benda's own emergence after the Liberation as a resolutely engaged fellow-traveler of the Left, defending the show trials in Stalinist eastern Europe on just the same grounds that he had once castigated in the moral "relativists" of the nationalist Right. What had then seemed the height of cynical irresponsibility—the alignment of some of France's best-known writers behind the cause of the nationalist Right to the exclusion of any concern with the truth about individual cases—now became the very definition of responsible engagement when attached to a similarly exclusive resort to collective authority now advanced by the internationalist Left.

Most twentieth-century French intellectuals, then, are not a very instructive guide to what was happening in the France of their times, since so much of their writings merely reflected back into the public sphere the country's own long-standing political divisions. With the abusive assistance of hindsight, however, we can perhaps recast the chronology of intellectuals and politics alike, availing ourselves of the notion of responsibility with which intellectuals from Zola to Sartre were indeed familiar, but assigning it a distinctly different and more normative meaning from that conventionally employed in histories of intellectual behavior, where it is taken as synonymous with "engagement."[2]

2. This topic is adumbrated in my earlier book, *Past Imperfect* (Berkeley and Los Angeles: University of California Press, 1992), but only in relation to a group of writers whose "irresponsibility" (in this sense) was my concern there. The subjects of the present book took the notion of responsibility altogether more seriously, which is why they are so interesting.

From the end of World War I until the middle of the 1970s, French public life was shaped and misshaped by three overlapping and intersecting forms of collective and individual irresponsibility. The first of these was political. Reading the history of interwar France, one is struck again and again by the incompetence, the *insouciance* and the culpable negligence of the men who governed the country and represented its citizens. This is not a political observation, in the partisan sense, but rather a cultural one. The *députés* and senators of all parties, the presidents, prime ministers, ministers, generals, civil servants, mayors, and party managers, from Communists to monarchists, displayed a striking lack of understanding of their times and their place. The policies they advocated—when they had something to advocate—were partisan in the narrowest sense, which is to say that they drew only upon the traditions and interests of a narrow segment of the community and made no serious effort to appeal beyond that segment when presenting themselves for election or appointment.

Why this should have been so is an interesting question, since France had not lacked for imaginative and forceful national leaders in earlier years. The Third Republic before 1918 had brought forth Gambetta, Ferry, Jaurès, Poincaré, and Clemenceau. But the ossification of political institutions, reinforced by the national trauma of World War I, gave to the interwar Republic a petrified quality, like a rabbit caught stunned and motionless in the headlights of history. In domestic affairs the country was torn between a yearning for t... (misremembered) prosperity and stability of the prewar years and a promise of reform and renewal to be paid for out of German financial penance. Halfhearted postwar attempts at radical change, backed by widespread mass pressure for improved working conditions and social services, fell victim to a polarized political culture in which any institutional or economic reform was treated as a zero-sum game and thus energetically and effectively opposed by a coalition of presumptively threatened interests. The rhetoric of the Popular Front, and the response it aroused in its nervous, credulous opponents, took this polarization to ever greater heights.

As for foreign policy, this rested first on the illusion of French postwar power (itself drawing on the no-less-illusory proposition that France had somehow emerged from the war a victor); then, when the withdrawal of

the Americans and the disengagement of the British left the French diplomatically vulnerable, on the fond hopes of collective security through the
League of Nations; and finally, the League having proved a rubber crutch,
upon a retreat by the French military and political leadership not so much
to a position of hopeful appeasement (which implies a degree of strategy
and initiative) as to one of disabused pessimism—of which the most telling
symbol was Edouard Daladier returning from Munich in 1938, aware that
he had abandoned Czech and French national interests alike and expecting
a torrent of patriotic abuse, only to be greeted upon his return, to his utter
amazement, by cheering crowds of his relieved fellow-citizens. The defeat-
ist, cynical, weary response of the French governing elite to the German
military victory in 1940 was inscribed in the way they had governed the
country for the previous two decades. The tired relief with which many of
its elected representatives abandoned the Republic in July 1940 was at first
a shock to some observers, but upon reflection they did not find it so very
surprising.

The political irresponsibility of the rulers of Vichy France is well docu-
mented now, depending as it did upon a wilful refusal to look honestly at
their own weakness, the true aims of the occupiers, or the increasingly pre-
dictable consequences of their initiatives and concessions. But no less remarkable was the continuing inadequacy of a significant part of the political class *after* the war, despite much talk of renewal and some serious efforts
to implement it. The damaging political tactics of the French Communist
Party were a distinctive problem, since by its very nature the PCF operated
under criteria of responsibility and rationality that were not determined by
French national interests or local political considerations. But the failure
of the Socialists to rethink their doctrine and program, the widespread inability on all sides to recognize the changed and reduced place of France in
a postwar world, the chronic parliamentary divisions and bickering, and
the disastrously inadequate response to demands for independence in
French colonies, all bespeak a continuing political failure to think disinterestedly about the national interest.

That postwar France was saved from its political leaders, in a way that
it could not be saved a decade earlier, was thanks to major postwar changes
in international relations. A member of NATO, a beneficiary of the Mar-
shall Plan, and increasingly integrated into the nascent European community, France was no longer dependent upon its own resources and decisions

for its security and its prosperity, and the incompetence and errors of its rulers cost it far less than they had in earlier days.

If the era of political irresponsibility in France lasted from 1918 to 1958, the age of moral irresponsibility may be said to have begun in the mid-thirties and endured for the best part of four decades. At first sight, this seems an odd proposition, at least so far as it concerns intellectuals. Surely, between antifascist engagement, wartime resistance, postwar political idealism, and anticolonial agitation, the French, or at least some of them, were never more morally involved and committed than in these years. But the difficulty with that response is that it treats of this era of "engagement" exclusively in the terms in which it was experienced, notably by those whose writings at the time and since have set the contours for our understanding of their behavior.

The most unambiguous example of apparent "moral responsibility" is that of intellectual antifascism in the thirties. It certainly represented a moment of political commitment on behalf of the forces of good against those of evil, as understood by those who made that commitment. But there were considerable numbers of men and women, including not a few intellectuals, who were as committed *to* fascism, whether in Italy, Spain, or even France itself, and for some of the same reasons. And since some of them would later reprogram themselves as intellectual *anti*fascists during and after the war, we do well to recall that what most characterized intellectual "responsibility" in pre–World War II Europe was not commitment to the Left, but commitment per se.

It is because the victors write the history that the degree of intellectuals' engagement before World War II on the side of integral nationalism or ideological fascism was rather forgotten for many years following the fascist defeat. Knowing this, and knowing the extent of the political and intellectual emigrations from Left to Right before 1940 and from Right to Left after 1942, we might do better to think of political engagement as a characteristic of the whole period.[3]

---

3. Many intellectuals themselves had good reason to ignore, or rewrite, the history of their own commitments in earlier days. This is far from being a distinctively French story, of course—witness the troubled (and until recently largely unacknowledged) history of writers in interwar Romania, most of them admirers and advocates of the most unpleasant sorts of fanatical and anti-Semitic nationalism. This would not matter so much had not some of them—Cioran and Eliade most notably—been so successful in presenting themselves to the West after the war in a quite different light.

In that light, the concept of moral *irresponsibility* begins to make sense. It could take many forms. According to Jean-Paul Sartre's own version, in his notebooks from the "phony war" period, he spent the interwar years culpably unaware of what was happening around him, clinging to the apolitical pacifism born of World War I. Hence his later hyperengagement, a reaction above all to the risk of once again missing the vessel of History as it steamed past him in the night. Sartre's motives may have been personal, but the pattern was widespread. Adrift and uncertain in the storms of the thirties, some intellectuals and public figures avoided or neglected to cast in their lot with the defense of democracy; some made choices, but the "wrong" ones; others made the "right" choices, but late.

For any of the decisions thus taken, moral criteria were certainly in play. Men and women who declared themselves "defenders of Western civilization" or "antifascists," "resisters," "progressives," "anti-imperialists," and the like were making a moral judgment about the world and their responsibility in it, even if the particular political community to which they affiliated preferred to legitimate its claims in historical, or economic, or aesthetic terms and officially abhorred "moralizing." But once the decision was taken, the moral initiative was almost always abandoned, at least for a while. Political engagement, on any side, carried a price: the duty to pursue the logic of one's choice, in the face not just of opposition but of the unwelcome company in which one traveled and the troubling actions of one's own side.

This was the situation of intellectuals who went to Spain after 1936 and saw a little too well what their Communist or Franquist allies were doing; of idealists for national renewal who saw the National Revolution of Laval and Pétain at close quarters; of resisters who watched the inadequate, partial, and often unjust score-settling that followed the Liberation of France; of fellow travelers who tried to swallow the defense offered for show trials and gulags in the socialist homelands; of anticolonialist writers who explained away the dictatorial and corrupt regimes that replaced ousted imperial authorities; and of *tiers-mondistes* of the sixties and seventies constrained to understand and justify Mao's Cultural Revolution and Pol Pot's Cambodia.

One can, of course, recite a litany of examples of men and women who retained the intellectual courage and moral initiative to bear witness against the betrayal of their commitment: Georges Bernanos, for example, or Margarete Buber-Neumann, George Orwell, Arthur Koestler, Ignazio Silone, and Czeslaw Milosz—entries from the Almanach de Gotha of European intellectual integrity in our times. What is perhaps harder to accept is that many of the better-known French intellectuals, not to speak of the lesser known, never made it onto this list.

I have written of intellectuals because they mattered in France, and because the moral liabilities that followed in the wake of political engagement were most readily associated with intellectuals, given their own emphasis upon the ethical dimension of their choices—and the presentation of such decisions *as* choices. But the abandonment of individual judgment and initiative, in the name of political responsibility—to a collective or political allegiance that comes over time to eviscerate and undermine the very notion of any distinctively *moral* responsibility at all—is not necessarily an attribute of intellectuals alone. Others were no less exposed to risk: Politicians, civil servants, soldiers, teachers, students were all vulnerable, in those years more perhaps than before or since.

There is, however, a distinctively *intellectual* sort of irresponsibility, which seems to have marked the whole period under consideration, though reaching its apogee in the postwar decades. This has less to do with the public choices intellectuals made, or the moral mess they got themselves into because of those choices, than with the very business of being an intellectual—the things that scholars, writers, novelists, journalists and others chose to think about and to invest their energies in understanding. And this brings us back to my earlier observation about the propensity of twentieth-century intellectuals in France to reflect and echo in the most conventional way the political and cultural fissures and conflicts around them, rather than contributing to the redirection of national attention on to other, more promising tracks.

The problems facing France in the first two-thirds of this century were camouflaged from common view for many reasons, some of which I have tried to suggest. But they were not inherently obscure, and their pathological symptoms were manifest, as any conventional account of recent French history can show. Foreign policy, military policy, economic policy were frequently adrift, often incompetent, and aggressively and destructively contested for much of this period. The constitutional dilemma distorted public life. The doctrinal divide—where ideological warfare substituted for attention to local realities, so that everything was politicized while few paid serious attention to politics—monopolized analytical attention. The radical fallacy—in which the search for ultimate solutions displaced sustained attention to the costs of economic or social stagnation or the limits upon political action—continued to captivate writers and polemicists until the very eve of François Mitterrand's election to the presidency in 1981.

Why did most intellectuals pay so little attention to such matters until quite recently? In part, to be sure, because for the first half of this century public intellectuals were predominantly men of letters: novelists, poets, essayists, philosophers, whose contribution to public debates was often inversely proportional to their knowledge of the matter under discussion. But in the course of the 1950s the literary intellectual was steadily replaced by the social scientists—historians, sociologists, anthropologists, psychologists—without any obvious gain in the quality of public conversation. Whatever specialized knowledge might have been contributed by the growing prominence of men and women with academic expertise in various disciplines was neutralized by the expectation that, as intellectuals, they should be able to speak about anything. Moreover, their continued engagement on one side or another of a politicized and divided culture meant that, however dispassionate the analytical objectivity they applied to their own work, their public pronouncements were keyed to a polemic in which expertise took second place to political or ideological affiliation.

In any case, the scholarly world itself was far from immune to polemical and doctrinal alignments, so that the most prominent, and thus influential, representatives of the academic community were not necessarily the subtlest practitioners of their disciplines. The distorting effect of this process was most evident in and around 1968, when the visibility and influence of certain prominent participants in debates over education, the media, and the national condition were a function of their popularity and their appeal to fashion inside the politicized academy itself.

The counterexamples to this pattern—scholars who concerned themselves with the contemporary problems of France, who brought formal expertise to bear on the analysis of national dilemmas or processes that others had not even noticed, and whose work prompted public recognition—were rare enough that their most influential writings form unusual and curious features in the national intellectual landscape, like windswept menhirs on a Breton hilltop: J.-F. Gravier's *Paris et le désert français* (1947), Henri Mendras's *La Fin des paysans* (1967), Michel Crozier's *La Société bloquée* (1970). And even so it is unlikely that these or comparable works were much read by the better-known Parisian intellectuals.

This situation changed after the mid-seventies. The topics that had once excited and monopolized intellectual attention no longer seemed to matter very much, or had been damaged by the changed political climate, where the threshold of tolerance for violence and terror had been markedly lowered in the aftermath of the *gauchiste* fantasies of the late sixties. There followed, to be sure, an interlude during which the electronic media feasted on intellectuals' own absorption with the crimes and errors of men and ideas they had once idolized; but for most of the past two decades the more interesting thinkers in France have been seriously engaged with the choices and difficulties facing the country and the world they now live in.[4]

This book is about three Frenchmen who lived and wrote against the grain of these three ages of irresponsibility. They were very different men and would have been surprised to think of themselves as a group, yet they have something rather distinctive in common. All three played an important role in the France of their lifetime but lived at a slightly awkward tangent to their contemporaries. For much of his adult life each was an object of dislike, suspicion, contempt, or hatred for many of his peers and contemporaries; only at the end of their long lives were Léon Blum and Raymond Aron, for quite different reasons, able to relax into the comfort of near-universal admiration, respect, and, in some quarters, adulation. Camus, who had experienced all three by the age of thirty-five, died twelve years later an insecure and much-maligned figure; it would be thirty years before his reputation would recover.

All three were cultural "insiders"; but their views and their pronouncements were frequently at odds with their time and place. And in certain

---

4. Those French intellectuals who have nothing of interest to say on these matters now typically say it to—and for—Americans.

crucial respects they were also "outsiders." Blum and Aron were Jews. Though neither saw any reason to deny this, they made little of it; Aron, however, became more conscious of his Jewish identity and troubled by it as he advanced in years. But their Jewishness was not a matter of indifference to their many enemies, and in Blum's case his unsolicited role as a lightning rod for modern French anti-Semitism makes his trajectory central for any understanding of this most neglected of national political passions. Camus came from Algiers, which made him an outsider in more than one sense in the world of Parisian left-wing intellectuals where he found himself after his arrival in France early on in the war. He also lacked the mandarin educational credentials that defined and distinguished the leading edge of the French intelligentsia whose hero and spokesman he nevertheless, briefly, became.

But despite these marks of difference and distinction, and others that I discuss in the essays that follow, all three men forged a place for themselves at the heart of modern French public life. Blum was not only a presence on the fin de siècle Parisian literary scene and a reasonably prominent Dreyfusard intellectual by the age of twenty-six; he was also of course the leader of the French Socialist Party throughout the interwar era, the prime minister of a Popular Front government on two occasions in 1936 and 1938, the most important political enemy of the Vichy governments, condemned to prison, trial, and deportation, a postwar prime minister, and France's most respected elder statesman until his death in 1950.

Raymond Aron outshone his intellectual contemporaries at the Ecole Normale Supérieure in the twenties (Sartre among them) and was the most promising young French philosopher of his generation until the war years, spent in London with the Free French, interrupted his academic progress. After the war he reestablished an academic career that culminated in a chair at the Collège de France while writing dozens of books and essays and many thousands of daily and weekly articles for Le Figaro and L'Express. When he died in 1983, having just published his intellectual memoirs at the age of seventy-eight, he was perhaps the best-known writer, essayist, sociologist, political commentator, and social theorist in France.

Albert Camus, despite his modest "colonial" origins and unfashionable provincial education, rose from obscurity to nearly unequaled political celebrity in postwar Paris thanks to two novels (*L'Etranger* and *La Peste*), an essay *(Le Mythe de Sisyphe)*, and his editorials in the new postwar daily *Combat*. He was widely regarded as the peer, companion, and counterpoint to Sartre and Simone de Beauvoir—what he lacked in intellectual fire-power he more than made up in charisma and moral credibility, having played a real and not merely "virtual" part in the Resistance. Despite a falling out with the Sartreans and his growing isolation from the main-stream left intellectual community over Communism and Algeria, Camus's standing abroad continued to grow, and he was awarded the Nobel Prize for literature in 1957. His death in a car accident two years gave an iconic dimension to his relatively short life (he was born in 1913), and even though it has taken the French a long time to rediscover him, he is now widely regarded in France, as he has long been elsewhere, as a national treasure.

In the essays that follow, however, I have chosen to highlight the trou-bled, conflicted nature of the relations that Blum, Aron, and Camus main-tained with the France of their time. In part this is because what makes these three men interesting is their shared quality of moral (and, as it hap-pens, physical) courage, their willingness to take a stand not against their political or intellectual opponents—everyone did that, all too often—but against their "own" side. They paid a price for this in loneliness, in reduced influence (at least for much of their life), and in their local reputation, which rarely matched the one they had gained among friends and admirers abroad. In a country where the pressures of political and intellectual con-formity were unusually strong during their lifetimes, this willingness to court unpopularity—among politicians, the public, fellow left-wingers or one's intellectual peers—was a rare and attractive characteristic and would alone justify writing about them.

But there is another, and from the perspective of French history a more compelling, reason to devote some attention to these three men. The par-ticular grain against which they went, the current they sought to reverse or at least to challenge, was irresponsibility as I have defined it; the propensity in various spheres of public life to neglect or abandon intellectual, moral, or political responsibility. There is a paradox here that their many critics and enemies would have been the first to notice. Was it not precisely Léon Blum whose almost religious identification with the goals of the Socialist movement contributed to the political divisions and instability of interwar

France, by his insistence on placing the interests of a political party over those of the country? Was it not Albert Camus who reduced himself to silence by his refusal to take sides in the Algerian imbroglio and thus stood apart from the most divisive and morally wrenching crisis of postwar France? And did Raymond Aron not take a near-monastic vow of noninvolvement in public affairs, the better to comment dispassionately upon them, with the result that his cool realism lacks direct engagement with some of the difficult choices that Frenchmen faced in his lifetime?

The charge against Aron is unfair, as I argue in the essay on him, though the implicit association of "engagement" with "responsibility" is a clue to the age. Camus most certainly did suffer terribly and lost many friends and admirers through his refusal to support Algerian independence (which was matched by his equally well attested opposition to the practices of French colonialism). But his Algerian dilemma followed upon a decade of openly avowed and deeply unfashionable disagreement with prevailing intellectual opinion: on postwar score-settling, on the death penalty, on the idea of "revolution," and on the practice of Communism. His Algerian silence drew upon the same instinctive sense of moral obligation —including the duty to be quiet when you have nothing to say—that had shaped these earlier pronouncements and engagements. That it should have had unfortunate and easily misinterpreted outcomes was something about which he could do little; Camus's version of responsibility (in contrast with that of Aron) entailed dismissing that sort of consideration.

The case of Blum is more complex. His contribution to the political crisis of 1930s France is indisputable; precisely because of his great influence over the inflexible Socialist Party of his era, he should have known better than to encourage all its worst instincts for political irresponsibility and detachment. Since the Socialist Party was by 1936 the largest political organization in France, Blum's failure to lead it away from sectarian habits and toward postdoctrinal political alliances and programs inevitably makes him partly responsible for the political dénouement to which the Socialists' earlier mistakes contributed.

The trouble is that Blum's role in the Popular Front and its subsequent downfall has distorted discussion of his broader contribution to public life. He was, after all, the only prominent French Socialist to have the courage openly to abandon pacifism, collective disarmament, and appeasement in the face of the international realities of the late thirties. He was one of a small group of French Socialists who opposed Pétain from the start, and he used his consequent incarceration to rethink, at the age of seventy, a substantial part of his long-held socialist beliefs—*without* abandoning the moral premises and social critique that had brought him to those beliefs in the first place.

In this he was quite distinctive, as he was in his long-standing interest in constitutional and governmental reform and in his post-1945 efforts to renew the French Left and refound it upon modern and rational principles. His failure in *these* matters, in contrast to his better-known shortcomings as prime minister in 1936, speaks well of him, since it shows just how much he was thinking and working against the mental and institutional habits not just of his own past but of a whole political tradition. Blum, I shall suggest, made many mistakes. But it was his special quality to be able to see them *as* mistakes, to acknowledge them and to attempt a public recasting of his political heritage, sometimes at great personal risk and always at the cost of a popularity and public success that could have been his. That sense of political responsibility was in short supply in his generation of politicians and statesmen, which is also why many of them disliked and resented him so intensely.

In addition to the qualities of courage and integrity already alluded to above, Blum, Aron, and Camus have something else in common. They were all anti-Communists. In itself this is uninteresting—there were many anti-Communists in France, and anti-Communism, however justified, hardly constituted in itself a distinctive stance, much less a guarantee of responsible behavior. It is the way in which they were anti-Communists that makes them helpful to an understanding of their country and their times.

Blum, whose speech at the December 1920 Congress of the Section Française de l'Internationale Ouvrière (SFIO) where the Leninist scission was consummated is still one of the best accounts of just what distinguished Lenin's revolution from the venerable tradition of European social democracy, was a *political* anti-Communist. From the start he was uncomfortable with the Russian Revolution. A socialist, he felt, could not condemn a revolution made in the name of socialist ideals, and for this misguided reason he refused all his life to treat Communists as the enemy, even though they saw in him little else. But Leninism was a mistake, he insisted—at best a throwback to earlier, well-forgotten traditions of insurrection and dictatorship, at worst an invitation to install terror and repression as the central principles of postbourgeois government. Communism would betray both its ideals and its followers, he noted with some prescience in 1920; and in so doing it risked bringing down with it the whole worthy edifice of socialist achievements and aspirations. As he wrote in 1941, Leninists in other lands could only ever be spokesmen for the interests of the Soviet Union—he famously dubbed the French Communists a "foreign nationalist party"—and were thus condemned to betray the interests of their own country as well as those of their supporters and voters.

Blum's absolute clarity on the Communist question—Raymond Aron, who was otherwise not very charitable toward what he regarded as Blum's moralizing naïvetés, conceded that with regard to Communism he had been "clairvoyant" from the very start—made him the political anchor for a Socialist vessel swaying unsteadily among competing currents. In Blum's view the non-Communist Left must never, ever, concede the political game to the Communists or (which came to the same thing) agree to a reunification with an unrepentant Communist party. But nor could the Socialists reject their past and quit the ideological terrain altogether. If Communists were claiming the inheritance of the French Revolution, Socialists must insist that they, too, were its legitimate heirs. Communism was not the enemy—unlike many younger Socialists Blum recognized that in the circumstances of interwar France one could not identify the Communists as one's primary enemy without moving de facto across the political spectrum to the far Right—but it had no legitimate claim upon the Left either.

This was an impossible position to sustain in practice—made worse by the Socialists' need to distinguish themselves from the Radical republicans by insisting on their own revolutionary credentials—and the doctrinal contortions he engaged in to shore it up made Blum vulnerable to critics at the time and since. But without it, without Blum's leadership and example, the French Socialists would almost certainly not have recovered from the split of 1920, and the shape of interwar French history would have been quite different and not necessarily healthier. The French Communists were absolutely right to see in Léon Blum the principal moral and political impediment to their monopoly of radical politics in France—both in the thirties and again from 1945 to 1948. Blum intuitively appreciated that preserving French Socialism from the Scylla of Communism and the Charybdis of absorption into the Radical center was the necessary condition for the maintenance of a democratic public space in republican France. Few of his fellow Socialists understood this, and his political opponents gave him no credit and begrudged his every achievement. In an age of distinctly irresponsible politicians and politics, Léon Blum bore the burden of political responsibility almost alone.

Albert Camus's anti-Communism was driven by quite different considerations. He had passed briefly through the Communist Party in Algeria in the mid-thirties, but by the time he arrived in France in 1940 he was immune to the political appeal of organized parties of any kind. To be sure, in the immediate post-Liberation months Camus, like most other participants in the Resistance coalition, was unwilling to attack the PCF, convinced that cooperation with Communists was necessary for a postwar renewal of French public life and institutions. In his case, however, this suspension of disbelief did not last very long. But when Camus broke with the *bien pensant* progressive consensus in France—first in his private notes, then in a series of articles and essays, and finally in *L'Homme révolté* (1951), his major critique of the revolutionary illusion—it was for a quite distinctive reason.

What Albert Camus found distasteful and ultimately intolerable about the "anti-anti-Communism" of his friends and colleagues was its moral ambivalence. One could not, he felt, claim to have entered upon a public existence, to have taken a stand in history, on grounds that were inevitably moral—however camouflaged by talk of "necessity" or circumstance—and then focus the lens of one's judgment upon one-half of humanity alone. If discrimination and repression was wrong, then it was as wrong in Moscow as in Mississippi. If concentration camps, a regime of terror, and the aggressive destruction of free peoples constituted the crimes of Fascism, then the same things were no less reprehensible when undertaken by one's "progressive" comrades. Camus knew perfectly well how such bifocalism could be justified—he had offered justifications of his own in earlier years. But the linguistic, intellectual, and ethical contortions— the silences and half-truths—that were required were ultimately beyond him.

Thus, while Camus was sympathetic to the Blumist idea that Communism was a political crime against the non-Communist Left, a polluting agent that would ultimately corrode all decent forms of radical politics, this was not what drove his determination to speak out against it. He simply could not tolerate the hypocrisy of his own side, having devoted some of his life and much of his writing to exposing the equal and opposite hypocrisy of his and their enemies. It was this refusal to take up sides and use his judgment to dampen his intuitions that made Camus seem so pridefully stubborn, as well as politically naive.

Forced to choose, as it seemed to him, between political engagement and ethical consistency he finally opted for the latter, to his own discomfort and social disadvantage. It was a choice made more out of acknowledged psychological necessity than from calculated analytical premises—another reason why it seemed so at odds with its times. Camus's contemporaries had come to Communism, or to "progressive" positions, from what they habitually understood as historical logic or political necessity; when they abandoned the Party, or their efforts to befriend it from outside, it was often on similar grounds. Some could not accept the perverted reasoning of the show trials; others were offended by Soviet foreign adventures; others still found Leninist doctrine less convincing the closer they looked. Camus was different—he looked in the mirror of his own moral discomfort, disliked what he saw, and stepped aside.

Raymond Aron certainly saw through the hollow pretensions of Communism's utopian promise, and he had no peer when it came to revealing the ideological and moral contradictions at the heart of intellectual "engagement." Indeed, *L'Opium des intellectuels* was credited after the fact by many French intellectuals with having first opened their eyes to the unsustainable inconsistencies of their own convictions. But Aron was indifferent to the moral dilemmas of intellectual political affiliation—the very obsession with the subject itself seemed to him a symptom of the French disease. His own anti-Communism had quite different sources. As a student and admirer of Marx he had no quarrel with those who took a sustained interest in nineteenth-century social theory. The problem was that most French leftists, starting with Sartre, had no such sustained interest and were in fact grotesquely ignorant of the very theories they purported to defend and illustrate.

In short they were not serious, or *konsequent* as the Germans say, and it was this lack of intellectual seriousness that Aron found most grievously wrong with French public discussion. French intellectuals talked about books they had not read, they advocated doctrines they did not understand, and they criticized the policies of their rulers while lacking any reasoned alternative of their own to propose. This would have been bad enough if a dilettantish propensity among scholars and essayists to write first and think later had been confined to their own self-regarding communities. But in France such men and women had an audience that extended beyond their own circle of friends and admirers; in Aron's opinion what they were engaged in was thus not merely self-indulgent but intellectually irresponsible. The task of the observer, of the commentator and the engaged thinker, was first of all to understand the world as it was—a point brought home to Aron by his own observations of the terrifying course of events in early 1930s Germany.

The wilful failure of his colleagues and friends to do just this seemed to Aron, in 1932 and for the rest of his life, the height of recklessness. The state of the world in Aron's lifetime did not allow, in his view, for speculative musings upon ideal solutions, for the search for ultimate resolution in exotic locales or hyperrational abstractions from metahistorical premises. Aron knew whereof he spoke: his own early scholarly interests had led him to devote a lot of thought to the philosophical underpinnings and paradoxes of just such ways of reasoning. But he devoted his public career to the understanding and critique of the uncomfortable minutiae of political and economic reality—and to the skillful exposing of the vapid and irresponsible escapism of his peers. Communism, for him, combined both concerns; it was *the* problem of the age—and an escape from the problems of the age.

It is on account of their unconventional relationship to their times that Léon Blum, Albert Camus, and Raymond Aron are of interest today. They were, in Hannah Arendt's felicitous description of other "awkward" figures in the European past, "men in dark times." They were not marginal figures—had they been, their influence would have been less and their interest to a historian of France correspondingly smaller. But they were misunderstood in their lifetime to the degree that they themselves sometimes understood so much better than their contemporaries what was happening around them. The appreciation and self-understanding of their community, like the owl of wisdom, came only at dusk. We, too, can perhaps find in these men some assistance in understanding the times through which they passed.

ONE

The Prophet Spurned

LÉON BLUM AND THE PRICE OF COMPROMISE

*L*éon Blum today is a half-forgotten man. To be sure, there is a good-sized square named after him in the Eleventh Arrondissement of Paris; and just as elderly Londoners as late as the mid-1980s would speak of collecting "the Lloyd George," the retirement pensions introduced by the British chancellor of the Exchequer before World War I, so two generations of grateful Frenchmen and women associated their annual paid vacation with the reforms of Blum's first Popular Front government in 1936. But in his day Blum was a strikingly controversial figure: the leader and exemplar of French Socialism in all its doctrinal fidelity and contradictions; the head of the Popular Front government of 1936, from which so much was expected and feared; France's first Socialist prime minister and its first Jewish one at a time of widespread anti-Semitism; the chief target of Pétainist revenge following the installation in 1940 of the Vichy regime, as well as "enemy number one," as Blum himself put it, of the French Communist Party. That such a man, around whom swirled and stormed for three decades the anger, the hatreds, and the political divisions of his country, should now be the object of benign neglect is an index of the changes that have taken place in France since the 1950s.

For many years after his death in 1950, at the age of seventy-seven, Léon Blum's reputation rose or fell according to historiographical and political fashion, much of which attached itself to conflicting interpretations of the brief life of his first Popular Front coalition government from June 1936 to June 1937. Was the Popular Front a "missed revolutionary opportunity"? Was Blum right to support, however reluctantly, nonintervention in the Spanish Civil War that broke out within a month of his arrival in power? Or, from a different perspective, were Blum and his companions economically illiterate, worsening the economic crisis that greeted them and then blaming it on factors beyond their control? Did the Popular Front, despite

Blum's best intentions, contribute further to the moral and political undo-
ing of France and help pave the way for the collapse of 1940? Was Blum,
in the words of the least forgiving of his recent foreign critics (his domestic
opponents were considerably fiercer), "an economic innocent, and a vain-
glorious phrasemaker for whom the betterment of mankind coincided un-
erringly with the dictates of factional interest"?[1]

The Popular Front passed through its sad agonies six decades ago.
Since then there has been such a transformation in the history of the European Left, such a whittling away of its illusions, that some of these questions now seem as dated and misconceived as the policies with which they
charge Blum himself. The SFIO (Section Française de l'Internationale Ouvrière), the French socialist party to which Blum devoted half his life, is
now gone and with it many of the factional and intradoctrinal disputes
with which Blum was associated. We know, too, a lot more about the political and ideological sources of Vichy, as well as the circumstances of the
German victory of 1940, and Blum's responsibility for the course of events
in France from 1934 to 1944 seems marginal.

But far from casting Léon Blum himself onto the ash heap of history,
a forgotten man among the many justly forgotten men, these changes help
us see him in a different and more interesting light. Why was this man—
this aloof, literary figure from an earlier age, a secular Jew with no great
personal ambition and distinctly reasonable and accommodating opinions,
whose political successes and failures were as moderate as the man himself—the "most hated man in France"? What can we learn about the
French twentieth century by looking once again at the person who, more
than anyone else, drew down upon his person and his opinions the hopes,
the fears, and the wrath of his contemporaries?

Léon Blum was born in Paris in 1872, into a moderately successful
lower-middle-class commercial family of semiassimilated Jews. In the
course of his life he would follow three utterly different careers. It was universally acknowledged, even (indeed, especially) by his most vicious enemies, that Blum was a man of unusual gifts, who could have turned his
precocious talents in any one of a score of different directions—of a prize-

1. Stephen Schuker, "Origins of the 'Jewish Problem' in the Later Third Republic,"
in The Jews in Modern France, ed. Frances Malino and Bernard Wasserstein (Hanover,
N.H.: University Press of New England, 1985), pp. 135–81.

winning philosophy essay he wrote at the age of seventeen, one of his teachers at the Lycée Henri IV commented, "If a youngster of seventeen wrote that he is a monster." He was admitted into the Ecole Normale Supérieure in 1890, but despite passing through it like a "meteor" (Elie Halévy) he found it too restrictive and dropped out a year later, enrolling instead in the Faculty of Law.[2]

Meanwhile, however, Blum was already embarked on the first of his three public careers, writing literary and theatrical criticism for the small reviews and journals that flourished in fin de siècle Paris. By the mid-1890s, and still in his early twenties, Léon Blum was an established presence on the Parisian scene, acknowledged as a gifted and unusually original critic by established writers like Anatole France as well as by younger ones, notably André Gide. He would maintain his literary interests, and his presence in Parisian literary circles, well into the first decade of this century, even publishing a study of Stendhal just before the outbreak of war in 1914. But at the same time he was building a parallel career as a skilled and influential jurist. In 1895 he had been appointed to the Conseil d'Etat, the highest tribunal of administrative law, as an *auditeur;* by the time he resigned from the Conseil d'Etat in 1919, to take up a parliamentary seat for the first time, he was a *commissaire du gouvernement* and had written into French administrative jurisprudence a series of important and enduring judgments and recommendations, many of them expanding and confirming the role of the Conseil d'Etat as a rampart against arbitrary state action.

It was as a jurist that Blum was called upon to play a small role, preparing the defense case at the trial of Emile Zola, in 1898, his first involvement in the events surrounding the Dreyfus affair. Hitherto he had shown no active interest in public affairs, though Fernand Gregh, in his memoirs, claims that as early as 1892 Blum had confided to him an intention to devote himself to "politics." But the cynicism and the injustice of Dreyfus's treatment, and his own despair at the public mood of the time, changed his views. Commenting nearly forty years later on the circumstances of his entry into political commitment, he quoted from *War and Peace:* "Everything was so strange, so different from what he had hoped." Impressed and

2. For the comment on Blum's school essay, see Joel Colton, *Léon Blum: Humanist in Politics* (New York: Knopf, 1966; rpt. Durham, N.C.: Duke University Press, 1987), p. 8.

convinced by Jean Jaurès, Blum became not only an active Dreyfusard but a committed socialist.[3]

If we are to believe Blum's own account of his first intimations of socialist reasoning, it came rather earlier; as a *lycéen*, he was reading a book on contemporary theater and came across a line in which a character in a play remarks that the use of intelligence to amass riches is not controversial; the difficulty is, that whereas wealth can be inherited, intelligence cannot. In Blum's words, "Isolated from working life by my 'bourgeois'— my very petit bourgeois—origins and by my education, it was to these few lines of comedy that I owed my first sense, my first critical awareness of the present laws of society."[4] Be that as it may, it was to the palpable injustice of the Dreyfus case, and Jaurès's powers of example and persuasion, that Blum owed his first engagement with the French Left, and both factors were to remain a lifelong source of his socialist allegiance.

But it was not until the assassination of Jaurès on the eve of war in July 1914 that Blum took on active political responsibilities. Until then his engagement with Socialism was confined to enthusiastic personal support for Jaurès's ultimately successful efforts to unite, in 1905, the disparate and often antagonistic strands of French Socialism into a single party, a process whose early stages are well described in Blum's own contemporary narrative published in 1901. And it was only after the war, in 1919, at the age of forty-seven, that Blum was elected to the Chambre des Députés as a Socialist representative from Paris and chosen by his colleagues to serve as secretary of the Socialist parliamentary group, beginning a third and highly visible career as a national politician. As he would later note, in the preface to a 1930 reissue of his 1914 essay "Stendhal et le beylisme," his earlier career as a literary critic seemed now very far away indeed: "Since then I have changed my existence, about as completely as a man can do. . . . This book is by a me to whom everything binds me and yet whom I hardly recognize. In truth, I feel as though I were exhuming the work of a dead brother."[5]

3. Fernand Gregh, *Souvenirs*, vol. 1: *L'Age d'or* (Paris: Grasset, 1947), p. 114; Léon Blum, "Souvenirs sur 'l'affaire,'" in *Oeuvres*, vol. 4, pt. 2 (1937–40) (Paris: Albin Michel, 1965), p. 559.
4. "L'Idéal socialiste," *Revue de Paris*, May 1, 1924, in *Oeuvres*, vol. 3, pt. 1 (1914–28) (Paris: Albin Michel, 1972), p. 348.
5. "Les Congrès Ouvriers et Socialistes Français," (1901), in *Oeuvres*, vol. 1 (1891–1905) (Paris: Albin Michel, 1954), pp. 391–493; "Stendhal et le beylisme," preface to 2d ed., 1930, in *Oeuvres*, vol. 2 (1905–14) (Paris: Albin Michel, 1962), p. 464.

The distance between the younger Blum and his mature self was a measure not only of his changed interests and commitments, but also of the speed with which he had risen to prominence both in his party and on the national scene. Within a year of his election to the Chambre, Blum found himself the spokesman of those French Socialists opposed to the proposal to attach the SFIO to the newly formed, Moscow-based Third International. At the Eighteenth Congress of the SFIO, held in late December 1920 in the provincial town of Tours, Blum made a stirring and famous speech in defense of French democratic Socialism, "the old house," and against those who would go adventuring after the sirens of Bolshevism. He did not succeed in holding his party together—like socialist parties all over Europe at the time, it split, at Lenin's explicit behest, in two: those (the majority) who believed in the prospects for an imminent French imitation of the October Revolution or were mesmerized by the romance of the Russian example formed the Communist Party; while those who saw themselves as remaining loyal to the Jaurèsian past, or to conventional Marxist interpretations of the Russian Revolution as a "premature coup," remained in the Socialist camp.

Blum's example, and his arguments against Leninism, were adopted only by a minority of the SFIO. But from December 1920 until his death thirty years later Blum was the unquestioned moral leader of his party, as well as its outstanding intellectual and parliamentary presence. From 1921 to 1936, as his party recovered from the scission to become the largest political organization in France, Blum devoted himself to nursing the SFIO back to health and confidence. He kept the party clear of alliances and governmental responsibility until, in the elections of 1936, it was returned with more parliamentary representatives than any other group and was in a position to take office.

The Popular Front government that was formed in June 1936, born of the Communist-Socialist-Radical alliance forged in 1935 in response to the apparent threat from the neofascist leagues, was at once moderately successful and a dramatic failure; and both its successes and its failures contributed directly not only to its own downfall a year later but to the frustration, anger, and ultimate revenge of the Right. By 1939, when war broke out, the Popular Front was in tatters; the Communists, who had only ever agreed to support the Blum government but not to participate in it, had withdrawn their backing quite early and had opposed Blum and his Radical successors in office, over economic policy, nonintervention in the Spanish Civil War, and Munich.

The Radical Party, led by Edouard Daladier, had from the start been nervous about the revolutionary implications of the strikes, factory occupations, and social reforms of 1936, despite Blum's reassuring moderation and his insistence that the Popular Front government had no revolutionary ambitions. The Socialist Party itself was torn apart, first by Blum's very moderation (the left wing of his party had dreamed of a revolutionary seizure of power in the street, favored if not led by the new government), then by Blum's own growing awareness of the need to stand up to the threat posed by the dictators; the antiwar sentiment of nineteenth-century French socialism had been massively reinforced by the memory of Verdun and the feeling that peace must be preserved at any price, a view that Blum himself had long shared but that he abandoned with regret in the course of the 1930s, as the nature of the European situation became clear to him.

The defeat of 1940 and the collapse of France into the arms of Pétain, Laval, and their allies thus found Léon Blum lonely and vulnerable, the object of left-wing suspicion and right-wing hatred. He was one of just eighty parliamentarians (forty of them Socialists) who voted in July 1940 not to hand full powers to Philippe Pétain. His own position was clear and unambiguous—"I consider France to be dishonored," he wrote in his unpublished 1940 memoirs of the turmoil of that year.[6] Blum was imprisoned by Pétain on September 15, 1940, and kept there until February 1942, when, along with Daladier and General Gamelin, he was put on trial at the little town of Riom (near Vichy) for his purported contribution to the decline and fall of his country.

Despite being isolated, ill, and in considerable danger, Blum put on a forensic performance at Riom so stunningly successful that the German authorities discouraged Vichy from continuing the trial for fear that Blum's courtroom achievement—turning the tables and assigning responsibility for the French tragedy to his accusers—would have disastrous public consequences. Blum was duly returned to his prison cell, whence he was deported, in March 1943, to the concentration camp at Buchenwald. Blum survived two years in concentration camps, first Buchenwald and later Dachau, through remarkable strength of will and because, as the war went badly for the Nazis, they began to see him as a possible hostage for use in

---

6. "Mémoires," in *Oeuvres*, vol. 5 (1940–45) (Paris: Albin Michel, 1955), p. 62.

surrender negotiations and accordingly kept him in comparatively decent conditions.

After a final, harrowing transportation by the SS to the "Tyrolean redoubt" in April 1945, Blum and his wife were rescued by what remained of the regular German army, then by Italian partisans, and, at last, by American troops. Returned to France in May 1945, Blum served his country once again as prime minister of a brief interim government in December 1946, as emissary to the United States in vital commercial negotiations, and as the moral spokesman and éminence grise of his Socialist Party, rebuilt from the rubble of 1940. Despite the authority and grace conferred on him by his experience and his suffering, Blum was unable to carry his party with him in an effort at doctrinal and moral renewal, and he spent his final years warning, in the daily articles he wrote in the socialist newspaper *Le Populaire*, of the need for fresh thinking and more resolute political leadership on the Left and in France generally, in the face of the threat from totalitarian Communists and authoritarian Gaullists alike. It was ironic, but not wholly unrepresentative of his career, that Blum should have died, just before his seventy-eighth birthday, advocating change and renewal to the men of the Fourth Republic, some nearly half his age, who were determinedly clinging to the ideas and practices of the past.

It is tempting to think of Léon Blum as a sort of serial Renaissance man, passing through a variety of interests and incarnations, from literary aesthete to republican Dreyfusard, from skilled jurist to Socialist leader and, in his last years, on to a valedictory role as the moral and political critic of French national shortcomings. This is how his biographers present him, and it certainly reflects the shifting emphases at different moments in his long and unusually active life. But in order to understand the complexity of the man, and one cannot begin to estimate his strengths and weaknesses until then, it may be more helpful to think of his various concerns and interests as always present, but in changing proportions and configurations; it is the distinctive interweaving of all the various Blums that accounts for the attitudes and actions that characterize Léon Blum at any one time.

As we shall see, it was one of Léon Blum's great political strengths that he was a compelling, even a seductive presence. He was not a great speaker—he lacked Jaurès's rich, powerful voice, Clemenceau's virile forcefulness, or de Gaulle's classical rhetorical cadences. His voice was thin and rather high. He was a tall man but appeared fragile, always in some measure the ascetic dandy of his early years as critic-about-town for the *Revue blanche*. If he moved men, it was not by his charisma, in the conventional sense, but by the power of argument, the logic and depth of his own convictions clearly and convincingly conveyed to even the most hostile and alien audience, whether in parliament, on a platform, or in a newspaper column. And it is striking to note that it was this aspect of the man, his dependence upon argument and reason rather than emotion or imagery or personality, that sensitive readers picked out even in his earliest works of criticism.

André Gide, who knew Blum well and observed him closely, once described him to his diary as having "la tête la plus antipoétique du monde," by which he meant that Blum was not only no poet himself, but too given to analysis and argument; he was temperamentally unsuited to the comprehension and appreciation of poetic style. Gide was right: Blum himself was an admirer of Stendhal (at that time quite out of fashion) for what he saw as his very *English* clarity, his way of reasoning and explaining not through psychological insights but through the accumulation of description. In an early review of *Northanger Abbey* he praised Jane Austen for just these qualities and for the her abstention from redundant authorial intervention. Contemporary French writers, he complained in 1897, are pretentious and empty, mistaking symbols for reality and preferring "languid descriptions of dull allegories" to clarity and intelligibility.[7]

What Blum found most admirable in other writers—clarity of description and exposition producing the desired impact with minimal authorial decoration or affect—was also what his contemporaries found most distinctive in his own work. Pierre Vidal-Naquet's grandfather, upon receiving in 1905 a copy of Blum's collected reviews, *Au théâtre*, wrote to the author that "your reflections are of a quality at once so rare and so precious that one is led to question one's own taste and to let oneself be seduced by that of the critic." Blum's early writings all display this quality—they combine a confident and sometimes provocative aesthetic preference (for Stendhal, for the early over the later Barrès, for obscure and now forgotten contemporary playwrights and essayists) with a delicate, rationalistic, almost

7. André Gide, *Journal 1887–1925* (Paris: Gallimard, 1996), January 24, 1914, p. 763; for Blum's comments on French writers, see "Nouvelles Conversations de Goethe avec Eckermann," November 26, 1897, in *Oeuvres*, 1:226; for Blum's review of Austen, see ibid., p. 65.

forensic process of argument, which asks of readers not that they share the author's tastes or emotions, only that they follow his logic.[8]

If Blum abandoned literary criticism for political journalism and for politics, he never altered his style or his way of reasoning. He was a republican, in the very particular sense that this word had in the France of the Third Republic, because it was the natural and obvious and reasonable stance for a man of good faith and optimism to take if he was born in France at that time. To be sure, Blum was an enthusiastic reader and admirer of Michelet and Victor Hugo (his uncompromising sympathy for the work of Hugo is one of the few instances in which we might now find Blum's taste curiously dated and time bound),[9] but his arguments for the Republic were strictly rationalist and owed little to images of the people-in-arms or the romance of revolution.

Like Clemenceau, Blum took the Revolution as a "bloc": the Terror of 1793 was inseparable from the achievements of Mirabeau and Danton; the Commune, too, "that brief, disorderly outburst" was part of the great republican and revolutionary movement of the era, the worthy if incomplete legacy of Gambetta. It was, in Blum's view, simply contrary to reason to question the necessity of the Republic (and thus of the Revolution without which it could not have come into being). The point was to defend the achievements of the Republic—equality, laicity, freedom, justice—and to educate the citizenry such that they would defend and advance the process that had brought these things forth.[10]

In his uncritical, positivist admiration for the undifferentiated "Republic" Blum was of course indistinguishable from many of his contemporaries. It accounts for his heartfelt anger in December 1927 when the conservative daily Le Temps (anticipating François Furet by half a century) suggested that the time had come "to put the Convention and the Committee of Public Safety behind us" in their troubling ambivalence. How, Blum exploded, could a republican newspaper even dare suggest such a thing? The

---

8. See Pierre Vidal-Nacquet, Mémoires. La brisure et l'attente, 1930–1955 (Paris: Seuil/La Découverte, 1995), p. 33.

9. See, e.g., Blum's remarks on the occasion of the Hugo Jubilee in 1935: "a poet whose only equals are Dante and Shakespeare," in Le Populaire, May 24, 1935, in Oeuvres 4, pt. 2:475.

10. See Blum's review of Paul and Victor Marguerite, La Commune, in La Revue blanche, rpt. in Oeuvres, 1:166–68; on the pedagogic responsibilities of the Republic, see Le Populaire, June 21, 1922.

Revolution was a whole and must be taken all in all. But the same unquestioning allegiance also explains his courage and determination in 1940 and
again at the Riom trial. For Blum the Republic was untouchable as achievement and objective—in his last effort to form a government, at the height
of a national political crisis in November 1947, he concluded his unsuccessful appeal to the National Assembly with a peroration from the Giron-
din Vergniaud—"May we be forgotten, that the Republic be saved!"[11]

What marked Blum out from the mass of French republicans, however,
was his characteristic pursuit of reason and logic a stage further. If a Republic is a good thing, it is because it is just. But for a Republic to be truly just
it must secure not only political and civil justice for all, but social justice
as well. And so Léon Blum, like Jean Jaurès, was a socialist *because* he was
a republican. Of course the "rational" case for Socialism was declaimed as
self-evident with no less enthusiasm in Britain or Germany or Italy than in
France. But it was one of the distinctive features of French socialist argument—and one of the sources of its political dilemmas—that the *political*
form of a socialist society already existed in France, thanks to "the Revolution." The fortunate French—unlike most other peoples in the world—
already had a republic; all that remained was to invest it with the logically
(and morally) appropriate social content.

Blum brought to the case for Socialism the same energy and reason
that he had brought to the exposition of Stendhal's style or to a judgment
in the Conseil d'Etat. Socialism, as he explained in a turn-of-the-century
review of Anatole France's *Crainquebille*, is "the result of a purely rationalist
conception of society. . . . Socialism wishes to bring social justice into con-
cordance with reason, to line up positive institutions with rational conviction."[12] If the state can bring coherence and justice to social disorder by
establishing monopolies, or by helping science to conquer nature to everyone's advantage, then human beings will no longer be the servants of nature. In which case, more power to the socialist state. Why would anyone
wish matters otherwise?

Convinced by his own arguments—and by those of Jaurès—Blum
could not imagine why any reasonable person would not be similarly con-

11. Quoted by Vincent Auriol in the diary of his presidency, *Mon septennat 1947–1954* (Paris: Gallimard, 1970), entry for November 21, 1947.
12. *Oeuvres*, 1:89.

vinced. It was for this reason, and not from any deep conviction about the primacy of class interest or class struggle, that Blum supposed that people who were not socialists either had direct personal motives (they did very well from present arrangements) or else had not yet been exposed to the case for socialism. In either case, he seems to have felt a very powerful sense of duty to present, again and again and again, the irrefutable case for socialism to all who would read or hear his pleas: "[Socialism] has this in common with religion, that it takes advantage of every opportunity in its pursuit of souls of good will." As he explained to his readers in a 1919 pamphlet, "There is no truth more obvious once you have thought of it. The only astonishing thing is that so many great thinkers have passed by it without realizing, like navigators who used to pass near by unknown continents without knowing they were there."[13]

Despite, or perhaps because of his optimistic assumption that most people, especially most republicans, were not socialists only because they had not yet been made aware of the case for socialism, Blum was not an ideologist, in the reductive, mechanical sense that was true of many of his contemporaries—in the Socialist Party of Great Britain, for example, or the Kautsky wing of the German Social Democrats. He was a moralist. He called himself a Marxist on occasion, and he certainly believed that socialism was the logical and necessary future outcome of the historical process, but its inevitability was not an aspect of the case for socialism that much preoccupied him. It was good that socialism would come anyway, and this was an additional weapon in his logical armory. But the main argument for socialism was simply that it was a good thing.

The moral dimension of Blum's outlook is sometimes a little difficult to discover for two reasons. In the first place, he was temperamentally unsentimental, as his aesthetic distaste for the more self-indulgent fancies of French modernist literature suggests, and he always emphasized the rational case—for a book, a play, a legal decision, a political choice, or a historical interpretation—in preference to the moral case. But in fact his whole world picture was powered by moral assumptions. In his "Nouvelles Conversations de Goethe avec Eckermann" (1897–1900), where Blum imagines a renascent Goethe into whose mouth he places his own thoughts, Goethe upbraids Rousseau for regretting his decision to place his children

13. "L'Idéal socialiste"; and "Pour être socialiste" (1919), in *Oeuvres*, 3, pt. 1:22–42.

in the care of others. The state, "Goethe" asserts, has moral duties and tasks: to support the indigent, educate the young, protect the old, and so forth. In Blum's thought the "state" is an evolving, living entity, entertaining responsibilities and having purposes, a position that is as unambiguously present in his last writings as in his earliest ones. The distinctively *Socialist* state exists immanently in *all* states; thus part of the goal of Socialism is to moralize the state so that it in turn may moralize society. His reading of the French Revolution, showing uncritical empathy with all its forms and moments, was perfectly consistent with this.[14]

The second source of difficulty in identifying Blum's moralized approach derives from his ambivalent relationship to his own background. Blum was not embarrassed or ashamed to be of (petit) bourgeois origin— he was certainly in good company in the French socialist party of his time—but in a movement whose elective affinity, if not its electoral support, lay with the industrial proletariat, men like Blum were under some pressure to abjure their background by paying lip service to the importance of manual work, of the "masses," of the primacy of class conflict, and so on. In Blum's own case, though, his distinctive appearance and style, his clothes, his association with the refined world of the literary magazines, his work at the Conseil d'Etat, his notorious (and, in its time, daring) essay *On Marriage* (1907), all marked him out as an "individualist," not just bourgeois but "bohemian."

Even his early socialist sympathies were eclectic and unorthodox. According to Elie Halévy, Blum was one of the very, very few socialists at the Ecole Normale Supérieure around 1890—"but his socialism was singularly tinged with Boulangism, with Barrèsism, with Disraélism."[15] Blum's later insistence upon the importance of doctrine, of party discipline, of unity, and, in the ideological sense, of conformity were all to some degree compensations, however unconscious, for this earlier dilettantism. He was certainly vulnerable to the accusation that he lacked conventional socialist background and training and had come from nowhere to lead a party prematurely deprived of Jaurès, its natural leader. Hence Blum was not disposed to display his moral concerns overmuch, except on special occasions;

---

14. "Nouvelles Conversations de Goethe," July 13, 1900, 1:320–21.
15. Elie Halévy, letter to Charles Andler, August 24, 1929, in Halévy, *Correspondance 1891–1937* (Paris: Editions de Fallois, 1996), p. 697.

his instinctively rationalist style and political prudence alike constrained him to conform to the habits of a party whose natural language was heavily invested with positivism and "historical materialism."

In particular, Blum took it upon himself to ensure that the SFIO would not "move to the right" as a consequence of its break with the Communists in 1920, lest such a move hand the whole of the "revolutionary tradition" over to the Communists, who claimed it for themselves by right. This fear of a *déviation de droite* would ultimately make Blum the apologist for French Socialism's refusal and failure to take power and participate to the full in the life of the Republic before 1936; but it also ensured that the French Left—before and after 1940—would have at least one leader who undeviatingly defended what passed at the time for a firm left-wing position. This Blum consistently did, and it explains why millions of voters and party members who had absolutely nothing in common with the man instinctively recognized in him the heir to the great radicals of the previous century.

There is another side of Blum that shapes no one part of his life but informs all of it. It is captured in Halévy's telling allusion to "Disraélism." The fact that Léon Blum was a Jew is central to any understanding of the man and his times. It was, as we shall see, the chief source of the widespread hatred and aggression to which he was subject in France, under the Republic and Vichy alike. It may account for his special emphasis on "justice" when describing his personal vision of Socialism—as he wrote of Bernard Lazare and his contribution to the cause of Dreyfus: "There was in him a Jew *de la grande race*, of the prophetic race, of the race that speaks of '*Un juste*' where others speak of 'a saint.'"[16] But Blum's own identification with his Jewishness was more complicated than this conventional association.

Like many prominent French Jews of Alsatian background (both of Blum's parents came from Alsatian families), Léon Blum was what Pierre Birnbaum has called a "Juif d'Etat": secularized Jews devoted to the public service of their country who, integrated into French society by and through the Republic, identified completely with the laic universalism of the modern French state. Blum was in one sense utterly representative of this group, even to the extent of specializing in administrative jurisprudence; but his devotion to Jaurèsian Socialism distinguished him from the more charac-

16. "Souvenirs sur l'affaire," p. 518.

teristic Radicalism of men like Lazare or Joseph Reinach, whom he other-wise closely resembled.[17] But unlike Marc Bloch, another Jew of eastern French origin with a strong sense of service to the Republic, Blum retained a clear awareness of his own Jewishness. Bloch, in a famous passage in *Strange Defeat*, took his distance from all ethnic identification—"A stranger to all credal dogmas, as to all pretended community of life and spirit based on race, I have through life felt that I was above all and quite simply a Frenchman." Blum, on one of the rare occasions when he felt constrained to respond to charges that his primary loyalties were to "international Jewry," expressed himself a little differently. Addressing the French Chamber in 1923, he informed his parliamentary colleagues: "I was born in France, I was raised in French schools. My friends are French. . . . I have the right to consider myself per-fectly assimilated. Well, I nonetheless feel myself a Jew. And I have never noticed, between these two aspects of my consciousness, the least contra-diction, the least tension." As he told a packed and slightly hostile audi-ence at the Luna Park in Paris thirteen years later, on September 6, 1936, "I am a Frenchman, proud of his country, proud of its history, nourished in its tradition as much as anyone, and in spite of my race."[18]

It needs to be emphasized that for a Jewish Socialist, the controversial prime minister of a divided Catholic nation, so unambiguously to "assume" his background in public in this way not only took considerable courage (of which more below) but a high degree of self-awareness. For Blum was in a difficult position. He knew that even left-leaning men of unambiguously republican credentials saw in him first and foremost "a Jew." There is a marvelous letter from Elie Halévy to the philosopher Emile Chartier ("Alain"), dated August 23, 1936, in which he takes his correspondent to task for his obsession with Jews. "Your antiurban, peasant philosophy is degenerating into an anti-Jewish one," he writes. "And when you write, 'It

17. On the subject of secularized Alsatian Jews, see Annie Kriegel, "Un Phénomène de haine fratricide: Léon Blum vu par les Communistes," in *Le Pain et les roses. Jalons pour une histoire des socialismes* (Paris: Presses Universitaires de France, 1968), pp. 235–55, in particular p. 253.

18. Marc Bloch, *Strange Defeat*, trans. Gerard Hopkins (New York: Norton, 1968), p. 178, originally published as *Etrange Défaite* (Paris: Editions Franc-Tireur, 1946); Blum is quoted by Pierre Birnbaum in *Les Fous de la République. Histoire politique des juifs d'etat de Gambetta à Vichy* (Paris: Fayard, 1992), p. 209.

is a pity that Blum is a Parisian,' it would be almost more picturesque to say: 'It is a pity that he is a Jew.'"[19]

But Blum could not merely "assume" his Jewish origins and move on, even if he had been entirely oblivious to the degree of anti-Semitism in the country at large. He was untroubled by his own Jewishness (when he visited Prague as deputy prime minister in 1937, he made a point of visiting the old synagogue there), but he was an acerbic critic of the French Jewish community. In "Souvenirs sur l'Affaire" (1935) he castigated "the rich Jews, the Jews of the middle bourgeoisie, the Jewish civil servants who [were] afraid of the struggle engaged on behalf of Dreyfus exactly as they are afraid today of the struggle against Fascism. They thought only of going to ground and hiding themselves." He was contemptuous of those, like the grand rabbi of Paris, who in 1936 apparently sought to bribe him with a life pension if he would only agree not to compromise his fellow Jews by taking office as prime minister. And in 1938, as chairman of a meeting of the Ligue International contre l'Antisémitisme he reflected, "There was nothing in the world more painful or shameful than the spectacle of French Jews striving to close France to Jewish refugees from other lands."[20]

It was because of this awareness of the Jewish condition at large, and his strong sense of justice and a shared responsibility, that Blum, unlike most French Jews of his background and advantages, was sympathetic to the Zionist project. As early as 1925 he was a member of the France-Palestine Committee, together with four other past or future prime ministers: Aristide Briand, Edouard Herriot, Paul Painlevé, and Raymond Poincaré. He was a delegate in 1929 to the constitutive conference of the newly expanded Jewish Agency, representing the Ligue des Amis de la Palestine Ouvrière. There he described himself as "Zionist, because I am French, because I am a Jew, because I am a Socialist, because modern Jewish Palestine is an unexpected and unique meeting of humanity's oldest traditions and its newest and strongest strivings for freedom and social justice."[21]

Blum seems never to have been seriously alarmed by indigenous

19. Halévy, *Correspondance 1891–1937*, p. 733.
20. "Souvenirs sur l'Affaire," p. 557; for the grand rabbi's offer, see André Blumel's comments in *Léon Blum chef de gouvernement, 1936–1937* (Paris: Armand Colin, 1967), p. 46; see also Pierre Birnbaum, *Un Mythe politique: La "République juive"* (Paris: Fayard, 1988), p. 275.
21. Quoted in Birnbaum, *Les Fous de la République*, p. 117.

French anti-Semitism (except in Algeria), preferring to think of it, at least until the late thirties, as Parisian, literary, "mondain." But he recognized early on the hopeless condition of Jews in other places and the opportunity Zionism represented for them. After the war he wrote articles to this effect, understanding that Jews who had never known life in democracies might welcome the offer of a homeland of their own—while painstakingly explaining to suspicious correspondents that none of this had any bearing on his own continuing loyalty to France.

That he *was* so loyal to France is a tribute to the strength of his republican faith. For France was decidedly unloyal to him. To be a Jew in France after 1934 was to feel the growing discomforts of domestic anti-Semitism and its echoes of racism across the Rhine. To be a prominent Jew—and the leader of a self-styled "revolutionary" political party—was to invite opprobrium and dislike even in respectable quarters. To be a Jewish Socialist advocating a firm stand against Hitler was to invite left-wing criticism and whispered suggestions that you favored a "Jewish" war. To be a Jew in Vichy France, even a French Jew, was to be at permanent risk. And to be Léon Blum was to be handed over by Vichy to the Germans for despatch to a concentration camp. But Blum, like de Gaulle, believed in a "certain" France—in his case one where anti-Semitism, racism, injustice, persecution, and prejudice were mere passing epiphenomena. The true France, the France of the (Socialist) Republic lived on in Blum's heart, and he remained loyal to it and thus to its inadequate earthly embodiment.

His last contribution to this topic came in February 1950, just two months before his death. Too weak to attend a banquet in honor of Israeli president Chaim Weizmann, Blum contributed a written encomium: "When I met him [Weizmann] I knew nothing of Zionism. He introduced me to it and won me over. . . . A French Jew, born in France of a long line of French ancestors, speaking only the language of my country, nourished above all in its culture, having refused to leave it when I was most in danger, I participate nonetheless with all my soul in the admirable undertaking—miraculously transported from dream to historical reality—which henceforth assures a free, equal and dignified national existence to all those Jews who did not have my own good fortune to find such an existence in their place of birth."[22]

22. "Hommage à Weizmann" February 1, 1950, in *Oeuvres*, vol. 6, pt. 2 (1947–1950) (Paris: Albin Michel, 1963), p. 442.

For a man who achieved so much in such a variety of undertakings, Léon Blum would seem an odd candidate for a study in failure. But just as his various incarnations and commitments—aesthete, critic, jurist, republican, socialist, statesman, Jew—combine fruitfully in the making of the man, so they, and traits of personality and personal psychology that they reveal, often worked against the sort of single-minded political realism required for success in the only activity that truly counted for Blum during much of his mature existence—the leadership of a national political party. For even if we attribute to circumstances many of the shortcomings of the Popular Front government, it remains true that as a politician Blum—a man who by near-universal (retrospective) acknowledgment was one of the most impressive and competent Frenchmen of his age—was not a success. Why?

Léon Blum was not really interested in power. He did not seek to wield it and he did not fully understand it, though he wrote a lot on the subject. It is thus ironically appropriate that most of the circumstances of the Popular Front, the era with which he will forever be associated, lay beyond his control. This observation applies with equal force to the successes of the time and to the failures. For most of the period from the end of World War I until 1936, France had been governed by coalitions of the center-right, even though left and left-center parties had actually won parliamentary majorities in the elections of 1924 and 1932. The Communists' unwillingness to compromise or to work with any other party and the "principled decision" of Blum's Socialists not to participate in any governments led by "bourgeois" parties meant that only parliamentary coalitions of the center and center-right could command a steady majority.

This, together with the political reaction that had set in following the unsuccessful strike movements of 1919–20, had left France with an unbalanced political culture: compared to Britain, Germany, or the Benelux countries, French social services and welfare provisions were woefully inadequate, the economy was chronically deflationary and underproductive, and one-half of the country—the working-class, small peasant, white-collar, and state-employed supporters of the non-Communist Left—felt excluded from power and from access to public policymaking.

All this changed in 1934: the French Communists, at Stalin's behest, offered to work in coalition with other "anti-Fascist" parties; Blum's Socialists, thoroughly frightened by the events of February 6, 1934, when a right-wing mob nearly succeeded in occupying the National Assembly and the Radical government of Edouard Daladier resigned in terror, decided to collaborate more closely with Radicals and Communists in building a political alliance. In the ensuing national elections, in January 1936, thanks to the workings of the two-round electoral system and without any significant increase in net votes for the Popular Front parties, they were voted into office with an unexpectedly large majority.

This was the first unanticipated outcome of the Popular Front coalition, whose program had been kept deliberately vague, as befitted so ill suited a trio of political bedfellows. The second was that it was Blum's SFIO that got the most votes—hitherto it was the Radicals that had been the largest party of the traditional Left. Against expectation, then, Blum and the Socialists were now invited to form a government. The third unwonted consequence of the election victory was a series of mostly spontaneous sit-ins and strikes during May and June 1936 by a national workforce frustrated for nearly two decades of even the most modest reforms and driven to heights of optimism and confident anticipation at the prospect of a Socialist-led government.

For all these reasons Blum was able to push through, at the Matignon Accords of June 8, 1936, more reforms than had been seen in France in a generation: generous wage increases, a forty-hour working week, paid vacations, and the right to collective bargaining. Once the strikes had ended, the sit-ins been abandoned, and the *patronat* recovered its nerve, there were to be no more such easy social conquests, though Blum did manage to pass other long-overdue changes—in the administration of the Banque de France, the regulation of wheat prices and the management of the national railways in particular. But the major successes of the Popular Front—the mere fact of its existence, the appointment for the first time of a Socialist-led government, and the passage at great speed and under extraordinary conditions of a variety of social and administrative reforms—were a product of Blum's own efforts only in part.

As to the Popular Front's failures, these too were in some measure unavoidable. The initial successes brought a subsequent backlash in the form of *patronal* intransigence and conservative stonewalling in the Senate, where the Popular Front had no majority. Blum's Radical allies, who had not anticipated the developments of May and June 1936, began to bethink themselves and warned of social "conflict" if further reforms were at-

tempted. The Communists, for all their tactical moderation and their refusal to participate in the government itself, were a burden for Blum,
allowing his opponents to label him as their prisoner. And it was Blum's
misfortune to take office at a tragic time in the affairs of Europe.

Although Blum was initially convinced of the wisdom as well as the
propriety of selling arms to the beleagured Spanish Republican government, he was truly constrained; not only at home, where conservatives and
Radicals alike counseled caution, but abroad, where the Conservative government of Britain, France's only strong ally in a hostile continent, urged
him not to "intervene." Léon Blum's admiration for Britain went beyond a
taste for English literary style, as expressed in many of his early critical
writings; as we shall see, he was also a fervent admirer of the British system
of government and administration, especially when contrasted to what he
had long regarded as the dangerously dysfunctional parliamentarism of the
Third Republic.

He was also deeply aware, and had been since the early twenties, of
France's vulnerable international situation. In one of his many critical forays against Poincaré's occupation of the Ruhr in 1923 he had written that
to dissociate French policy from that of Great Britain was "to isolate
France, to isolate her diplomatically, financially and morally."[23] How much
more was this the case in 1936, with Hitler in power and allied to Mussolini, the Rhineland remilitarized, the League of Nations discredited, and
Russia a distant and unreliable partner. From the diplomatic point of view,
the only statesmanlike decision was to hold fast to the British, even if this
meant abandoning the Spaniards to their fate.

Blum was also, and unavoidably, influenced by the widespread French
aversion to any suggestion of the necessity, much less the inevitability, of
a future war. Himself an unconditional advocate of negotiated collective
disarmament throughout the twenties and early thirties, Blum was well
placed to know just how difficult it would be to carry even his own party,
much less the rest of his country, behind a policy of resolute firmness with
Hitler or Mussolini. If the majority of Socialists favored "arms for Spain"
on emotional grounds, they would certainly not have supported any confrontation with the dictators that might have resulted—as their enthusiasm for the Munich agreement just two years later was to show. The best
Blum could do was stay out of foreign entanglements and quietly pursue a

23. See Le Populaire, August 5, 1923.

policy of rearmament at home—and as he was able to demonstrate at Riom in 1942, he did this with more energy and imagination than any of the conservative governments that had preceded him in office.

The one arena in which Blum, as prime minister, had some control over his and his government's fate was in economic policy. Here, decidedly, the responsibility for failure was his. But Blum's confused economic policy—demand-led reflation largely vitiated by a foolishly delayed devaluation and clumsily administered limits on factory working hours—was widely supported at the time by his party and his allies. His opponents on the Right, who had been responsible for the previous four years of deflation and an overvalued currency, could attack him for undermining production with his reduction of the working week and his wage increases, but few of them had anything better to propose, and they used their majority in the upper house to deny Blum the sorts of financial decree-powers that they readily accorded his successors once the Socialist government had fallen.

Nevertheless, the economic policy of the Popular Front *was* a disaster—as Raymond Aron and others noted at the time. And it need not have been—both the principles and the instruments of a moderately reflationary program of currency devaluation and increased productivity were to hand. To be sure, Blum was in some measure a prisoner of the expectations of a frustrated working population on the one hand and a recalcitrant, unimaginative, and self-satisfied bourgeoisie on the other. But nonetheless, as Jean Paulhan wrote to René Etiemble in March 1938, the Popular Front was a great disappointment—its majority divided against itself, its policies disastrously self-defeating, its initial popularity in shreds. All this was all the more mysterious "in that everything seemed to be in our favor: intelligent ministers, honest men, circumstances that could easily have been foreseen." For such a perfect failure there must surely be a "single, simple explanation."[24]

Blum himself understandably attributed the Popular Front's demise—his own government lasted just one year and the Radical-led coalitions that succeeded it introduced no further reforms—to the weight of circumstances. He admitted, at his party's 1937 national congress, that "many of our estimates proved incorrect" and that the experiment had proven a dis-

24. Jean Paulhan to René Etiemble, March 9, 1938, in Paulhan, *Choix de lettres 1937–1945* (Paris: Gallimard, 1992), p. 47.

appointment. But peace, at least, had been preserved. As to the charge that he should have overruled senatorial objections and pressed on with financial and economic reforms "regardless," Blum's response is both characteristic and instructive; it had not been the moment for a "revolutionary offensive": "placed before such a choice, considering the domestic state of our country, its political condition, its psychological condition, considering the external threat, we said 'No, we don't have the right to do that, we don't have the right vis-à-vis our party, we don't have the right vis-à-vis our country.'"[25]

Blum was correct, of course. A "revolutionary offensive," whatever that might have meant in the circumstances, was not only politically impossible but utterly beyond the scope or imagination of Blum and his party. And yet a revolutionary offensive somehow represented for them a hypothetical alternative—something that under other circumstances might have addressed and resolved the Socialists' dilemma. And there, not so much in what Blum said to his fellow Socialists but in the assumptions that lay behind his reasoning, is to be found Paulhan's "single, simple explanation"—not so much for the rise and fall of the Popular Front as for the tragic political trajectory of Léon Blum and the French Left.

The history of the French Socialist movement was one of unusual division and contention even by the fissiparous standards of the European Left. It was not until 1905 that Jaurès had succeeded in imposing a fragile, formal unity upon the various strands of the French socialist Left—a unity that lasted only until the Communist scission of 1920. Blum was not just conscious of the ever-present risk of scission in his party, he was obsessed by it. His 1901 study, "Les Congrès Ouvriers et Socialistes Français," published at a time when the unification was far from certain or complete, closes with these words: "In spite of mistakes, bitterness, conflicts, socialist unity was under way." Later, assuming the task of continuing the work of the dead Jaurès, Blum laid ever greater emphasis upon the primacy of political unity for French Socialists. "Only socialism," he declared in a 1917 lecture commemorating Jaurès assassination, "will take upon itself tomorrow the task of

25. See Blum's speech at the SFIO congress in Marseille, July 12, 1937, in *Oeuvres*, 4, pt. 2:42–64, quotation from p. 55.

national moral renewal, of defending the nation against a sort of industrial caesarism. That is why we [Socialists] must remain united."[26]

Thereafter, at every threat to a unified Socialist movement—from December 1920 to the "neosocialists" split from the party in 1933 in opposition to Blum's parliamentary tactics—Blum would make an impassioned plea for "unity." He himself, as he reminded a 1947 congress of his party, never joined any factional grouping within the movement, seeking always to stay above the fray and promote the larger, common cause. To the very end of his life he maintained his conviction that organizational unity was the necessary condition for any socialist politics and thus for any social transformation.

In France, Socialist unity had been exposed to two contrasting threats. In 1899 an independent Socialist parliamentarian, Alexandre Millerand, had accepted an invitation from René Waldeck-Rousseau to join his government. Millerand's "indiscipline" (he had not sought the approval of his parliamentary colleagues) was exacerbated by the presence in Waldeck-Rousseau's cabinet of an officer who had played a part in the 1871 repression of the Commune. His action fissured the fragile accord that had been established among Socialists in response to rumors of an antirepublican coup by the clerical and monarchist Right. Thereafter, and especially once formal unification had been achieved in 1905, it was understood that no Socialist would enter any government led by others except under very restricted conditions and with explicit party permission. With the exception of the special circumstances of the wartime governments of national unity, this tactic was pursued diligently until the formation of the Popular Front, and Blum, who knew very well how fragile the unity of his party truly was, took extraordinary care to keep it out of office for just this reason.

The other threat to Socialist unity came, and had of course already come, from the Left. After his unsuccessful attempt to maintain the integrity of his party at the December 1920 Tours congress, Blum turned to the Socialist delegates there who were voting to join the Third International and advised them that "we are deeply convinced, while you chase after adventure, that someone has to stay and keep the old house." The old house in question was not just the Socialist Party but its accumulated baggage of traditions, tactics, practices, doctrines, and articles of faith. Among

26. "Les Congrès Ouvriers et Socialistes Français"; "Idée d'une biographie de Jaurès," speech delivered in Paris, July 31, 1917, in *Oeuvres*, 3, pt. 1:3–21.

these were the conviction that Leninism, whatever its passing victories, was little more than a revived nineteenth-century insurrectionist illusion—"blanquisme à la sauce tartare," as someone described it—and that the SFIO remained the true repository of the revolutionary heritage.

If he was to keep faith with that tradition—and in Blum's understanding fidelity, like unity, was a hallmark of the qualities of real Socialism— Blum had to keep his party from slipping to the right, from chasing the rewards of office, from compromising with "bourgeois" parties and thereby giving hostages to Communist propaganda. In one of his characteristically personal newspaper editorials in the Socialist *Le Populaire*, taking his readers into his confidence, Blum confessed the difficulty of walking this thin line—refusing the ultraradical separatism of the Communists while conceding to them none of the revolutionary high ground: "The great difficulty of our tactic, in the last ten years, has been to maintain our progress between the Communists and the bourgeois parties, without ever leaning to one side or the other."[27]

It was thus perhaps unavoidable that, after nearly two decades of holding his party together in the mined and obscure terrain between governmental participation and too close an identification with the Communists—and it was an article of faith for Blum that while Socialists must defend the Russian Revolution against its "reactionary" critics, they must no less resolutely maintain that Socialism and Communism were utterly distinct—Blum should have come to judge his political career above all by the degree to which he had succeeded in this thankless undertaking. As he reminded his prosecutors at Riom, in 1942, it would have been easy for him to have been accepted as a national statesman—all he would have had to do was "betray those who trusted me." But he had not betrayed them. Describing the difficulties of his Popular Front government to his fellow Socialists at their July 1937 congress, he concluded that the main thing to remember was that he and his fellow ministers had not "dishonored the party. . . . It was hard, it was difficult, but all the same we did credit to socialism [nous avons bien mérité du socialisme]."[28] The party had survived the experience of government intact.

Blum's distinctive contribution to the survival of his party, beyond his

27. *Le Populaire*, December 19, 1929.
28. Speech at the SFIO congress in Marseille, July 12, 1937, in *Oeuvres*, 4, pt. 2:42–64, quotation from p. 48.

inexhaustible enthusiasm, cajoling, encouragement, and of course example, lay—or so he and his admirers always supposed—in his subtle recasting of its doctrine. At first sight this seems odd; in Eugen Weber's
words, Blum's was a "sophisticated intelligence, more subtle than profound," and he was not an original theorist. And indeed, what others
thought of as socialist doctrine he instinctively preferred to describe in almost religious terms: "The socialist faith is the only version of that universal instinct [for justice and solidarity] that corresponds precisely to the present conditions of social and economic existence. All others have been
overtaken by the passage of time. . . . Socialism is thus an ethics and almost
a religion, as much as a doctrine."[29]

Nor was Blum a Marxist thinker, even though it was de rigueur, especially after the Communist scission, for French Socialists—Blum included—to pay frequent lip service to the unimpeachably Marxist character of their theory and practice. In his earlier years Blum had actually been
quite scathing of the Marxist groupings, especially those followers of Jules
Guesde who had opposed Jaurès at the time of the Dreyfus affair: "Among
thoughtful socialists it is well known that Marx's metaphysics are mediocre
and that his economic doctrine is coming apart daily."[30] But in later years
he was more circumspect, adopting for himself the Jaurèsian "synthesis" of
"reform and revolution" and affirming the primacy of class struggle, the
inevitable fall of capitalism, and the primordinate role of the organized
working class in preparing it. As he advised those right-wing socialist critics
in 1933 who insisted that Jaurès would not by then have refused the chance
to participate actively in government today and who blamed Blum's tactical "rigidity" on his ideological convictions: "To oppose Jaurès to Marx is
absurd. Jaurès was a Marxist. In the present state of affairs, an anti-Marxist
socialist would no longer be a socialist and would rapidly become anti-
socialist."[31]

Even in 1948, by which time Blum was a forthright critic of those in
the SFIO who would cling to outdated "Marxist" clichés, he justified his
own advocacy of parliamentary politics (against those who sought some
more "radical" strategy) as truly Marxist in its emphasis upon political participation above all else. As he wrote in the preface to a new, centennial

29. "Pour être socialiste," p. 23.
30. Revue blanche, January 1, 1900.
31. Le Populaire, August 14, 1933.

edition of the *Communist Manifesto*, "The whole essence of Marxism is contained in the *Communist Manifesto*, and, tested over a century, Marxism is more alive, more active, more influential than ever."[32] Blum was not above adapting his language to his audience. In an editorial in December 1938, defending himself against the charge that his opposition to Nazism had blinded him to the need to preserve France from war, he reminded readers that as prime minister he had even consented to receive Hjalmar Schacht and had said to him: "You know who I am, you know that I am a Marxist and a Jew. Now let us sit and talk." On trial for his life at Riom, on March 11, 1942, he repeated the story in the same words. But when he recounted the same event in August 1947 to the parliamentary commission investigating the developments of the years 1933–45, he reported the conversation thus: "I reminded him [Schacht] that I was on the one hand a socialist and on the other a Jew."[33] Marxism was for Blum always an elective affinity, not a way of thought.

What Léon Blum actually contributed to socialist doctrine was not something that would have been recognized as "theory" either by Marx or by any of Blum's contemporaries among the socialist thinkers in Germany, Italy, Austria, or even Britain. Indeed, it is a revealing indication of the impoverished state of left-wing political argument in twentieth-century France that Blum's contribution should have acquired such passing significance, for what he did was provide little more than a rather original linguistic camouflage for interwar Socialist parliamentary tactics.

In order to convince his party and its supporters that the present refusal to enter government did not entail a refusal *ever* to soil their hands with power, Blum in the late 1920s began drawing a complicated distinction between what he called the "exercise of power" and the "conquest of power." The purpose of Socialism, he explained in dozens of editorials and at the 1926 congress of his party, is not to conquer power for its own sake— that is what other political parties (the Communists included) seek, not us; but the conquest of power is nonetheless the precondition for the making of a socialist society. "I have always thought—or else I wouldn't be a socialist—that the social transformation, which is properly speaking the revolution, was neither possible nor conceivable without full control of

---

32. *Le Populaire*, July 9, 1948; April 13–14, 1948.
33. "Déposition devant la Commission Parlementaire d'Enquête," in *Oeuvres*, 4, pt. 2:357–417.

public power, that is to say without the conquest of political power by the proletariat."[34] However, until circumstances are ripe, any such "conquest" of power is premature and can only lead to dictatorship and/or defeat—of which French history could furnish several sad examples. In the meantime, however, it may become necessary (in the event of a crisis) or possible (in the event of a Socialist electoral victory) to *exercise* power in the context of bourgeois society.

Such an exercise of power is not something we Socialists seek to avoid, Blum insisted. It has propaganda value—we can be seen to govern and govern well—and it can be the occasion for legislating real reforms. But the exercise of power, like the conquest of power, is not to be sought as an end in itself. And thus, for the sake of our autonomy, our unity, and our political integrity, we (the SFIO) should not envisage it unless and until we are the dominant party and can control our own agenda.

This isn't a strikingly original set of arguments, and in retrospect it has a mildly specious air, depending as it does on categories and distinctions that existed mostly in Blum's own head. It reveals the rather banal, evolutionist cast of Blum's historical understanding ("the Revolution, as we understand it, is in accordance with the theory of the evolution of living species, as today professed by Darwin's heirs"). Note, too, the ease with which he could substitute verbal concordances ("for us Socialists the apparent contradiction between Reforms and Revolution has long since been resolved") for real contradictions.[35] But Blum's reasoning had a powerful impact upon its intended audience.

Socialist voters in France from 1919 to 1936 were, after all, being asked to elect a party that would almost certainly refuse to share in the government of the country (since the prospect of the SFIO topping the polls was inconceivable for most people before January 1936), while at the same time they were being assured that the party had no intention

34. *Le Populaire*, July 1, 1935.

35. See "Radicalisme et socialisme," in *Oeuvres*, 3, pt. 1:440–50; "Bolchevisme et socialisme," in *Oeuvres*, 3, pt. 1:451–60. These pamphlets were originally published as a series of articles from January to March 1927. But note Blum's earlier condemnation of just this sort of "scientific" methodology in Zola: "Zola is inclined to absorb everything living and complex into the single notion of science. He thinks that science alone incarnates human progress and that it alone is preparing a future of justice and goodness. . . . An old idea, this, once overhasty and now rather dated, which as I have said before constituted the basis of Renan's optimism" ("Nouvelles Conversations de Goethe," May 19, 1900, 1:304).

of seizing power by unconstitutional means. Socialist parliamentarians, of whom there was a growing number as the party recovered from the loss of the Communists in 1920, were understandably frustrated at being excluded from the prospect of office *sine die*. At the same time the SFIO's militants, still a significant and ideologically rigid presence in the interwar years, resolutely opposed any departure from the hard, "antibourgeois" line of earlier days. Blum's smooth compression of these contradictions into a single, integrated tactical stance did not resolve the dilemma, but it buried it for a while.

In the same way, his acknowledgment that the SFIO was not "in principle" opposed to dictatorship—"une vacance de légalité"—allowed Blum to justify in practice the SFIO's firmly constitutional stance. When the time comes to make the final move to revolution, it *may* be necessary to inaugurate a proletarian dictatorship; after all, "if socialism bound itself definitively to a sworn respect for legality, it would expose itself to the risk of playing into the hands of others." But not a dictatorship as the Communists envisage it. "It should be, in Vergniaud's words, active and clear as a flame. All individual wills should participate in it, it must derive its nourishment and its support from popular life, which is to say from democratic activity more spontaneous and more intense than ever."[36] It is hard to believe that Blum was doing more than paying lip service to a cliché here, and his witty suggestion at a later date that Socialists believe in *all* roads to the revolution—*even* legal ones!—reveals a degree of unseriousness. In his heart he simply didn't believe that the issue would ever arise, and he was striking the doctrinally correct pose in his own distinctive style.

If there was conviction behind Blum's tactical elucubrations, it derived from his experience not only of the hard-won road to party unity before 1905, and the ongoing battles with the Communists, but also of the 1924–26 Cartel des Gauches, when Blum and the Socialist parliamentary group supported the weak Radical governments of Herriot and Painlevé from the outside and got little but frustration in return. Henceforth, Blum assured the SFIO national congress in April 1927, we fight our own fights and take part in no battles except those that move us and where we are in charge. Moreover Blum was skeptical of the workings of parliamentary and administrative life in Third Republican France and saw little advantage in merging the public identity of his own party with that of the short-lived,

36. "L'Idéal socialiste"; *Le Populaire*, August 2, 1922.

incompetent, and often corrupt ministries and parties that attempted to govern the country between the wars. Better to err on the side of empty revolutionary rhetoric.

It is thus not so very surprising that Blum should have initially judged the success or failure of the Popular Front by its impact on his party and its practices (later he would be harsher in his self-criticism). We exercised power, he asserted, we avoided both compromise and illusion, we retained our revolutionary credibility. Nonetheless, judged by any other criteria, the Popular Front was not only a political failure but a national trauma. The revolutionary rhetoric of the Socialists, for which Blum was partly responsible, aroused unrealistic expectations, despite his frequent reminders of the limits of the "exercise of power." Disappointment and anger ensued, contributing to the cynicism and detachment with which so many left-leaning French men and women viewed the sad collapse of the Republic just three years later. Meanwhile, Socialist rhetoric, which some on the Right truly believed and which others exploited to political advantage, drove a significant part of the mainstream conservative electorate toward the mood of nervous insecurity that Pierre Laval exploited so successfully in 1940.

Moreover, the SFIO's refusal to ally with the Radicals and others in governments where Socialists would be in a minority effectively manacled the republican Left and center-Left in France for a generation, from the end of one world war until shortly before the next. It drove the center of gravity of French public and parliamentary life farther to the right than was necessary or prudent in the age of the Fascist dictators and left a vacuum where social-democratic politics might have been. Léon Blum cannot be held responsible for the fall of France or what followed. But he and his party bore some share of responsibility for the political condition of republican France, for the ease with which a divided country slipped into authoritarian rule. Why did Blum not see this at the time?

In the first place, Blum was a hostage to his party. The young Charles de Gaulle, who visited Blum in October 1935 in a vain effort to convince the Socialist leader of the need for military reforms, would later tell Georges Duhamel that Blum was simply unable to conceive of a change in French strategy: "He raised his arms to the ceiling and said to me, 'How do you expect me, a socialist, to embrace the idea of offensive warfare?' Clearly, he could not. He was paralyzed by his party." If de Gaulle meant that Blum was constrained by his party in the sense that his loyalty to its past and to its doctrines prevented him seeing things as they were, he is surely right. As Blum would later concede, on the related subject of the SFIO's opposition to voting military credits: "The socialist parliamentary group, by ritual fidelity to an ancient symbol, continued to refuse military credits so long as it knew they would be approved in any case, a gesture not without an element of hypocrisy."[37]

But Blum was not innocent in these matters. There was something curiously intoxicating in his manner of reasoning, and he was its first and lifelong victim. It was not the intoxication of rhetoric, the self-induced inebriation born of the exuberance of one's own verbosity of which Disraeli famously accused Gladstone; it was something altogether more subtle and integral to Blum's personality. André Gide noticed it first. Reflecting on the brilliant sheen of Blum's theatrical and literary criticism, he concluded in 1907 that "he judges men and things according to his opinions, not his taste. He holds the latter less reliable than the former and would rather belie his taste than seem inconsistent with himself. Of the things he says he likes one is not, perhaps, always perfectly sure that he really does like them, but rather that he thinks he does and knows why."[38]

This rings true. For the best part of twenty years Blum surrounded himself with men who were his intellectual inferiors—many of whom, it later transpired, often resented and even hated him for just that reason. He made himself the spokesman for arguments and ideas, at the level of doctrine and faith, which he would have dismissed with disdain had he encountered them in his earlier work at the Conseil d'Etat. He put his name and his person at the service of a political movement that was sometimes narrow-minded and always a little parochial; and he devoted his immense talents and energies to an objective—the socialist revolution—that he himself consigned to the cloudy future even as he knew, better than most of his contemporaries, the problems that his country faced in the present. He was able to do this because he deployed his unmatched clarity of exposition and argument, in pamphlets, articles and speeches, to the task of convincing people that these men must be good, this doctrine must be true, this movement must be sacrosanct, and the future must be as he willed it. And the first person he convinced of all this was himself.

37. Charles de Gaulle, Lettres, notes et carnets, juin '51–mai '58 (Paris: Plon, 1985), interview with Georges Duhamel, October 1954, p. 219; "A l'echelle humaine" (1941, first pub. 1945), Oeuvres, 5:409–95 (see pp. 454–55).
38. Gide, Journal 1887–1925, January 5, 1907, p. 547.

Why was Blum so susceptible to his own arguments? It is, after all, one thing to use reason to overcome taste in literary judgment, quite another to deploy it so successfully for the purpose of denying one's own access to social or political reality. Part of the answer lies in Blum's thoroughly Panglossian personality; he simply denied for as long as he could whatever he preferred not to see. He assured readers of the Socialist press in 1932 and into January 1933 that Hitler would not come to power and if he did he would be unable to do much harm. He remained convinced well into 1934 that collective disarmament was the best solution—and therefore a possible one—to all Europe's woes. He was convinced in July 1939 that were Hitler to go to war it would spell the end of his regime, overthrown from within after "a few" weeks.

On August 23, 1939, he even wrote an editorial half welcoming the Molotov-Ribbentrop Pact: "a new hope of peace has appeared"; Hitler will now appear so successful to his domestic audience that he will no longer need to threaten his neighbors (but he had the grace to concede that readers might "mock me once more for my crazy optimism"). After the war Blum was among the last to admit the inevitability of the division of Germany and Europe—though he noted in a mournful editorial, conceding the likely failure of the 1947 foreign ministers' meeting in Moscow, that "only a few crazy optimists like me insisted on expecting a success *and perhaps felt obliged to do so.*"[39]

Some of these optimistically inaccurate forecasts can be attributed to Blum's consistent failure to understand the workings of international power politics. Just as he confused governmental office with power in his writings on socialist doctrine, so he treated relations between states as something that ought to be conducted along logical and ethical principles and could therefore be analyzed as though they were indeed so conducted. But beyond this there was Blum's naturally optimistic view of the world, something he was unable to square with the need to see things in their contingently pessimistic actuality. He had too much faith in people to understand the collapse of political civility in 1930s France—the men he appealed to for support and understanding, across the floor of the Chambre or in his newspaper editorials, were the very ones who would call for his Jewish blood a few years later. He could not imagine that Fascists might aspire to conquer

---

39. Emphasis added. See Blum's editorials in *Le Populaire* throughout the thirties and again from 1945 to his death.

or dominate half of Europe—"One cannot ascribe such absurd, such de-
mented plans even to a Hitler, even to a Mussolini." Blum never fully accepted, in Voltaire's words, that "le mal est dans le monde."[40]

This chronic lack of psychological or political realism, the wish to find
good in men and events fathering the thought that it was there, was of a
piece with Léon Blum's essential decency. He was not particularly ap-
proachable—one did not readily *tutoyer* him—but he was unusually kind
and generous of his resources and his time. He had an inexhaustible fund
of goodwill toward almost everyone and innocently supposed that it would
be reciprocated in most cases. Disagreements could be resolved, misunder-
standings explained. In his unpublished wartime prison notes he reflected
self-critically on this aspect of his political style: "I tried to ennoble everything, to dignify everything. Maybe that was my mistake. If I had a gift that
was it. Maybe I believed too much in virtue; conciliation through reaching
for a more exalted level."[41] Here, at least, the occupations of his early years
served him ill; as he wrote of Stendhal, "It is never without cost that we
confine our apprenticeship in life to books, and to books alone."

In addition to being both unrealistic and pathologically optimistic (as
his prison companion Edouard Daladier sourly observed in 1942),[42] Léon
Blum had so intertwined his feeling of duty and commitment to the SFIO
with his own sense of self that he came not only to speak of the party as his
"family" but also to treat it as one, as an extension of his thoughts and
feelings. He used the party press, public meetings, party congresses, and to
a lesser extent the Chambre des Députés itself as forums in which to reveal
his scruples, confess his errors, and admit to all manner of doubts. The un-
calculated advantage of this disarming self-revelation was that many
French men and women, even those who never voted for his party, instinctively understood and appreciated him as more honest, more open,
more direct, and far more interesting than other Third Republican politicians. But there were disadvantages too.

Having with some difficulty overcome his scruples at leading his party

40. See in particular a series of articles in *Le Populaire* from November 1930 to February 1931 entitled "Les Problèmes de la paix," published in 1931 and reprinted in *Oeuvres*, vol. 3, pt. 2 (1928–1934) (Paris: Albin Michel, 1972), pp. 139–237.

41. From the *Fonds Blum*, at the Fondation Nationale de Sciences Politiques, quoted
in Jean Lacouture, *Léon Blum* (Paris: Seuil, 1977), p. 497.

42. See Edouard Daladier, *Journal de captivité 1940–1945* (Paris: Calmann-Lévy,
1991), entries for August 2 and August 19, 1942.

into government, and his fear of "misleading" the working class into believing he could deliver more than was possible, Blum left office with an almost audible sigh of relief—and then spent a good part of the remainder of the 1930s half confessing in public to the mistakes and miscalculations of his ministry. Even his defense of his actions as prime minister often took this form. In a speech to the June 1938 congress of the SFIO, in which he defended his decision to devalue only in September 1936 (rather than in June, when the move would have had more impact and a better chance of success), he acknowledged that "we undertook a devaluation that did not secure all possible benefits on the technical level because we did it in such a way as to limit the economic and human injustices that it would cause. That is true. That failure, that defect, I admit them."[43]

There was much more in similar vein. Years later, a few days after the Communist coup in Prague in February 1948, Blum wrote an editorial for *Le Populaire* explaining why the coup should be a *cas de conscience* for French Socialists: did we do enough for our East European Socialist comrades? "They wanted to work with the local Communists, and we encouraged them. At their behest we turned a blind eye to what was really happening, we withheld support from anti-Communist exiles or the victims of Communist intolerance. For the East European Socialists' *own* sake we should have been more critical."[44] The confessional tone, the recognition, but after the fact, of his own purblind naïveté, the moral admonition directed at himself and his fellow French Socialists are all classic Blum.

Blum's need to share with the widest possible audience his sense of guilt, of shared suffering at the cost of his own errors and those of others, is well known, thanks to the famous "Munich" editorial of September 20, 1938, in which he confessed his own relief at seeing peace preserved but acknowledged that the way it was done "affords me no joy, and I find myself torn between a cowardly solace and shame [un lâche soulagement et la honte]." The following day he pursued his theme, bemoaning the way in which French-Czech relations and treaties had been trampled upon: "Can you blame me for thinking of them? Is it surprising that I feel today a sense of degradation as I reflect that they have been betrayed in spirit and maybe even in the letter?"

43. June 7, 1938, speech to SFIO congress at Royan, in *Oeuvres*, 4, pt. 2:134–66.
44. *Le Populaire*, February 29, 1948.

Yet Blum was not responsible for Munich—he had long since been out of office, and we have no way of knowing how he would have handled the Sudeten crisis in Daladier's place. But in spite of this, and in spite of his sense of shame, he voted in the Chambre to approve the Munich accords. When his younger Socialist colleague and friend Jules Moch warned him that he, Moch, planned to vote against the accords, Blum turned upon him the full force of his moral authority and personal charm: "Jules, how can you do that to me, *you* do it to *me!*" Suitably chagrined, Moch withdrew his opposition.[45]

But it is striking that Blum should have used the occasion to insist, in effect, that Moch not betray him by refusing to share Blum's own pain in voting for the Munich accords—though in his wartime essay "A l'échelle humaine," Blum confessed somewhat belatedly that he had avoided taking a clear line over Munich not because he did not know what was right, but because the SFIO was so divided that any clear choice or categoric language would have revealed the split in the party and torn it apart.

Jean Lacouture, Blum's French biographer, is certainly right to see Blum's public agonizing as a species of *angélisme*, altogether inappropriate in a statesman. And noting Blum's public grief over his painful decision to advocate nonintervention in the Spanish Civil War, he cruelly observes that "the value of a policy should not be measured by the suffering it inflicts upon the man who conceived and implemented it."[46] But it may be that Lacouture misses something much more fundamental in Blum's makeup than *angélisme*. Blum was not trying to be "holier" than his critics, inside his own party and elsewhere. He was not even seeking sympathy from readers and listeners for his own pain at the mistakes of French policy, whether under his government or that of his successors.

He was, it seems to me, seeking not so much forgiveness as empathy. Léon Blum, a man who naturally sought out friendship and companions in his private life, was one of the loneliest public figures of his day. He was alone in his party, very few of whose senior figures shared his background, interests, or taste. He was alone in the Chambre, admired by many but hated and abused by as many again. He moved in many worlds but was in some measure a stranger to all of them, just because he was so very cosmo-

45. Jules Moch, *Une Si Longue Vie* (Paris: Laffont, 1976), p. 149.
46. Lacouture, *Léon Blum*, pp. 396, 583.

politan in his range. And he suffered the debilitating political weakness of wanting to be liked. He made no moral compromise with his opponents for the sake of their affection, but he sought it nonetheless. He reached out across the airwaves, the soapbox, the lectern, and his writing table to show his audience what he was thinking, why he was thinking it, what he had done and with what consequences. He debated his decisions in public and then described the pain of that debate in retrospect. In so doing he sought understanding for his dilemmas and his choices. And if he were understood, he would be liked.

This need to be liked is not a particularly rare trait among politicians and other public figures. For some it is what drove them onto the public stage in the first place. Franklin Roosevelt had it in some measure. But Blum, characteristically, took it much further and had prepared for himself no retreat, no withdrawal into arrogant self-confidence in moments of crisis. As a result, he suffered quite a lot, both at his mistakes and at the fear that they would lead those to whom he felt close to misunderstand and mistrust him. That is why a man who was actually quite decisive and even overpowering to many who came into contact with him could seem at times so uncertain and rudderless when placed in an unexpected position of power, as he was in 1936. Blum understood his weakness better than most of his friends and admirers; at the turn of the century, in the guise of "Goethe," he commented ruefully upon the cost of seeking the affection of all: "this need, this love of being loved, which has been the source of true gratification, has also brought me the sharpest of pain."[47]

"Léon Blum is never sure, he is always seeking; too much intelligence and not enough character." André Gide passed this judgment on his young friend when Blum was just seventeen years old and Gide himself was not yet twenty-one. It shows remarkable insight. But Blum's lifelong search for the truth, his transparent honesty and unabashed public self-questioning, while they opened him up to occasional ridicule, were also a source of his strength and influence. He could carry an audience by the sheer force of his personality and quality of his mind. As his friend, the French president Vincent Auriol, said of him at his funeral in 1950, "Blum's was an elo-

---

47. "Nouvelles Conversations de Goethe," August 1, 1897, 1:204.

quence that enveloped you bit by bit, penetrating you, gripping you, seduc-
ing you."[48]

The appeal was by no means limited to his colleagues and friends. All
accounts of his public performances in the interwar years agree that Blum
had an almost mesmerizing effect on even the most hostile of audiences
from any walk of life. Joseph Paul-Boncour, an erstwhile Socialist politician
who later left the SFIO and was by no means an unconditional admirer of
Blum, once described the difficult ambiance of political gatherings in the
1920s, with aggressive and often violent interruptions and heckling from
Communists and right-wingers alike: "When we did manage to speak, it
was wonderful to see this man, endowed with no special physical resources,
whose voice was weak and who never resorted to crude crowd-pleasing
techniques, dominating by the sheer superiority of his intelligence and the
precision of his analysis." Jules Moch and others have recorded similar impressions, noting the awe and admiration in which Blum was held by even
the most untutored provincial listeners.[49]

There was nothing patronizing about Blum's style. He deployed his
skills no differently in an electoral meeting in a wine-growing constituency
in Narbonne than he would in a Socialist pamphlet or a Chambre speech.
If he established a bridge to audiences of peasants and workers, it was in
spite of the gulf that separated him from them—what he said of Jean Jaurès
in July 1917 was true of Blum himself: "He was a socialist, but—and in our
party it was one of his distinguishing features—he had not been brought
to socialism by abstract reflection upon economic phenomena, nor by
working experience, nor yet by troubled feelings [une commotion sentimen-
tale]. He did not come from the people. He did not know the people until
afterward."

Blum's rhetorical artistry lay in the absence of art. Gide again, this
time in 1907: "One can conceive of no account more precise, clearer, more
elegant and confident than that which Léon Blum can deliver, at the drop
of a hat, whether it concerns an event, a book or a play. What a wonderful
rapporteur he must make at the Conseil d'Etat! If only his thoughts were not

48. Gide, Journal 1887–1925, January 1890, p. 115; Vincent Auriol, "In memoriam,"
in Blum, Oeuvres, 1:ix–xiii.
49. See Joseph Paul-Boncour, Entre deux guerres (Paris: Plon, 1945), pp. 71–72, also
cited in Lacouture, Léon Blum, p. 202; Moch, Une Si Longue Vie, p. 57.

so intent upon politics, what a distinguished critic he would be!"[50] Blum's rigorous clarity depended not only upon an unusually well-ordered and logical mind—he could compose a speech or an editorial in his head and then write or deliver it without pause and in perfect, unbroken sequence—but also upon an unequaled control of his material, a skill he had honed and deployed for nearly a quarter of a century in his legal work.

One can see this quality at work in the countless parliamentary speeches he delivered over the course of the years 1919–48. From his very first intervention in December 1919, a complex and detailed argument for state control of certain loss-making public services, through his well-informed criticisms of the moral and economic damage wrought by Poincaré's foreign policy and the deflationary financial practices of the Right, to his spectacular indictment at Riom of pre-1936 French military and industrial planning and on to his deposition to the postwar Commission D'enquête sur les Évenements Survenus en France de 1933 à 1945, Blum displayed a command, unrivaled in his generation, of military or technical detail as well as political and administrative history; marshaling information into columns of unassailable and reasoned conclusions, he could bring his supporters to their feet while rendering his opponents frequently speechless with impotent fury.

It is perhaps difficult today to appreciate to the full Blum's particular gifts. But in an age before loudspeakers and microphones, when radio was in its infancy and newspapers thrived, when the Chambre des Députés still mattered and its proceedings were widely followed, Blum's capacity to hold an audience or a readership by the power of knowledge and reason alone was distinctive, and it counted. And at a time when most French politicians were either mediocre provincial worthies or else phrase-making Parisian businessmen and lawyers cynically unconcerned with ideas or ethics, Blum stood nearly alone.

As for the Socialist Party, while it could boast a few men capable of holding or moving a left-wing crowd, and a handful of Parisian intellectuals who graced its membership lists and parliamentary group with their presence, it had no one remotely comparable to Blum when it came to combining intellectual, moral, and political assets in a single person. That is why

50. Gide, *Journal 1887–1925*, January 5, 1907, p. 547.

he was the party's "natural" leader, and that is why so many of his colleagues tolerated his leadership even as they envied and resented his gifts.

One of Blum's distinctive assets, curiously rare in its day, was his skill at weaving domestic and international developments into a single narrative or argument. As we have seen, he could be quite wrong in his international analyses, particularly when engaging in prediction. But between the wars—and again for a while after the Liberation—many French politicians and thinkers retreated from unpleasant international reality into a sort of reassuring *nombrilisme*, an obsession with their own affairs to the exclusion of much interest in how these might be affected by what was happening across their frontiers. This, after all, is the background not only to the tragic accumulation of errors in foreign and military policy before 1940, but also for the ostrichlike frame of mind with which much of the national elite followed Pétain into Vichy.

Blum was different. His critiques of the deflationary policies of the Bloc National from 1920 to 1923, for example, were always tied closely to his disapproval of the Versailles clauses, the occupation of the Ruhr, and the impact of these, in their turn, upon prospects for social reform in France. He long favored peace and disarmament at almost any price, not just in the name of a venerable party tradition but because he worried as much about the prospects for democracy and socialism in Germany and central Europe as he did in France. His vacillations and errors in office derived in part from this same unusually cosmopolitan perspective—he was nervous about the British alliance, about the growing strength of the dictators, and about the need for friendly relations with the United States, at a time when most of his colleagues and supporters had eyes only for domestic revolution, or the next parliamentary vote.

This broader field of vision helped Blum see some things sooner than other people. In July 1928 he wrote an editorial condemning the then widespread French admiration for the achievements of Mussolini: "There is something worse in this world than the abuse of force; it is the servile complaisance that such force encounters when it is successful, that obsequious adulation which forgets the crime in order to flatter the success." It is ironic that he could as well have been speaking of the adulation of Pétain after 1940—or of the fawning affection for Stalin that swept the Parisian intelligentsia a decade later. In prison in 1942, he anticipated that French ignorance of international reality would lead public opinion in the country to "exaggerate rather presumptuously the role that France will play" after the war—which is just what happened, and not only to public opinion but to many leading politicians as well.[51]

Most of all, Blum's instinct for seeing French affairs in an international light made him a steady and unwavering analyst of the PCF, the French Communist Party. To be sure, it took no great insight to understand that the French Communists, like Communists everywhere, were tightly bound to Moscow and to Soviet policy and interests—that bondage, after all, was what Lenin had sought in 1920, and the decision to accept or reject it was the explicit basis for the split between Communists and Socialists at Tours. And we now know, from Soviet sources, what had long seemed self-evident to disinterested observers: that the strategy, the tactics, and the day-to-day decisions of the PCF were *téléguidé* from Moscow for most of the party's first seventy years.[52]

But these matters were not always so obvious to everyone at the time. Communist militants, and even some of the less well informed Communist leaders, fondly imagined themselves to be pursuing an autonomous policy in pursuit of the interests of the French proletariat, interests that just happened to coincide with those of the Soviet state. Some Socialists who longed for reunification with the PCF liked to think so too. Many intellectuals, especially in the era of anti-Fascist mobilization during the thirties, were reluctant to hear or speak ill of the PCF—and confusedly regarded any accusations of Moscow-centrism as somehow slanderous, despite their own admiration for the Soviet achievement.

Léon Blum was certainly sensitive to the appeal of left-wing unity and always sought the agreement and support of the Communists when he thought it was to be had. He welcomed the Communist-sponsored Popular Front alliance and stood on podiums and platforms and street corners arm in arm with Maurice Thorez and other Communist luminaries. Even after the Liberation he was reluctant to admit the coming of the iron curtain and supported coalition governments with the PCF as long as these were possible. But he suffered no illusions about his fraternal allies.

51. See *Le Populaire,* July 19, 1928; letter to the French in London, dated May 1942 and smuggled out by Edouard Froment, in *Oeuvres,* 5:349–61.
52. See Annie Kriegel and Stéphane Courtois, *Eugen Fried. Le grand secret du PCF* (Paris: Seuil, 1997).

In his speech at Tours in December 1920 Blum summarized his understanding of the distinguishing feature of Bolshevism and its French admirers: "For the first time in the history of socialism you are thinking of terrorism not merely as a final recourse, not as an extreme measure of public safety to be imposed on bourgeois resistance, not as a vital necessity for the revolution, but as a means of government. It is this, this emphasis on dictatorial terror, on the Russian model as a grid to be applied willy-nilly to France, together with the slavish, unquestioning obedience to Moscow that it presumes, that distinguishes you from us and always will."[53]

Blum's response to the twists and turns of PCF domestic tactics remained firmly focused upon the broader Soviet context. He never doubted the fraudulence of the Moscow trials of the thirties, nor the blatant self-interest of the Soviets in instructing their French puppets to turn after 1934 from attacking social democracy as "social fascism" to an anti-fascist alliance with their Socialist "brothers." Yes, he wrote in October 1939, we knew what the Communists were about in 1936, but it was worth the risk anyway: to save the Republic, to revive the working-class movement, and maybe even to have some impact on the PCF as a result of the experience. He was depressed but not surprised by the relative ease with which French Communists switched their line again in the aftermath of the Molotov-Ribbentrop Pact—though he tried without success to stop Daladier from banning the PCF in September 1939, making of it a martyr just when its errors were bringing it to the point of collapse.[54]

It was Blum who, in his prison essay "A l'échelle humaine," first described the PCF as a "foreign nationalist party," and Blum, too, who wrote from prison to warn de Gaulle of the inadvisability of giving the Communists a special status in the emerging Resistance coalition: "It is a great mistake, to which your personal representatives seem disposed, to consider Communism as the only popular force [in the Resistance]. It is a signal error to offer your hand to the Communists over the head of the Socialists. It is wrong to deny legitimacy to political parties in the one case and to concede it in the other."[55] And it was Blum who remarked most insistently,

53. Speech to SFIO Tours congress, December 27, 1920, in Oeuvres, 3, pt. 1:137–60, quote from p. 155.
54. See Le Populaire for September 26 and 27, 1939; October 4, 1939.
55. See Jean-Louis Crémieux-Brilhac, La France libre (Paris: Gallimard, 1996), where Blum is quoted on p. 512.

in the last years of his life, on Stalin's interest in exploiting de Gaulle's anti-Americanism as a weapon that could be turned to Communist advantage, in France and in the European arena.

Léon Blum was not, of course, the only Socialist to see the French Communist Party for what it was, in an age when many observers at home and abroad were swept away by anti-Fascist enthusiasms, before and after the war. Socialist leaders in his generation knew from bitter experience what it was like to deal with the PCF—some of them had even passed briefly through it, in the early, innocent enthusiasms of the post-1917 years. But it was Blum who most consistently and insistently drew a distinction between the moral and political traditions of the French socialist Left and those of Leninism; and it was Blum who, at Tours, had argued that case with enough force and conviction to save his own party and limit the domestic damage wrought by the rise of the Third International. Little wonder the Communists hated him so.

When he was not involved in the affairs of his party, Léon Blum devoted quite a lot of attention to the problem of government in France. The failings of the Third Republic were no secret. Born of a compromise vote in 1875 in the aftermath of the collapse of Louis-Napoléon's empire, the Republic's system of election and of parliamentary government had been shaped by the fear of authoritarian rule—whether by imperial usurpers, overpowerful presidents, or military adventurers. As a consequence, the executive branch was kept deliberately weak, and parliamentary majorities were difficult to form and almost impossible to sustain, since there was no sanction in place for those who brought them down. Political parties were little more than occasional combinations of local political and economic interest, brought together for electoral advantage. Coalition governments, top-heavy with untalented men given office as a perk or a sop to sectional interest, were chronically incapable of devising or implementing a program, and there was no presidential office to compensate for legislative inertia. Except in moments of national crisis, Third Republican France was reasonably well administered, but it was to all intents and purposes ungoverned.

Most French politicians in the years before and after World War I were quite content to allow matters to rest there. Socialists, especially, saw little point in attending to the deficiencies of a bourgeois republic whose very legitimacy they questioned; their task was to undermine and replace it with a socialist one. Left and Right alike were deeply set in their ways—echoing an electorate that by the 1930s was instinctively backward-looking (in 1936 fully 67 percent of the French population was over twenty, the oldest in Europe). But Blum, who had formed strong views on administrative reform during his years in the Conseil d'Etat, was not content with postponing change to the Socialist *calens*, and in 1918 he published a little essay on governmental reform (reprinted in 1935 on the eve of the Popular Front's election to office) in which he laid out some practical suggestions for improvement.

His recommendations were quite straightforward. The prime minister should have more executive power (on the British model) and should not run one or more ministries at the same time while heading a government, as was common in the Third Republic. The "Orleanist constitution" of 1875 was not sacred and should be subjected to scrutiny and reform—a contentious point to make in France, where "constitutional reform" had been the rallying ground of authoritarian antirepublicans since Boulanger and would form the basis in 1940 of the "respectable" face of Pétainism. But Blum insisted that the case for strong and efficient government should not be held hostage to fears of "caesarism."[56]

In office, in the difficult circumstances of 1936, Blum was in no position to implement most of his thinking; he did, however, appoint fewer ministers than usual and inaugurated a prime ministerial office and secretariat, with experts and specialized advisers—something that would become a model for post-war and especially Fifth Republic governments and ministers. And the Popular Front government promoted more, and more important, legislation than all other interwar French governments combined. For all its ideological rhetoric and controversial outcome, it was in the prosaic tasks of managing government and passing legislation that Blum's first Socialist administration set a precedent for postwar France.

During the war Blum reflected further on this subject. In his prison writings—the unpublished memoirs, the prison notes, the essay "A l'échelle humaine"—he returned again and again to the failings of French parliamentary democracy, and to the Socialists' and his own mistake in confusing the practices of French parliamentarism with the broader principles and requirements of a modern democracy. What would be required in postwar France was *both* a stronger executive, perhaps on the U.S. model (so that

56. See Blum, "La Réforme gouvernementale" (1919), in *Oeuvres*, 3, pt. 1:507–75; also *Le Populaire* for October 20, 1934.

the country could actually be governed), *and* decentralization of administrative and political life, to encourage public initiative and to counter the chronic French tendency, in moments of crisis, to hand centralized power over to authoritarian rulers. This was a problem for France as a whole, he wrote in a letter to his fellow Socialists smuggled out of his prison at Bourassol in March 1943; but it was also a task for Socialists, if they wished to play a credible role in the reconstruction of their country.[57]

His interest in a move to presidential government, and his understanding of wartime political realities, made Léon Blum initially more sympathetic to the Gaullist project—and to de Gaulle himself—than most other members of the Socialist resistance, in France or abroad. Indeed, Blum's support was an important asset for de Gaulle in his London exile; the imprisoned Socialist smuggled a number of letters to the embattled general, assuring him of his backing and encouraging others to place their faith in de Gaulle's leadership. According to Jean-Louis Crémieux-Brilhac, who was in London at the time, "No other French politician undertook such a commitment during the war. Nor did any one else address to de Gaulle such a closely reasoned correspondence: Blum, with the authority of age and experience, exercised at the time a dominion that neither de Gaulle nor the historians of Socialism have since cared to recall."[58]

Blum went to great lengths to try and convince his fellow Socialists of the qualities of de Gaulle, as well as the advantages of a stronger executive. But he never hesitated to insist to de Gaulle himself that a postwar democracy would need political parties—"we must modify them, we must renew them, but we must not eliminate them." And it was only when de Gaulle, during and especially after his brief period in postwar office, began to display a scornful and dismissive distaste for the daily practice of party-political democracy in the Fourth Republic, that Blum reluctantly turned away from him. By 1947 he was criticizing de Gaulle's newly formed Rassemblement du Peuple Français as a gathering place for all the antirepublican, ex-fascist, and reactionary elements in the nation. As for the general himself, he had become, in Blum's words, "un personnage plus qu'un citoyen." And as a result, and however reluctantly, Blum "put back in the drawer and repressed in my own thinking the idea of presidential power."[59]

---

57. See Blum, "Note au parti," dated March 1, 1943, in *Oeuvres*, 5:392–93.
58. Crémieux-Brilhac, *La France libre*, p. 511.
59. *Le Populaire*, October 4, 1947; December 31, 1947.

Whether or not Blum was right to abandon so readily the case for a presidential republic, it is noteworthy that he had no hesitation in admitting his error. In some of the contexts discussed earlier in this essay such open self-criticism shaded into the remorse of the confessional. But his ability to change his mind openly, to appeal to his opponents by acknowledging his own past faults, was also what made Blum, on occasion, a statesman. In March 1938, in the midst of the international crisis brought on by the Anschluss, he made a moving appeal to the center and right-wing parties in the Chambre to join him, despite all their ideological and personal differences, in a national government.

"Gentlemen," he began, "I speak here at this moment as a man who feels responsible for human lives," and then laid out before the last legislature of the Third Republic the case for understanding the drift of international developments, the changes that had taken place in a few short years, and the need to put behind them past squabbles and conflicts. Realizing that he would not succeed in convincing his audience, Blum concluded on a note of quiet hopelessness: "I tell you that at this moment I feel a sense of desperation and of tragedy at the thought that my voice, which once found so much resonance among the members of the [Popular Front] majority, can no longer find an echo among you."[60]

In June 1938, at the SFIO congress of that year and three months before the Munich crisis, Blum spoke no less directly to his own party, now deeply divided at the prospect of rearmament and the growing threat of war. Socialists can no longer fall back to the moral high ground of our opposition to Versailles and our long-standing desire to see the treaty revised, he told them. We are facing an imperial threat to Europe. One of the few hopes *now* of preventing war is to convince certain states that by attacking others they risk facing a united Europe. In November of the same year he warned his own party again of the risks of trying to keep its hands clean by refusing to take responsibility for the nation's affairs in the worsening international situation. You can keep on saying that "we didn't vote for the Versailles treaty," he wrote, "but don't fool yourselves; that is the attitude of spectators, not participants. And don't forget that uncaring spectators can sometimes become accomplices."[61]

60. Speech in Chambre des Députés, March 17, 1938, in *Oeuvres*, 4, pt. 2:80–90.
   61. June 7, 1938, speech to SFIO congress at Royan, in *Oeuvres*, 4, pt. 2:134–66. See also *Le Populaire*, November 2, 1938.

Neither Right nor Left responded to his appeal, each indifferent in its own way to the common national cause of France. By the spring of 1940 the moral and political decadence of France had reached a point where most public men preferred to settle old scores rather than face the national disaster looming just ahead. In the debate on March 21, 1940, over Paul Reynaud's proposed new government, observers were shocked at the partisan, hate-filled, blinkered mood of the French legislature. In the words of Charles de Gaulle, "Only Léon Blum, to whom, however, no ministerial job had been offered, raised the tone of the debate."[62]

It is fitting that de Gaulle should have thought it worth remarking that it was Blum above all who raised the tone of the debate, when feelings ran high and when most other men were running for cover. Léon Blum was an extraordinarily brave man. Of his moral and intellectual resolution—his willingness to go against fashion, even against his own party and his colleagues when he thought they, or he, had been wrong—we have seen many examples. Like Raymond Aron, he followed the logic of his reason wherever it took him, for good and ill; for this reason (again like Aron) he was willing as late as the autumn of 1942 to forgive Pétain, despite everything that had happened, if the marshal would throw himself now into the Allied camp—"I declare firmly that for my part I would willingly close my eyes to his past crimes and his present self-interested calculations; in any such recantation I would see only its contribution to a quicker and more secure final victory."[63]

Pétain did no such thing of course. But even so, in 1945 Blum—who had every reason to wish Pétain nothing but ill—admonished the Communist leader Jacques Duclos for demanding that the marshal's trial be conducted with "a holy hatred." No, he responded, a judge must not hate. "He must keep in his mind both a vigorous detestation of the crime and a scrupulous impartiality toward the accused man. That is the terrible dilemma of all political justice."[64] In the revenge-filled atmosphere of post-Liberation France, such legal and ethical scruples were at a steep discount.

But more even than his moral integrity, it is Léon Blum's sheer bravery that stands out. He was, after all, a marked man. Just how marked is a little

62. Charles de Gaulle, *Mémoires de guerre*, vol. 1: *L'Appel* (Paris: Plon, 1955), p. 25.
63. Blum, "Letter to London," August 15, 1942, smuggled out by Daniel Mayer and "Capitaine Rolland," in *Oeuvres*, 5:357–61.
64. Quoted by Lacouture, *Léon Blum*, p. 511.

easier to grasp now than it would have been only a few years ago. The intensity of racist and anti-Semitic sentiment in interwar France was not much discussed in the decades following the Liberation; after all, even the anti-Semitic aspects of the Vichy regime itself were largely ignored until the 1970s. Today it is widely acknowledged that Vichy played an active role in facilitating the deportation and extermination of many thousands of Jews; but even so, rather less attention has been paid to the moral and cultural circumstances that prepared the way for the collaboration of Pétain and his colleagues in this aspect of the Nazi project. Vichy, after all, did not come from nowhere. The things that were said and done in France in the years 1940–44 were said and done by men who had been publicly active long before 1940, and who had in their turn been influenced by things written and spoken by other men of the Third Republic. In gaining some understanding of the opprobrium cast upon Léon Blum in the interwar decades we are also in a better position to place this aspect of the Vichy years in its historical setting.

Anti-Semitism, "respectable" anti-Semitism, was hardly new. Blum himself had written about it in his "Souvenirs sur l'Affaire," but like most observers before 1914 he dismissed it as an aberration, associated with Edouard Drumont, the Panama scandals, and the brief nationalist hysteria surrounding the accusations against Dreyfus. Like most assimilated Jews he simply assumed that anti-Semitism in its harmless, "cultural" form, was endemic to French life and should be ignored. And he ignored suggestions that he might himself be a distinctive object of anti-Jewish feeling. But even Blum's youthful acquaintances and admirers were not above invoking his Jewishness against him. André Gide, who was so shrewd an observer of Blum's talents, confided to his diary in 1914 that Blum's interest in things Jewish "comes in the first instance from the fact that a Jew is especially sensitive to Jewish qualities; but above all it is because Blum considers the Jewish race to be superior, as though entitled to dominate having for so long been dominated, and he believes it is his duty to work for its triumph and to help it with all his strength."

Gide did not stop there, but ruminated further about the "Jewish" qualities of Blum's personal mannerisms: "At a dress rehearsal, in the corridor of a theater where he comes upon you by chance, he takes you by the waist, the neck, the shoulders, and even if you haven't seen each other for a year he would have people believe he saw you just the night before and has no more intimate friend. . . . But why do I speak here of his defects? It is enough for me that the qualities of the Jewish race are not French ones."[65] André Gide did not hate Léon Blum—he rather liked him. But he, like so many lesser men, saw nothing amiss in thinking of Blum as a Jew, and ascribing his character traits and defects, as he imagined them, to his Jewish roots.

Blum knew nothing of Gide's private thoughts at the time. He did know about hatred, of course—as he himself noted, French political life was peculiarly subject to moods of affection and dislike, and the greatest public figures of his era had taken great abuse. Georges Clemenceau, Blum wrote on March 3, 1899 (the year after Clemenceau's courageous publication of Zola's "J'Accuse" in his paper *L'Aurore*), "was the most contemptibly, falsely calumnied man of our time." Eighteen years later, reflecting on the buildup of malice and slander that paved the way to the murder of Jean Jaurès, Blum remarked that "it was such a distinctive hatred that, as Jaurès once said, had he looked to it as the measure of himself, he would have been led to commit the sin of pride."[66]

But neither Clemenceau nor Jaurès was a Jew. Once Blum entered public life in 1919, the tone of political aversion descended to a key more menacing and contorted than anything to which Clemenceau or even Jaurès had ever been exposed, as though all the undercurrents of French self-doubt after the war—the fear of foreigners, a sense of national decline, and the fruits of a generation of semirespectable racist literature—merged and converged upon the person of Léon Blum. There were other Jews in politics, of course, but none was as prominent as Blum; few of them were writers or intellectuals, and most were associated with conservative political groupings: they were thus spared the association between Jewishness, cultural "elitism," and the threat of radical social change that so many critics made when they thought about Blum.

It is not possible here to do full justice to the sheer vulgarity and verbal violence to which Blum was exposed—a few examples will have to suffice.[67] In December 1920, writing in Charles Maurras's *Action française*,

65. Gide, *Journal 1887–1925*, January 24, 1914, pp. 662–63.
66. "Nouvelles Conversations de Goethe," March 3, 1899, 1:259; lecture on the anniversary of Jaurès's assassination, July 31, 1917, in *Oeuvres*, 3, pt. 1:7.
67. Unless otherwise indicated, citations in the paragraphs that follow are from Pierre Birnbaum's pathbreaking study of political anti-Semitism in twentieth-century

Léon Daudet set the tone, informing his readers that "a simian little yid like Blum is utterly indifferent and even hostile to French interests." A decade later the same Daudet, noting Blum's widely quoted remark that he was not a heavy drinker, seized upon this "un-French" quality to refer to him in the same paper as "that indescribable androgyne . . . the circumcised, oenophobe Blum."

Blum's exaggerated "sexuality," his sinuous, sensual mannerisms (real or imagined), were an obsessive theme for his enemies—aided by the exaggerated notoriety of *On Marriage*, an essay in which the young Blum had advocated greater premarital freedom and experience for men and women alike. His spontaneous humanity and his distinctive, slightly dandified, fin de siècle sartorial tastes laid him open to vicious slanders. Charles Maurras himself described him in a January 1936 article as a sadist and inveterate pederast—"who never encounters a friend without taking him by the waist, fondling him, flattering him, turning and inverting [retourner] him in every sense"—a theme taken up by many others.

For his enemies, Blum's sexuality was polymorphous. When he wasn't being accused of pederasty he was presented—in articles and cartoons—as a woman. "Léon Blum," wrote Pierre Dominique in a March 1927 article, "appears under the guise of a prophetess, something like Deborah or the witch of Endor of whom the Bible tells us. He has, too, something of Judith in him: we saw him on May 11, 1924 [the date of the election of the Cartel des Gauches] penetrate the republican camp, fragrantly perfumed, to make love to the Radical Holofernes before, having inebriated his lover, severing his head at the end of the night." Blum, wrote another right-wing journalist in March 1936, "is a hysterical, possessed woman, ripe for the padded cell and the straitjacket."

Blum's "Jewish femininity"—or else his seductive wiles—were a staple of conservative and far-right vituperation. Cartoons in journals like *Le Charivari* represented him as "La Juive errante." But though the threatening sexual connotations of Blum's Jewishness were an obsessive and revealing topic in their own right, it was the mere fact that he *was* a Jew that gave the greatest offense. Already a distinctive theme in attacks on Blum since his first election to parliament, this became a source of paroxysms of fury in the Popular Front years. How, his enemies howled, could such a

France, *Un Mythe politique*. I am deeply grateful to Professor Birnbaum for permission to draw upon his work in this essay.

man represent French interests? "That M. Léon Blum can be the *député* for Narbonne, and in that capacity be allowed to play a role—and what a role!—in the French parliament, shows the extent of the tragic absurdity of our electoral system," exclaimed an editorialist in *Je suis partout* in October 1934.

The prospect of Blum actually becoming prime minister was too much. Here, declared Maurras, is "a man to shoot down, but in the back ... human detritus who should be treated as such." On the day Blum presented his government to the Chambre des Députés, Xavier Vallat (later to become Vichy's first Commissioner for Jewish Affairs) solemnly advised him, over the warnings of Edouard Herriot, the president of the Chambre, that "Your arrival, Mr. Prime Minister, is without question a historic date. For the first time this ancient Gallo-Roman land is to be ruled by a Jew.... To govern this peasant nation of France it would be better to have someone whose origins, however modest, lie deep in our soil, rather than a subtle Talmudist." Vallat was by no means the crudest or most virulent of Blum's critics; but it was an even more respectable figure, Joseph Caillaux, a former government minister, who orchestrated the Senate's overthrow of Blum's government the following year and who rejected Blum's attempts to form a national government in 1938. Someone else should make the effort, he explained to Blum: "Unlike Jaurès ... you don't have enough French soil on the sole of your shoes."

The fact that the prime ministerial office under Blum contained rather more Jews than was usual for a French government of the day drove his opponents to the edge of paranoia. Soon you won't even be able to get into Matignon (the office of the prime minister), wrote *Le Charivari* on July 11, 1936, without being frisked by Blum's cops and only after demonstrating, member in hand, that you are one of the tribe that governs France. "We are living today under the sign of M. Léon Blum, the sign of the pruning shears." The thirty-two [sic!] Jewish cabinet ministers have been "sacrés, consacrés, circonsacrés." The untranslatable quality of the pun does not make it any the less salacious.

Maurice Bedel, writing in the respectable and widely read periodical *Candide* the following year, described Blum thus: "The prime minister, coming from a wandering race, dumped in the Ile-de-France by a chance that might as easily have deposited him in New York, Cairo, or Vilna, feels put out at being the leader of a people foreign to his flesh." And Pierre

Gaxotte, who would later join Charles Maurras in the august halls of the Académie Française, reflected in April 1938 on Blum's premiership in the following terms, which can stand for many similar articles from less renowned pens: "To begin with, he is ugly. On the body of a disjointed puppet there sits the sad head of a Palestinian mare. . . . How he hates us! He resents us for everything: for our blue sky and our soft air, for our peasants who walk in clogs across French soil and whose ancestors were not camel dealers, wandering in the Syrian desert with his Palestinian friends. Socialism rules us like those nomads who once seized the southern oases of Algeria, ruined the settlers, and then, gorged, moved on to further pillaging. Between France and this cursed man, we must choose. He is the very incarnation of everything that sickens our flesh and our blood. He is evil. He is death."

The idea that Léon Blum was "Asiatic," as Marcel Jouhandeau put it in *Le Péril juif*, published in 1936, was extraordinarily widespread. More precisely, it was widely asserted, and believed, that, in the words of *Les Nouvelles économiques et financières* in October 1937, "our ex–prime minister (and still minister) is called Karfunkelstein; . . . Léon Karfunkelstein, known as 'Blum,' was born in Vidine [Bulgaria], in 1872 and came to Paris in 1874 with his parents." According to Pierre Birnbaum the myth was strong enough to reach across the war years and into the 1960 edition of the *Petit Larousse illustré*, where readers were informed that "Blum" was a pseudonym for . . . Karfunkelstein.

To this charge, and to this charge alone, Blum felt constrained to reply. In an article in *Le Populaire* headed "I Am French" he reminded readers that all four of his grandparents were French, born in Alsace. "Ever since French Jews have possessed full civil status my paternal ancestors have carried the name that I carry today." Otherwise, he kept his feelings to himself. As he advised Jules Moch, facing slanderous accusations of his own, "Do not lower yourself to reply. I have been calumnied, insulted, attacked. . . . Let it go. You are above all that." But Blum cannot have been utterly impervious to the almost daily assaults on his name, his appearance, his personal habits, his tastes, and his race. When his interior minister, Roger Salengro, became the object of a cruel and unjust campaign based on the charge that he had deserted in World War I, Blum defended him in the Chambre. You'll get used to it, he told Salengro. But however much you ignore calumnies of this sort, however much you pretend they don't get to you, "a man's heart can be eaten away by such abuse."[68] Salengro never did "get used to it," and he committed suicide a week later. Blum was made of sterner stuff. He survived not only hundreds of verbal attacks but also a violent physical assault on February 13, 1936, by followers of Maurras who came across him on the Boulevard St. Germain as his car was held up by the funeral procession for Jacques Bainville, a right-wing historian and prominent figure in the Action française movement. Blum was seriously beaten and did not return to active politics for many weeks. In view of the vicious treatment to which he had been exposed, in press and parliament alike, for the best part of two decades it is only surprising that he had not been assaulted before.

But then the Third Republic, for all the overheated and deeply divided condition of public life (and the utter absence of any restrictions upon a venal press), was a state operating under the rule of law. Blum could be pilloried, slandered, libeled, insulted, abused, berated, and vilified, but he could not be killed or hurt with impunity, and he could not be forced to withdraw from politics. All that changed in July 1940. There are many accounts of the atmosphere in Vichy as Pierre Laval orchestrated the vote to overthrow the republican constitution and hand full powers to Pétain, but Blum's own notes provide one of the best short descriptions.

> Laval had offered people embassies and prefectures like so many [ancien régime] commissaires généraux and provincial governorships. At first, no doubt, he won over just a small number of accomplices. But as each one was ensnared, he became an ensnarer in his turn; as each became infected, so he became a source of infection for others. The corrosive suggestions were passed from ear to ear, and in the end the chains linked up, the snowballs gathering force beneath our eyes.... History has doubtless seen more awful spectacles, but I doubt whether it has witnessed anything more vile.[69]

Blum knew better than to try and intervene. As he recognized and his friends insisted, he stood for everything that Laval and his followers hated

68. Le Populaire, November 19, 1938; Moch, Une Si Longue Vie, p. 69; Lacouture, Léon Blum, p. 411.
69. Blum, "Mémoires," in particular pp. 84–101.

most, and over which they sought dominion and revenge. Blum's participation in the dying struggles of the Third Republic would be worse than useless. "To feel that you are not just a burden, a useless ballast, but also a factor that, thrown into the balance, would work to your adversaries' advantage; to know that your very presence and your words discredit the cause you most passionately wish to serve; these are cruel impressions, and they are starting to preoccupy me."

Looking back later in 1940, and imagining what his friends would say to him if he had tried to offer an optimistic perspective or speak out against the inexorable collapse, Blum described the situation in these prescient terms: "There is now just one ruler in France and that is Hitler. French governments are condemned to outdo one another in obedience and compliance. One day that will change, and the change will come from deep within the people, but until then that is how it is. Like it or not, the so-called French governments will seek to install in France the principles and methods of Nazism. They will have their Gestapo and their storm troopers; they will go from individual executions to collective persecution; they will hunt down socialists and they will humiliate the Jews; and you are at the same time a socialist, a Jew, and yourself into the bargain."[70]

At great personal risk, Blum went to Vichy and took part in the historic vote, joining just seventy-nine other members of the legislative body elected in January 1936 who now refused full powers to Pétain. Not long after that he was arrested and imprisoned. In retrospect it is remarkable that he survived the war at all. Other Third Republican politicians, Jewish or left-wing, were not so fortunate. Two former Popular Front ministers, Jean Zay and Marx Dormoy (who had succeeded Salengro as interior minister and was a target of far-right revenge for his success in averting a planned coup in 1938), were assassinated; Georges Mandel, who shared Blum's prison quarters at Buchenwald, was returned to France in June 1944 and executed in retaliation for the killing by the Resistance of Philippe Henriot. If Blum survived prison, concentration camp, and the last-ditch SS attempt to retreat into the Alps, it was partly because of his very prominence, his potential as a hostage, and partly through sheer courage and good fortune.

Although in the last years of his life, from 1945 to 1950, Blum was not subject to public attacks from the Right, he remained a controversial figure.

70. Blum, "Mémoires," pp. 55, 61.

Anti-Semitism was no longer respectable, and there were now laws regulating the behavior of the press, but, as one 1946 opinion poll revealed, 43 percent of those asked did not believe that a Frenchman of Jewish origin was an "authentic" Frenchman. Times had not changed so very much. As Blum explained to de Gaulle in January 1946, when the general tried to convince him to take over as prime minister, "I am old, I am sick, and I have been the most hated man in France . . . no." And although he agreed to serve for one month in December 1946 as head of a transitional government, Blum again resisted taking office when pressed to do so by President Auriol in November 1947.[71]

But this time he gave a slightly different explanation. I cannot form a government, he explained to Auriol. I am the man the Communists hate most of all. It was true. The French Communists never forgave Blum his achievement at Tours in December 1920 and afterward. Like their populist opponents on the far right, they, too, despised Blum for his intellectual airs, as well as his public visibility, his Socialist politics and in certain cases, though they could not openly say so, for his Jewishness. The rhetoric of Communist vilification of Blum echoes that of the anti-Semitic Right to a remarkable degree.

In 1928, at the time of a Parisian electoral campaign during which the PCF worked successfully to unseat Blum, the Communist newspaper *L'Humanité* described him as "possessed by Freudian wriggling. . . . Shylock Blum rubs his hands together gleefully." A prominent Communist journalist, Paul Vaillant-Couturier, accused Blum of displaying all the nervous symptoms of "intellectual degeneration." According to Pierre Birnbaum the Communists at this time, again like the Right, had a fondness for describing and portraying Blum as a woman of easy virtue, "a great flirt," "an old serving-girl of the bourgeoisie, an old *séductrice* of Radicals." In 1931, at the height of the so-called Third Period of Communist sectarianism, the poet Louis Aragon published his famous poem "Feu sur Léon Blum," an anticipatory echo of Maurras's demand for a bullet in his back.[72]

The rhetoric was scaled down during the Popular Front era, only to pick up with a fury after the signing of the Molotov-Ribbentrop Pact. In

71. For de Gaulle's request and Blum's reply, see Lacouture, *Léon Blum*, p. 525; for the 1946 IFOP poll, see Michael Marrus, "Are the French Antisemitic? Evidence in the 1980s," in Malino and Wasserstein, *Jews in Modern France*, pp. 224–42.

72. See *L'Humanité*, February 14, December 8, 1928; Birnbaum, *Un Mythe politique*, p. 214.

early 1940 the leader of the PCF, Maurice Thorez, published a pamphlet titled "Blum (as He Really Is)," in which the erstwhile comrade of the Popular Front years was described thus: "Blum has Millerand's aversion for socialism, Pilsudski's cruelty, Mussolini's ferocity, the cowardice of blood-soaked men like Noske, and Trotsky's hate for the Soviet Union." Thorez railed against Blum's "obsession with elegance, his language, his affected style . . . his unbearable and indecent public self-analysis . . . his bitter casuistry" and his "love of playing with ideas." Blum, Thorez concluded, is a "jackal . . . stinkingly hypocritical . . . given to repugnantly serpentine twisting and hissing."[73]

It is not surprising, then, that official representatives of the Communist Party should have sought permission in December 1940 to testify *against* Blum at the forthcoming Riom trial. Fortunately for the party's postwar reputation the offer was turned down, and official PCF historians long denied that it was ever made. But no one in the PCF ever pretended to like Blum. After the onset of the Cold War in 1947 he once again became an object of concentrated vilification. At the founding meeting of the Cominform, in September 1947, Jacques Duclos—seeking to convince his skeptical East European and Soviet comrades of the PCF's revolutionary bona fides—could come up with no better proof than his party's consistent attacks on the Socialist leader: "The Communist Party of France has never spared Blum. We have always attacked him."[74] For once Duclos was telling the unvarnished truth.

The Communists were not alone on the left in vilifying Blum, of course. Paul Faure, the SFIO's own general secretary from 1920 to 1940 and one of Blum's closest party colleagues for a quarter of a century, could not wait to be relieved, by the armistice of 1940, of the burden of their relationship to express the view, shared with many Munichois Socialists, that "Blum would have got us all killed for his Jews."[75] Doubtless many of Blum's past comrades had long felt similarly. But unlike his critics in the SFIO, the French Communists had no need to camouflage their distaste.

73. See Maurice Thorez, "Léon Blum tel qu'il est," *Oeuvres*, vol. 5, book 8, cited *in extenso* in Kriegel, "Un Phénomène de haine fratricide."

74. Jacques Duclos at Session 8 of the first meeting of the Cominform in Sklarska Poreba, Poland, September 26, 1947, in *The Cominform: Minutes of the Three Conferences, 1947/48/49* (Milan: Annali Feltrinelli, 1994), p. 271.

75. Faure is quoted in Hector Ghilini, *A la barre de Riom* (Paris: Jean-Renard, 1942), p. 125. See Birnbaum, *Un Mythe politique*, p. 291.

Between his opponents on the Right, his *frères-ennemis* on the left, and his own party comrades, Léon Blum was a solitary and courageous man indeed.

Blum's life and his public career are a mirror held up to his country, reflecting much that was best and worst in twentieth-century France. He stood firmly for the French ideal of a universal, egalitarian, civic-minded Republic. Blum truly believed what he wrote in "A l'échelle humaine": "It is with pride that I record that the harmony of patriotism and humanism comes more easily and naturally to a Frenchman than to any other citizen of the world, because the special temperament of France . . . has always understood and included the noble requirement to think and act for universal goals." He would have been particularly pleased to learn, as the Austrian refugee Manès Sperber wrote in his memoirs, that "neither before nor afterwards did political emigrants in France feel as much at home as they did during the first months of the victorious Popular Front."[76]

It was this inexhaustible faith in the universal qualities and obligations of France that made Blum a socialist, too; no Frenchman, he thought, could be faithful to his republican heritage without seeking to extend it further. It is true that he contributed his share to the partisan myopia of the French Socialist movement, and thus to the downfall first of the Third Republic and later of his own party. But in this, too, he was representative of his age; for most of this century France was divided by the rhetoric of ideological and historical difference. As Blum would recognize in retrospect, he might have done more to rise above this crippling inheritance; but there were real as well as doctrinal grounds for the great gulf separating the heirs of the Revolution from their opponents, and Blum could hardly ignore these. Indeed, given his social conscience and his driving sense of moral responsibility, his own political choices were perhaps unavoidable.

Léon Blum's failure to bring French socialism to its senses is part of a larger story, the longstanding inability of French social democrats to embrace their condition and their time. It was Blum's personal tragedy to understand this even as he chose to set that understanding aside in the name of fidelity and party duty. For he certainly *did* grasp things that others

76. "A l'échelle humaine," in particular p. 484; Manès Sperber, *Until My Eyes Are Closed with Shards* (New York: Holmes and Meier, 1994), p. 103.

missed: the dangerous inertia of the republican parliamentary tradition; the need to modernize government and administration in a country still run along early-nineteenth-century principles; the urgency, after 1945, of reconstructing the shattered continent on international, cooperative principles.

Above all, perhaps, and in contrast not only to his fellow Socialists but also to most other French patriots of his generation, Blum saw his country and its weaknesses without illusion. An early supporter of feminism, Blum was disturbed at the cynical opposition of Left and Right alike to the case for female suffrage. Once, he wrote in 1927, we were a model to other lands, the home of courage and of free thinking. Today we oscillate between the timorous conventions of false bourgeois morality and a mean, low mood of dismissive mockery. Twenty-three years later, in the very last article he wrote, a few days before his death, he was as forthright as ever. Despite his abiding faith in socialism and his deep wish to see France "neither Americanized nor sovietized," as he had put it in 1947, Blum could not help but warn his fellow Frenchmen once again of their chronic failings: "Whereas the law of American capitalism is 'let new businesses be born,' the law of French capitalism would seem to be 'let old businesses never die.'"[77]

For a man of the French Left those were curious sentiments (as indeed they would be today), un-French and unsocialist. They reveal just how much Léon Blum stood at a tangent to his own community. He was always willing, as we have seen, to "stand up and be counted." But mostly he simply stood up, alone. If Annie Kriegel is to be believed, this is what made him the natural leader of his party—the very fact that he came from outside the traditional avenues of promotion and competition and stood apart. Blum may not have sought this distinction—as we have seen, he strove mightily to be at one with the Socialist movement and preferred (as Gide had predicted) to repress his moral and even his political instincts where these appeared to conflict with his party duty. And he recognized that of the many Blums within him—the intellectual, the aesthete, the modernizing reformer, the romantic utopian, the Jew—some would have to suffer that others might thrive. As he warned in *Du mariage*, "Life does not lend

77. See *Le Populaire*, December 24, 1927; speech at Vélodrome d'Hiver, October 16, 1947, in *Oeuvres*, 6, pt. 2:103; *Le Populaire*, March 29, 1950.

itself to the simultaneous retention of all possible benefits, and I have often thought that morality consists uniquely perhaps in having the courage to choose."[78]

Perhaps Blum's hate-filled critics were in one sense right. This classically French moralist—a man of nineteenth-century commitments and habits who confronted the modern age with a moral measure that drew heavily on the moderate disinterest of a Montesquieu—saw his country with such unblinking honesty and impressed so many who met him with that honesty above all, because he was never completely at one with it. If he was no "rootless cosmopolitan," he was nonetheless always a wanderer between the different French identities that he shared at various moments. He was a fin de siècle intellectual, one of the leading critics of his age, who could not help preferring politics to literary criticism. He was a lawyer who thought that the point was to change the laws, not just understand them. He was a Socialist in an aggressively materialist Socialist movement who nonetheless thought instinctively and always in moral categories. He was a wartime resister who refused the easy anger and revenge of many other resisters (real or imagined) once the time came for retribution. He was a firm defender and spokesman of France and the Republic in all their historical and traditional glory who nonetheless wrote uncomfortably "counter-cultural" articles advocating change and modernization. And he was an assimilated French Jew on whom was brought to bear the intense beam of a deep nationalist antipathy and who insisted to the end that he was French *and* Jewish in spite of it.

Blum was not actively interested in such issues. His attitude to discussions of "Frenchness" were well summed up in his early, critical dismissal of Maurice Barrès's *Au service de l'Allemagne:* "When I see him propose that between the Frenchman and the 'German' there is a fundamental difference of kind, of nature, of essence, when I hear him speak of 'Germans' as an explorer returning from central Asia might speak of the foreign civilizations—or rather barbarisms—that he had encountered, I don't have the stomach to counter him with names, examples, or arguments. To object, to make the effort to refute, would be to admit the legitimacy, the very possi-

---

78. See Annie Kriegel, *Ce que j'ai cru comprendre* (Paris: Laffont, 1991), p. 690. Of Blum's relationship to the SFIO after his return from captivity and his efforts to change and modernize it, Kriegel writes: "Admired, respected, venerated, Blum was listened to—religiously. But he was not heard" (p. 342). For *Du mariage,* see *Oeuvres,* 2:21.

bility of a discussion that one can only dismiss in advance."[79] For Blum his own, or anyone else's, national identity—their "Frenchness," for example—was a given, not a matter for investigation or interrogation.

Nonetheless, in some way that Blum himself never directly conceded, he *was* an outsider; not just in the sense that de Gaulle was an outsider, or Churchill, taking control of their countries by force of will and able to do so just *because* they lacked conventional political standing, but a man who was never quite French in the sense that his contemporaries insisted on defining Frenchness. Blum could not say this of himself—perhaps because of the implications for his understanding of the precise meaning of "Jewishness" in republican France—but he had "Goethe" say it for him in the "Nouvelles Conversations de Goethe avec Eckermann," in November 1897: "I am unacquainted with that familial piety which binds so many men to a house or a plot of land; it is a source of weakness for all of humankind, the greatest obstacle to the changes that are required in the human condition." Blum would have said that this urbane perspective, the view from nowhere, was what made him a good socialist and no doubt he was right. His enemies would have seen in it proof of his fundamental difference—and they, too, were right. But it is also and above all what elevated him beyond the limited and limiting world of his contemporaries and made him a great Frenchman.

79. *Oeuvres*, 1:79.

The Reluctant Moralist

ALBERT CAMUS AND THE
DISCOMFORTS OF AMBIVALENCE

In a letter to her husband, dated May 1952 and reporting on her visit to Paris, Hannah Arendt wrote: "Yesterday I saw Camus: he is, undoubtedly, the best man now in France. He is head and shoulders above the other intellectuals."[1] In the light of their shared interests, Arendt of course had reasons of her own for believing this; but for her as for many other observers, French and foreign, Albert Camus was *the* French intellectual. In the immediate postwar years he had exerted great influence across a broad swathe of Parisian opinion, receiving thousands of letters weekly in response to his newspaper columns. His style, his concerns, his wide audience and apparent omnipresence in Parisian public life seemed to embody whatever was most characteristically French about the intersection of literature, thought, and political engagement.

But Arendt's assessment clashed uncomfortably with fashionable French opinion. In the very year that she was writing Camus's star was beginning to fade. By his death, in a car accident on January 4, 1960, his reputation was already in steep decline, despite the Nobel Prize for literature, awarded him just three years before. At the time of the award critics fell over one another to bury its recipient: from the right Jacques Laurent announced that in awarding the prize to Camus "the Nobel committee has crowned a finished oeuvre" while in the left-leaning *France-Observateur* it was suggested that the Swedish Academy may have believed it was picking out a young writer (Camus was forty-six when he died), but it had in fact confirmed a "premature sclerosis." Camus's best years, it was widely believed, lay far behind him; it had been many years since he had published something of real note.

---

1. Arendt quoted in Jeffrey C. Isaac, *Arendt, Camus, and Modern Rebellion* (New Haven: Yale University Press, 1992), p. 17.

For this decline in critical esteem, Camus himself was at least partly to blame. Responding to the fashions of the day, he had engaged in philosophical speculations of a kind to which he was ill suited and for which he was only moderately gifted—*Le Mythe de Sisyphe* (1942) has not worn well, for all its resonating aphorisms. In *L'Homme révolté* (1951), as we shall see, Camus offered some important observations about the dangers of lyrical revolutionary illusions; but Raymond Aron said much the same thing to vastly more devastating effect in *L'Opium des intellectuels*, while Camus's philosophical naïveté exposed him to a cruel and painful riposte from Sartre that severely damaged his credibility on the intellectual left and permanently undermined his public confidence.

If his literary reputation, as the author of *L'Etranger* (1942) and *La Peste* (1947), was thus unfairly tarnished by Camus's forays into philosophical debate, it was his role as France's leading public intellectual, the moral voice of his era, that weighed most heavily upon Camus in his last decade. His essays in the postwar paper *Combat* had given him, in Raymond Aron's words, a singular prestige; it was Camus whose conclusions set the moral tone of the Resistance generation as it faced the dilemmas and disappointments of the Fourth Republic and whose many readers had "formed the habit of getting their daily thought from him." By the late fifties this burden would become intolerable, and the sense of being at odds with his public alter ego had become a source of constant discomfort in Camus's writing and speeches.[2]

Long before then, in June 1947, he handed over to Claude Bourdet control of the newspaper *Combat*, which he had edited since the Liberation. As his notebooks and essays suggest, he was already exhausted, at the age of thirty-four, from carrying the burden of expectations placed upon him—"Everyone wants the man who is still searching to have already reached his conclusions." But whereas in the earlier years he had accepted the responsibility—"One must submit," as he put it in 1950—by the time of his last interview, in December 1959, his resentment is audible: "I speak for no one: I have enough difficulty speaking for myself. I don't know, or I know only dimly, where I am headed."[3]

2. See Raymond Aron, *Mémoires* (Paris: Julliard, 1983), p. 208; Paul Villaneix, *Le Premier Camus* (Paris: Gallimard, 1973), pp. 10–11.
3. See "L'Enigme" (1950), in Albert Camus, *Essais*, ed. Roger Quilliot (Paris: Gallimard, 1965), pp. 859–67; "Dernière Interview d'Albert Camus," December 20, 1959, *Essais*, p. 1925.

In the years following his death, Camus's standing continued to fall. Most people living in metropolitan France no longer shared his concern for Algeria and its communities. As for the intellectuals, their interests in the sixties and seventies were so far from those that had moved Camus as to make him an object of scorn, condescension, and, finally, neglect. He was overtaken by the radical and increasingly intolerant politicization of a younger generation, by the self-lacerating *tiers-mondisme* of the later Sartre and his followers, by the "antihumanist" vogue among scholars, by new fashions in literature, and most of all by the decline in the status of the writer. Looking back on his own time in the sixties as founder-editor of the *Nouvel observateur*, Jean Daniel would recall "quickly discovering that it was among the human sciences—history, sociology, ethnology, philosophy—that one had to look for the equivalent of the *littérateurs* who, in my youth, had served as *maîtres à penser*."[4] In the world of Barthes, Robbe-Grillet, Lévi-Strauss, and Foucault, Camus was *dépassé*.

Not that he was unread: *L'Etranger*, *La Peste*, and *Caligula* were established texts of the lycée and university curricula, as they were (and are) on the reading lists of millions of students abroad. Albert Camus had become, in his own lifetime or very shortly thereafter, a worldwide "classic." But this, too, was held against him. By the time of Hannah Arendt's own death, in the mid-1970s, Albert Camus was so far outside the circle of concerns and styles that now shaped Parisian culture as to seem almost a foreigner. Even today, as his reputation is slowly and partially recovering, he seems somehow unrelated to the world of his intellectual contemporaries. There is something untimely, even un-French about Camus. Given the ease with which he seemed to speak for and to incarnate the France of the post-Resistance era, this seems curious. How could it be?

Camus's rapid rise to prominence, during and after the Occupation, was partly the consequence of his Resistance work as a clandestine journalist, which laid the path for his postwar access to the press and the influence of his editorials in *Combat*. But it was also the product of his literary success: *L'Etranger* and *Le Mythe de Sisyphe*, both published in 1942, established Camus indelibly as an "existentialist"; with Sartre and Simone de Beauvoir, he formed part of the informal club of "engaged" philosophical writers who dominated cultural and political fashions in the postwar era. Whatever the label meant for Sartre, Camus always thought it was a mis-

4. Jean Daniel, *L'Ere des ruptures* (Paris: Grasset, 1979), pp. 29–30.

take in his own case. As he observed in February 1952, "I am not a philosopher and I never claimed to be one."[5]

This is slightly disingenuous. Certainly, Camus lacked formal philosophical training—Raymond Aron would later find his philosophical forays in L'Homme révolté "puerile." But "existentialism" in the forties was both more and less than a philosophy, and in its French variant certainly bore only an exiguous relationship to the German writings of Husserl and Heidegger on which it ostensibly drew. What made Camus an "existentialist" for his contemporaries were the tone of his most famous novel and the argument, or at least the aphorisms, of his essay on the myth of Sisyphus. Meurseault, the protagonist of L'Etranger, lived out what its author chose to present as the "absurdity" of the human condition: the absurd, Camus claimed, was born of "this confrontation between human need and the unreasonable silence of the world."[6]

Today, with the publication of Camus's various carnets and, recently, his last novel, Le Premier Homme, we have a better grasp of what he meant to achieve with the notion of the absurd. He was investing the word with many of his own very concrete and deeply personal experiences—in particular, his difficult relationship with his mother, an illiterate and almost silent presence/absence during his impoverished childhood in Algiers—and was above all trying to express the importance that feelings of place and physical sensation held for him, in contrast with the apparent void of the spiritual world.

Thus there is a passage in Sisyphe where Camus writes thus: "In a universe suddenly divested of illusions and lights, man feels an alien, a stranger. His exile is without remedy, since he is deprived of the memory of a lost home or the hope of a promised land. This divorce between a man and his life, the actor and his setting, is properly the feeling of absurdity." Just as Camus is known to have felt that commentators missed the point of the Algerian settings in La Peste and L'Etranger, so critics and admirers alike often both overinterpreted and lost the message of his nonliterary writings. His readers in the forties, however, took at face value the airy assertions in Sisyphe: Man is "the only creature who refuses to be what he

5. "Entretien sur la révolte," Gazette des lettres, February 15, 1952, rpt. in Camus, Actuelles II (Paris: Gallimard, 1953), pp. 51–68.
6. The Myth of Sisyphus, trans. Justin O'Brien (New York: Vintage, 1991), p. 28; originally published as Le Mythe de Sisyphe (Paris: Gallimard, 1942).

is," who both "assumes" his condition and seeks to overcome it; the "existential revolution" is hope springing up in a world without issue, and so on. Camus, hoist on the petard of these and other nebulous reflections on the human dilemma, "submitted" reluctantly to Paris and lived out the second half of the forties as a public representative of the existential, "absurd" vision of the modern condition. But he never pretended to know what it meant to be an existentialist; indeed, to the extent that the term implied any particular position in metaphysical or political debates Camus was a recusant from the start—"I have little taste for the all-too-celebrated existential philosophy, and to tell the truth I believe its conclusions to be false; but they do at least represent a great intellectual adventure [une grande aventure de la pensée]."[7]

In effect, Camus the writer had been forced to follow an important shift in French intellectual taste: the central place occupied by literature and men of letters in Parisian cultural life for much of the previous century was replaced from the end of the 1930s by the vogue for public philosophizing. Long before he came to Paris, while he was still reviewing for a newspaper in his native Algiers, Camus was already uneasy at the new fashion. His comments on Sartre's Nausée, written in 1938—many years before the two met—are illustrative in this regard: "The mistake of a certain sort of writing is to believe that because life is wretched that it is tragic. . . . To announce the absurdity of existence cannot be an objective, merely a starting point."[8]

The paradox of Sartrean "existentialism," for Camus at least, lay in its emphasis upon political engagement. If there are no external duties or reasons driving us to make choices, if our freedom is untrammeled except by our own decisions, why then take up one public position rather than another? Starting from the Sartrean perspective, the condition of the engaged intellectual is at best contradictory, at worst self-indulgent. Camus reached this skeptical conclusion about his former friend's outlook after the break occasioned by the publication of L'Homme révolté in 1951 and the response

7. "L'Enigme," p. 158; Camus article in Combat, September 8, 1945. Olivier Todd, his biographer, judiciously remarks that Camus was trying to say almost too much with the notion of the "absurd": "He employs it variously in the sense of contradictory, false, unreasonable. His reasoning seems hasty, loose, overemphatic. Unsuccessfully seeking a degree of clarity, he reflects the unease of the mid-century years." Olivier Todd, Albert Camus. Une vie (Paris: Gallimard, 1996), p. 297.

8. Camus in Alger républicain, October 20, 1938.

to it in Sartre's *Temps modernes;* but the grounds of his own distaste for public political stances can be found earlier and are rather different.

Camus always described himself as a "writer" and spoke in the third person of his dilemmas as those of "the artist." From the early postwar years, at the height of his public visibility and influence, through the late fifties, when the Algerian tragedy reduced him to silence, his published and unpublished writings are shot through with reflections on the pressures upon the artist to perform a public role, to be someone other than himself. Sometimes he spoke through his characters—Rieux in *La Peste* (1947) announces that he lacks the taste for heroism or holiness and wants simply to be a man. Sometimes he made ringing declarations of public involvement that seem to suggest a simultaneous wish to retreat: in a December 1948 speech at the Salle Pleyel, to an audience of intellectuals in the ephemeral Rassemblement Democratique Revolutionnaire, Camus asserted, "In the face of contemporary political society, the only coherent attitude of the artist . . . is refusal without concession."⁹ Mostly, at least until 1951, he confined such thoughts to his notebooks, recording his wish to retreat from the world, to overcome the "psychological debacle" of his public involvement.

By the fifties, however, the tension was explicit. Calling for a truce in the Algerian war, in January 1956, he wrote, "I am not a political man, my passions and my tastes call me to places other than public tribunes. I go there only from the pressure of circumstances and the idea I sometimes have of myself as a writer."¹⁰ Much of the animosity toward him at this time, and in the decades after his death, derived from this refusal to concede that the proper and necessary place for the artist-intellectual was in the street. From well before the Algerian war the Communists in particular held against Camus not so much his anti-Stalinism as his growing refusal to share political "positions" or get into public arguments (as recently as 1979 the Communist daily *L'Humanité* described him as an irresponsible *endormeur*).

For Camus, the condition of French writers from an earlier generation was thus enviable—he admired Roger Martin du Gard in particular for his

---

9. Quoted by Herbert Lottman in *Albert Camus: A Biography* (New York: Doubleday, 1979), p. 456.

10. See "Appel pour une trève civile en Algérie," speech delivered in Algiers, January 22, 1956, rpt. in *Actuelles III: Chroniques algériennes 1939–1958* (Paris: Gallimard, 1958), p. 170.

success in "merging" with his own work, while he, Camus, had been too *externally* visible and had duly paid the price in both his work and his peace of mind. In a lecture delivered at Uppsala in Sweden, in December 1957, he exhibited this concern to the point of obsession, provoked by the criticisms of his failure to take up a position over Algeria and more generally for his long retreat from political engagement since the publication of *L'Homme révolté:* "In 1957 Racine would be apologizing for having written *Bérenice* instead of fighting for the defense of the Edict of Nantes." Two months earlier he had given an interview to *Demain* in which he made the same point—writers cannot ignore their times, but they must also keep, or take back, some distance if they are to remain true to themselves.[11]

To his contemporaries, Camus seemed thus to have evolved from the engaged intellectual of the Resistance, through the *maître penseur* of the postwar years, into the disabused and increasingly frustrated artist of the later fifties. From his own point of view there had been no evolution, simply a gradually increasing tension between his private needs and his public image, a pressure that boiled over on the sensitive issue of Algeria where his personal and political sentiments could no longer be kept apart. But if there was a moment at which Camus's relationship to his world shifted definitively, when he went from being an insider to an outsider, so to speak, it came with the publication, in 1951, of *L'Homme révolté.* In this extended essay on the idea of man in revolt, embodying a direct attack on the revolutionary myths that sustained contemporary radical thought, Camus not only broke publicly with the mainstream French political Left with which he had remained associated hitherto; he revealed aspects of his outlook that placed him still further outside the conventional intellectual community of discourse of which he had until recently been a prominent representative.

François Mauriac once described Camus as having an *anima naturaliter religiosa,* and in the course of their public disagreement in 1945 over retribution for wartime collaborators he wrote of "the traces of suppressed Christianity in the young masters of *Combat.*" However polemical and ironic, the characterization is to the point, and it would be picked up by Czeslaw Milosz in

11. "L'Artiste et son temps," rpt. in Camus, *Discours de Suède* (Paris: Gallimard, 1958), p. 29; Todd, *Albert Camus,* 761.

his obituary essay on Camus in 1960, where he wonders whether *all* Camus's work, and not just his academic thesis on St. Augustine, wasn't marked by a suppressed theological bent.[12] Contemporary French critics of *L'Homme révolté*, notably Francis Jeanson in his review in *Les Temps modernes*, and Sartre in his subsequent open letter to Camus in the same journal, naturally attacked the book's moralizing condemnation of revolutionary violence; but they missed, in their emphasis upon the work's philosophical shortcomings, its distinctively religious core, so out of keeping with the mood of its time.

In *L'Homme révolté*, Camus attacked the "historicism" of his contemporaries—their invocation of "History" to justify their own public commitments and their indifference to the human costs of radical political choices. But in contrast with other critics of contemporary Marxism, he chose to treat this as the consequence of a "divinization" of history, the tragedy of a desacralized society that has made itself an ersatz of religion and thus an object of its own adoration. This was no casual thought for Camus; he developed it further in his 1957 essay on the guillotine, and it is clearly the underlying source of the essays on justice and political moderation published between 1946 and 1951 (*L'Homme révolté* itself had been some six years in the making). Today the argument is commonplace, and "Hegelian" critiques of the damage done by Hegel and his heirs to European political thought have been much in fashion in France in recent years. But in 1951 this was a radical and quite daring departure from the local norm.

Camus's essay had the special virtue of highlighting the distinctively *religious* form taken by radical politics in the century since 1848, and the manner in which "revolution" had consequently been assigned the historical task of putting an end to sin, at least in the social form in which contemporaries were willing to acknowledge it. Hence his account of his bitterest critics among Sartrean fellow travelers as the "Savonarolas" of *Les Temps modernes*—"they admit sin but refuse grace,"[13] a description repeated in *La Chute*. From this insight, Camus proceeded to build a remarkably prescient critique of what François Furet would describe two decades later as the revolutionary "catechism."

Anticipating the historiography of a later era, and in ignorance of the

12. See Czeslaw Milosz, "L'Interlocuteur fraternel," in *Preuves*, January 1960, p. 16.
13. Camus, *Carnets III* (Paris: Gallimard, 1989), p. 62: "Temps modernes. Ils admettent le péché et refusent la grâce. Soif du martyre." Entry for some time in 1952.

writings of contemporaries like Arendt or Jacob Talmon, Camus reversed the conventional intellectual defense of revolutionary terror then in vogue: it is not the Soviet Union's ambitions and actions that are rendered explicable and defensible by analogy with the achievements of the Jacobins; rather, it is the French Revolution, and the very notion of revolution itself, that is called into question by what we now know of the costs of terror and violence, and by the way in which latter-day revolutionaries invoke their French forebears in their own support and defense.

Camus went further: if Rousseau, Hegel, and Marx have forged a world in which the Terror and its successor terrors can be justified, then it is they who must answer for it—we cannot defend the history of the past centuries by reference to the claims such thinkers have made about the process of which it is but a part. The application of ethical criteria to regicide, terror, torture disqualifies the regimes and theories that depend upon these means, whatever story they tell of themselves and whatever Heavenly City they promise in the earthly hereafter. The moral measure that we bring to bear in condemning the death penalty or the violence of Fascist regimes is indivisible and has the same disqualifying effect upon the actions and regimes of the revolution and its children, however "progressive."

As he wrote in an open letter to Emmanuel d'Astier de la Vigerie in 1948, "I merely say that we must refuse all legitimacy to violence, whether it comes from raison d'état or totalitarian philosophy. *Violence is both unavoidable and unjustifiable.*" Camus was to develop this theme in his letter to *Temps modernes* following Francis Jeanson's review of *L'Homme révolté*. How can you justify violence, he wrote, or deny the application of universal criteria of justice and truth, if, as "existentialists," you don't believe in the certitude (or even, in principle, the likelihood) that History will come to your service and retrospectively justify past crimes?[14]

The crux of Camus's thought on this subject, and its main weakness, comes in that last sentence. Like Maurice Merleau-Ponty, in *Humanisme et terreur*, Camus recognized the inevitability of terror. But he refused to justify it. This left him exposed to the merciless logic of Sartre, who accused him of indulging and displaying his moral sensibilities while leaving the world to its own resources. *L'Homme révolté* itself has other weaknesses besides. It romanticizes "rebellion" in order to contrast it with "revolution,"

14. *Actuelles II*, p. 184; "Révolte et servitude," letter to the director of *Les Temps modernes*, June 30, 1952, rpt. in *Actuelles II*, pp. 85–124.

thus revealing a sentimental anarchism to which Camus was occasionally disposed; and its effort to bring together artistic, philosophical, and political "revolt" into a single story is a messy failure—"here," in the words of his French biographer, "he is very French." But none of this weakens the central force of Camus's insight—that the problem of totalitarian violence was *the* moral and political dilemma of our age, and that the USSR and its satellites were not only admired by *philosophes*, they were governed by them—the heirs and fulfillment *ad absurdum* of the Western philosophical dream.[15]

Camus had good reason to emphasize the dangerous sympathy for revolutionary violence that marked many of his intellectual contemporaries. Had he lived long enough to read Jean-Paul Sartre's (1961) preface to Frantz Fanon's *Les Damnés de la terre* he would have learned that "[t]o shoot down a European is to kill two birds with one stone, to destroy an oppressor and the man he oppresses at the same time; there remain a dead man and a free man; the survivor, for the first time, feels a *national* soil under his foot." As it was, *L'Homme révolté* and Camus's disdain for its critics brought down on his head the full wrath of Sartre in particular. Sartre's public condemnation of the book—and his patronizing dismissal of its author's limited abilities—wounded Camus deeply ("I am certainly paying a high price for this book. Today I am completely unsure about it—and about myself; we are all too much alike")[16] and undoubtedly accelerated his retreat from political writing and from public life. But its virtues and defects are a faithful mirror of the author, and Albert Camus surely meant it when he later assured Roger Grenier that of all his books, *L'Homme révolté* was the one he held most dear.

Camus once described *L'Homme révolté* as his "autobiography"; but much the same was of course true in one sense or another of *Le Premier Homme*, *La Chute*, and most of his other writings, fiction and nonfiction alike. At odds with his professional environment, he wrote in constant search of his

15. See "Entretien sur la révolte," pp. 51–64. According to Olivier Todd, Camus told Mamaine Koestler that the chapter on art and revolution in *L'Homme révolté* was his special favorite (*Albert Camus*, pp. 557, 762).

16. Jean-Paul Sartre, preface to *Les Damnés de la terre*, by Frantz Fanon (Paris: Maspéro, 1961); see Camus's letter to Francine Camus of September 5, 1952, cited by Todd, *Albert Camus*, p. 573.

home—or, rather, used his writings to describe in a variety of keys his sense of exile. In one of his very earliest writings—"L'Eté à Alger"—Camus writes that "a homeland is only ever recognized at the moment of its loss," and this sense of loss, the feeling of exile and misplacement, is the central theme of his life and work.

In *L'Homme révolté*, in the course of a lyrical disquisition on "Mediterranean" thought, he writes of the heart that asks itself ceaselessly "Where can I feel at home," while the self-hating narrator in his last novel, *La Chute*, confesses, "Even today Sunday soccer matches in a stadium full to bursting, and the theater that I loved with an unequaled passion, are the only places in the world where I feel myself innocent." More than any other French writer or intellectual of his age, Camus lived in the permanent purgatory of exile—physical, moral, intellectual; always between homes (in metaphor and reality alike) and at ease nowhere.

Just because you are from somewhere does not mean you cannot be an exile there, too—a point once made by Ignazio Silone in a conversation with Gustav Herling, and by Camus himself in both *l'Exil et le royaume* and *L'Envers et l'endroit*. Nonetheless, if Camus had a place of his own at all it was Algeria, and more particularly the city of Algiers, where he was born in 1913. In 1932, at the age of nineteen, he wrote to a friend, "I shall never be able to live away from Algiers. Never. I shall travel because I want to know the world, but I am convinced that anywhere else I shall always be an exile."[17] It was true. His last novel, unpublished until three decades after his death, reveals an unaltered conviction of the *rightness*, the special meaning of Algiers for him.

Of course, no reader of Camus could ever miss the importance of physical sensations and the world of the flesh throughout his work, from *L'Etranger*, where the omnipresent sun plays out its fateful role, to the Nobel Prize speech, where he spoke of never having been able to do without the light, the sense of well-being, the life of freedom in which he grew up. And like his early stories and essays, *Le Premier Homme* luxuriates in the sheer sensuality of the sun, the sea, of youthful bodies in the water and at the beach. But it goes further. Here more than anywhere else in Camus's writings one feels his pleasure in such things and his fateful ambivalence toward the other, cerebral world in which he had chosen to dwell. In *Le Premier Homme* Camus recaptured something he tried to explain in a much

17. Quoted in Todd, *Albert Camus*, p. 56.

earlier piece of writing, "Noces à Tipasa," the appeal of "a life that tastes of warm stone." The marginal notes to the novel that was to have been the first part of his bildungsroman show Camus's intentions: "the book must be heavy with objects and with physicality."[18]

Algeria, too, is physically present in Le Premier Homme, as in so many of Camus's occasional writings and stories—its smells, its sounds, the topography of Algiers itself on its magnificent bay, the adventures of Jacques (Albert) and his friends in the streets and the back country. Algeria of course was also a mixed memory for Camus, of a poverty-stricken childhood in a fatherless family and, latterly, of the growing division between Arabs and others. But its significance for the author is unambiguous: "So it was each time he left Paris for Africa, a quiet jubilation, his spirit opening wide, the satisfaction of someone who has just made a neat escape and who laughs when he thinks of the faces of the guards."

Climate, and the lost innocence of carefree youth, were certainly part of it. Jean Paulhan, meeting Camus in Paris in January 1943, noted how he "suffered" from his inability to return to Algiers to "his wife and his climate." Camus even attributed the distance between Sartre and himself (long before their breakup) to the "simple fact that our climates are incompatible. From the artistic point of view, let's just say that the sky over Le Havre is not that of Algiers."[19] But there was something else.

In 1940, shortly after arriving in Paris, Camus reported his impressions to Christiane Galindo back in Algiers: "Here the funny thing is that I see stacks of people, 'la plupart de faux grands hommes,' but I carry into their midst the private world that accompanies me. Never revealing the essential part of oneself—it gives a curious feeling of power."[20] The clue to Camus's distance from his new circumstances lies in the phrase "la plupart de faux grands hommes." From the very start Camus felt out of place in the Parisian intellectual milieu for a distinctively French reason—he lacked the educational credentials of most of his newfound companions.

Unlike nearly all of them he had not attended one of the elite Parisian

18. Speech delivered December 12, 1957, in Discours de Suède, p. 20; "Noces à Tipasa," first published in 1939, in Essais, pp. 54–60.

19. Jean Paulhan to Raymond Guérin, January 6, 1943, in Paulhan, Choix de lttres, 1937–1945 (Paris: Gallimard, 1992), p. 298. For the contrast between Algiers and Le Havre, see Camus's letter to René Lalou, dated November 8, 1949, and quoted in Todd, Albert Camus, p. 492.

20. Letter of February 22, 1940, quoted in Todd, Albert Camus, p. 245.

schools but had been a scholarship boy at the local lycée in Algiers. He had not gone on to the Lycée Henri IV or the Lycée Louis-le-Grand to study in one of the prestigious preparatory classes for entry to a *grande école*. He had not then taken the entrance examination and been accepted at the Ecole Normale Supérieure but had enrolled instead at the university in Algiers. He had not taken and passed the national *agrégation* examination, qualifying him to teach at the highest level in the French system and matriculating him into a self-conscious and restricted echelon of French academic mandarins (in Camus's case admission to the *agrégation* had been refused on medical grounds—his tuberculosis precluding him from a titular post in the educational system). In short, and unlike Sartre, Maurice Merleau-Ponty, Simone de Beauvoir, Raymond Aron, Emmanuel Mounier, and the majority of their friends, Camus was not of the educational and educated elite in Paris, and he felt it.

This is not to say that Camus was ashamed of his education. On the contrary, as he showed in some of the most moving passages of *Le Premier Homme* and in many private communications, he was proud of his achievement and grateful to the primary schoolteacher who first entered his life as a partial surrogate father and who encouraged his mother and grandmother to allow him to sit a scholarship exam, even though success (and acceptance to the local lycée) would deprive them of his earning capacity for many years. Albert Camus, more than any of his fellow postwar literati, was a pure product of the Third Republic; its system of free primary education and competitive secondary-school scholarships had been of inexpressible importance for him, as for so many others. Accordingly, the ethical and pedagogical ideals of that much-maligned Republic meant more to him than to most of his Parisian contemporaries. When his Nobel Prize acceptance speech was published in 1958, it was to his primary schoolteacher, M. Louis Germain, that Camus dedicated it.[21]

Nonetheless, Camus was at a severe intellectual and psychological disadvantage in the presence of the others. He preferred the company of sportsmen, actors, or men from his own educational and social background, and as he explained in a television appearance in May 1959, "I don't know

21. Even before the war Camus anticipated the coming self-abnegation of the educated classes: "Those who speak lightly of the uselessness of learning are the very ones who have most profited by it." See Camus's reportage from the Kabylie, "Misère de la Kabylie," first published in *Alger républicain* in June 1939 and reprinted in *Actuelles III* (Paris: Gallimard, 1958), pp. 31–91, especially p. 64.

why but in the company of intellectuals I always feel I should be apologizing for something."[22] In addition to his own sense of cultural inferiority (three times over—for his social background, his provincial birthplace, and his education), Camus suffered quite directly at the hands of his critics. Even Raymond Aron, who shared many of his views, was scornfully dismissive of his arguments.

Sartre, of course, barred no holds. His open letter to Camus (on the occasion of Camus's own defense of *L'Homme révolté* against the *Temps modernes* review by Jeanson) made his sentiments clear: "And what if your book bore witness merely to your philosophical incompetence? If it were composed of hastily gathered knowledge, acquired secondhand? If, far from obscuring your brilliant arguments, reviewers have been obliged to light lamps in order to make out the contours of your weak, obscure, and confused reasoning?"[23]

As it happens, Sartre was right, at least so far as the structure and arguments of Camus's book were concerned—and he was perceptive, too, in his cruel insight into Camus's personality: "Your combination of gloomy complacency and vulnerability has kept us from telling you the whole truth." But it was not just what Sartre said that caused Camus so much damage; it was that it was said with all the authority that attaches to a man who had graduated from France's premier lycée to the Ecole Normale Supérieure and had then gone on, like Aron, to come top in the national philosophy *agrégation*.

All Camus could offer in response was his private conviction that Paris was full of "faux grands hommes," the rueful reflection (consigned to his notebooks) that "Paris is a jungle full of seedy-looking beasts," and the famous image in *La Chute* of Paris as a pond full of piranha fish who can strip a work of art in five minutes for the simple pleasure of destroying it.

But the damage was done—for the next two decades it was de rigueur in Parisian critical circles to dismiss Camus—before and after his death—as a "philosopher for high-school children." In 1958, Raymond Queneau went to see Camus's production of *Les Possédés*: "Camus? He's like the schoolteacher who teaches Kant and then thinks he *is* Kant. . . . Appar-

22. Todd, *Albert Camus*, p. 659.
23. "Réponse à Albert Camus," *Les Temps modernes*, 82, August 1952, rpt. in *Situations IV* (Paris: Gallimard, 1964), pp. 90–126.

ently one has to say something about the play to its author after seeing it. Gaston [Gallimard] warned me: 'Just say, "Are you pleased with it?"' So, after the performance, I said to Camus: 'Are you pleased with it?' But he replied, 'Are you?' I was struck dumb."[24]

On the whole, and perhaps surprisingly, Camus avoided slipping into a sustained mood of *ressentiment* (though his protagonist in *La Chute*, faced with the prospect of a Last Judgment, replies sardonically, "Allow me to laugh respectfully. I await it unflinchingly: I've known the worst—the judgment of men"). As he explained in the 1958 preface to *L'Envers et l'endroit*, every artist has a single source that nourishes his life and work and without which his work "shrivels and cracks." For Camus that source was the "world of poverty and sunlight that I lived in for so long, whose memory still saves me from two opposing dangers that threaten every artist: resentment and self-satisfaction." But he paid a price nonetheless, that of double exile—not only from his home and source but an internal exile in Paris itself.

Such exiles are not necessarily destructive, nor even undesired. Camus could sometimes revel in his (anticipated) solitude—as when he wrote to Paulhan, on the occasion of his principled resignation from the Conseil National des Ecrivains in 1944, "You see, it is my first retirement, an anticipation of the great Silence that, frankly, tempts me more and more."[25] He wrote *La Peste*, appropriately enough, in the remote village of Le Chambon-sur-Lignon, whose isolated Protestant community saved so many Jews during the Occupation, and he doubtless empathized with Tarrou, in whose mouth he put the following: "Once I decided to have no part in killing, I condemned myself to permanent exile. Other people will have to make history."

The idea of judgment—of judging oneself, being judged by others, of the passing of judgments as an act of intellectual power and of retreat/exile as an escape from such judgments—is a constant of Camus's writing from *L'Etranger* to *La Chute*, and the latter can also be read as a brilliant, dyspeptic disquisition on the forensic habits of mind of the Parisian talking classes—of "those specialized cafés where our professional humanists sit."

24. Raymond Queneau, *Journaux 1914–1945* (Paris: Gallimard, 1996), p. 1990.
25. The comment to Paulhan in 1944 was reported by Roger Grenier and is quoted by Todd, *Albert Camus*, p. 371.

But much earlier, from 1949, Camus is constantly confiding to his note-books and his correspondence the virtues of honesty, of unpopularity, and of going against the current.

However, beginning with the self-induced "expulsion" from the community of left intellectuals brought about by his publication of *L'Homme révolté*, Camus's internal exile took on a harsher and more self-pitying tone—"everyone is against me, is remorselessly seeking a share in my destruction; no one ever proffers his hand, comes to my aid, shows me affection for who I am." To be sure, Camus suffered considerable ostracism thereafter among his former acquaintances, and his later work—the collection of essays in *Actuelles III* and *L'Envers et l'endroit*, or the stories in *L'Exil et le royaume*—received remarkably little critical attention. But Camus was not without friends, his work continued to sell well, and it was he, after all, who was awarded the Nobel Prize in 1957—not Sartre, nor even Malraux. If he suffered at the condescension of the inner circles of Parisian intellectual fashion, it was because part of him—even if it was only part—longed for *their* recognition and acceptance by *them*.[26]

But what Camus could never share with the *juges pénitents* of the Left Bank was their disgust at their own condition ("Existentialism. When they criticize themselves you can be sure that it is for the purpose of crushing others. Remorseful judges [*des juges pénitents*]."[27] This is Camus's first use of this phrase, which he later deployed in *La Chute*). The wellsprings of anger and self-hatred of interwar French writers like Drieu la Rochelle or Céline were transferred with remarkable fidelity to their postwar heirs; with this difference, that the antibourgeois spleen that was vented in narcissism, anti-Semitism, nihilism, and ultimately philo-fascism by Drieu (or Brasillach and Lucien Rebatet) was now diverted into metaphysical solipsism, *ouvriérisme*, and in most cases philo-Sovietism by Sartre, Simone de Beauvoir, Emmanuel Mounier, and their followers. Here Camus was a true outsider, "parachuted" by historical chance into the teeming, overheated, self-regarding milieu of Parisian intellectual life and utterly at odds with it.

From this vantage point, Camus noted not just the self-hatred of the bourgeois intellectual and his fascination with violence but also the enduring French intellectual prejudice that interprets a parade of cultural despair

26. For Camus's private remarks, addressed to his unpublished notebooks, see *Carnets III*, p. 50.
27. See *Carnets III*, entry for December 14, 1954, p. 147.

as a sign of higher intelligence—a remark addressed as much at Gide as at his own generation. He chided André Breton for admiring in *L'Homme révolté* its courageous critique of Marxism; the *real* problem, he insisted, is nihilism, and until we have learned to recognize and name that for what it is we shall not find a way out of the impasse. Camus did not despair of France, and just as he disclaimed the label *existentialist*, so he refused to identify with "root and branch" enemies of the present condition—"You cannot always be a painter of the absurd . . . and no one can believe in a literature of despair."[28]

Perhaps Camus's most abiding and painful exile was that which placed him at odds with *himself*. In the first place, he was the outsider in Paris, *étranger* in something of the sense used in his famous novel. It was not that he felt out of place in the role of the intellectual, except in the sense already noted, but rather that there were two contrasting personalities in play, only one of which was understood and appreciated by his colleagues. When, during the Algerian conflict, he tried to explain the other part and hence his own pained ambivalence, few understood: "the Mediterranean separated within me two universes, one where memories and names were conserved in measured spaces, the other where the traces of man were swept across great distances by the sandy wind."

This separation of worlds had always troubled Camus; in an early (1939) review of *Bread and Wine* he picked out for comment the passage where Silone's hero reflects on the risk of theorizing too much about the peasants and thereby coming to know them ever less.[29] Camus, too, worried throughout his life about the risk of losing touch, of severing one's roots even before one has found them. It is this intuitive grasp of the condition of the rudderless intellectual that gives Camus's ethic of limits and of responsibility their peculiar authority.

And yet, in spite of the reiterated insistence on the antithesis between the rootless, cold Parisian world and his own sunny, terrestrial, nonjudgmental Mediterranean sources, Camus was anything but a southerner in the conventional sense in which he himself occasionally used the term. His style was cool, distant, and (with the exception of some magnificent lyrical

28. "L'Enigme," pp. 859–67. See also "Révolte et conformisme" (November 1951), in *Actuelles II*, pp. 43–49, and "Homage à André Gide," first published in *Nouvelle nouvelle Revue française*, November 1951, and reprinted in Albert Camus, *Lyrical and Critical Essays*, trans. Ellen Conroy Kennedy (New York: Vintage Books, 1970), pp. 248–54.

29. *Alger republicain*, May 23, 1939.

passages in his last novel) studiedly unemotional. To be sure, it suited him to set off the virtues of southern "moderation" against the extremism (political, aesthetic) of the "North," to remind himself and his readers of the tactile sensuality of the South when compared to the gray, livid light of the North, and so forth.

But that same south—Algiers—is also a "terre d'exil," in his first writings and his last. It is one of the purposes of *Le Premier Homme* to remind the reader that Algeria, too, was but a passing residence. Camus's own father was exiled thrice over: he came from a family of immigrants from German-occupied Alsace, had moved from France to Algeria, and would return again to France, to die there on the Western Front and be buried in a remote town in Brittany. Camus's mother was descended from Minorcan immigrants, a Spanish connection in which he took great pride. North Africa, too, was thus at best a contingent home.

Camus, then, was a cosmopolitan, rootless. And like other rootless cosmopolitans he sought throughout his life to ground himself in something firm, knowing all the while that it was a hopeless exercise and that to be in exile just *was* his true condition. This gives a special piquancy to the elegant exercise in *La Chute*, whereby Clamence offers a damning critique of the intellectual humbug of which he is himself a prime example. Camus used the novel to invert the procedure of which he had been a victim in *Les Mandarins*, where Simone de Beauvoir transposed all Sartre's worst characteristics and acts onto the Camus figure in her roman à clef; Camus took his *own* failings as he saw them, generalized them across the spectrum of Parisian intellectual life, and then subjected them to cruel inspection and interrogation in the manner of his own intellectual enemies. By the end of the tale it is no longer easy to distinguish between Camus/Clamence and his/their antagonists, much as Camus himself could no longer always see clearly which was his actual self and which the one with whom he sought a passing identification.

Camus was an unpolitical man. Not that he was unconcerned with public affairs, or uncaring about political choices. But he was by instinct and temperament an *unaffiliated* person (in his romantic life no less than in his public one), and the charms of engagement, which exercised so strong a fascination for his French contemporaries, held little appeal for him. If it is true, in Hannah Arendt's words, that Camus and his generation were "sucked into politics as though with the force of a vacuum," Camus, at least, was always resisting the pull. This was something that was held against him by many; not only because of his refusal to take a stance in the Algerian imbroglio but also, and perhaps especially, because his writings as a whole seemed to run against the grain of public passions. For a man who had exercised such enormous intellectual influence, Camus seemed to his peers almost irresponsible in his failure to invest his work with a lesson or a message—it was just not possible to derive from a reading of Camus any clear political message, much less a directive as to the proper use of one's political energies. In Alain Peyrefitte's words, "If you are politically faithful to Camus, it is hard to see how you could commit yourself to any party."[30]

The response to *La Peste* is characteristic. Simone de Beauvoir castigated Camus for his assimilation of the plague to some kind of "natural" virus, his failure to "situate" it historically and politically—that is, to assign responsibility to a party or parties within the story. Sartre made the same criticism. Even Roland Barthes, who might have been thought a more subtle literary reader, found in Camus's parable of the Vichy years an unsatisfactory failure to identify guilt. This criticism still surfaces occasionally among American scholars, who lack even the excuse of contemporary polemical passion.[31] And yet *La Peste*, while it may not be Camus's best work, is not so very difficult to understand.

The problem seems to arise from Camus's transposition of political choices and outcomes into a resolutely moral and individual key—which was precisely the reverse of contemporary practice, in which all personal and ethical dilemmas were typically reduced to political or ideological options. It is not that Camus was unaware of the political implications of the choices men and women had faced under the German Occupation—as some of his critics well knew, his own record in this respect was rather

30. Arendt is quoted by Isaacs, *Arendt, Camus*, p. 34. For Peyrefitte, see *Camus et la politique*, ed. JeanYves Guérin (Paris: Harmattan, 1986), where he is quoted by Guérin on p. 22.

31. See, e.g., Susan Dunn, *The Deaths of Louis XIV: Regicide and the French Political Imagination* (Princeton, N.J.: Princeton University Press, 1994), notably chap. 6, "Camus and Louis XVI: A Modern Elegy for the Martyred King," where she takes Camus to task for portraying fascism [sic] "in terms of a nonideological and nonhuman plague" (p. 150).

better than their own, which helps account for the acerbity of their attacks. But Camus recognized something that many at the time still did not grasp: what was most interesting, and most representative of people's experience during the war (in France and elsewhere), was not simple binary divisions of human behavior into "collaboration" or "resistance," but the infinite range of compromises and denials that constituted the business of survival; the "gray zone" where moral dilemmas and responsibilities were replaced by self-interest and a carefully calculated failure to see what was too painful to behold.

In effect, Camus's work anticipated Arendt's own now well-known reflections on the "banality of evil" (though Camus was far too adroit a moralist to have used such a phrase). In conditions of extremity there are rarely to be found simple and comfortable categories of good and evil, guilty and innocent. Men may do the right thing from a mixture of motives and may with equal ease commit terrible mistakes and crimes with the best of intentions—or no intentions at all. It does not follow from this that the plagues that mankind brings down upon itself are "natural," or unavoidable. But assigning responsibility for them—and thus preventing them in the future—may not always be a simple business. At best, political labels and passions simplify and render crude and partial our understanding of human behavior and its motives. At worst, they contribute willfully to the very ailments they purport so confidently to address.

This was not a point of view calculated to make Albert Camus feel comfortable in the hyperpoliticized culture of postwar Paris, nor to endear him to those—the overwhelming majority—for whom political labels and passions were the very stuff of intellectual exchange. Three examples, drawn from debates and divisions in which Camus was at first deeply involved, may help illustrate his distinctive stance and his characteristic move from engagement to distance, from an easy (and usually popular) conviction to a feeling of discomfort and ambivalence, with all the attendant loss of public favor these moves entailed.

Camus emerged from the French Resistance, in August 1944, as the confident spokesman of the coming generation, unshakable in his faith in the great changes that the liberation would bring to his country—"This terrible birth is that of a Revolution." France had not suffered, and the Resistance made so many sacrifices, only for the country to return to the bad habits of its past. Something radical and radically new was called for. Three days after the liberation of Paris he reminded the readers of *Combat* that an uprising is "the nation in arms" and "the people" are that part of the nation which refuses to bend the knee.[32]

This lyrical tone—which had reached a high point in his *Lettres à un ami allemand*, clandestinely published in 1943 and 1944—helps explain Camus's influence at the time. It combined a traditional, romantic view of France and her possibilities with Camus's own reputation for personal integrity, remarkable in a man just thirty-one years old when Paris was liberated. What Camus actually meant by "Revolution" was even less clear than is normally the case when the term is invoked. In an article of September 1944 he defined it as the conversion of "spontaneous élan into concerted action" and seems to have had in mind some combination of high moral purpose with a new social "contract" between the French. In any case, it was Camus's moral authority, not his political program, that gave him his audience.[33]

In the retributive atmosphere of those months, when the country was much taken up with arguments about whom to punish for wartime collaboration and crimes, and how severely, Camus's influence was initially exercised in favor of a harsh and swift punishment for the men of Vichy and their servants. In October 1944 he wrote an influential and uncompromising editorial whose pathological analogies are instructive. "France," he asserted, "is carrying in her midst a foreign body, a minority of men who harmed her in the past and harm her still today. These are men of betrayal and injustice. Their very existence poses a problem of justice, since they are part of the living body of the nation and the question is how to destroy them."[34] Simone de Beauvoir, or the head-hunting purgers of the Communist press, could not have expressed it better.

And yet, within a period of weeks, Camus was already beginning to express doubts at the prudence, and even the justice, of the summary trials and executions advocated by the Conseil National des Ecrivains and other progressive groups—it was a sure sign of his backsliding at this point that he was attacked by Pierre Hervé, the Communist journalist, for indicating a degree of sympathy for a resister who had talked under torture. Camus the writer was especially disturbed at the ease with which the intellectuals

32. See *Combat*, August 23 and 24, 1944.

33. See *Combat*, September 19, 1944. On Camus's wartime reputation, see, e.g., Jean Paulhan to François Mauriac on April 12, 1943: "He is someone who is brave and reliable" (Paulhan, *Choix de lettres, 1937–1945*), p. 304.

34. *Combat*, October 25, 1944.

of the winning side were selecting the *intellectual* collaborators for special punishment. And thus, within three months of his confident recommendation that the guilty men be excised from the body politic and "destroyed," we find Camus signing the unsuccessful petition to de Gaulle seeking clemency for Robert Brasillach.

As a symbol, a representative of intellectual collaboration, Brasillach was almost too perfect. Born in 1909, he was of the same generation as Camus, but of very different background. After a gilded youth that took him from the Ecole Normale Supérieure to the editorial pages of *Je suis partout*, he moved comfortably within the literary and journalistic circles of Occupied France, writing, speaking, and making visits to Germany in the company of other collaborators. He never made any effort to hide his views, which included a virulent and oft-expressed anti-Semitism. Although it became fashionable after his death to cast aspersions upon his gifts as a writer, contemporaries of all parties had credited him with a major talent. Brasillach was not just a gifted and dangerous polemicist but a man of fine aesthetic sensibilities and real literary ability.

Brasillach was tried in January 1945. His was the fourth such trial of a major collaborating journalist: December 1944 had seen the cases of Paul Chack (a journalist with *Aujourd'hui*), Lucien Combelle (director of *Revolution nationale*), and Henri Béraud (a contributor to *Gringoire*). But Brasillach's talent far exceeded that of the other three, and his case was of much greater interest to his peers. In his trial, it was established at the start (with Brasillach's agreement) that he had been pro-Vichy and was anti-Communist, anti-Jewish, and an admirer of Charles Maurras. The issue, however, was this: was he a traitor? Had he sought a German victory, and had he assisted the Germans? Lacking material evidence for such a charge, the prosecutor placed the emphasis instead upon Brasillach's responsibility as an influential writer: "How many young minds did your articles incite to fight against the *maquis*? For how many crimes did you bear intellectual responsibility? In a language all would understand, Brasillach was "le clerc qui avez trahi."[35]

Brasillach was found guilty of treason, of "intelligence with the enemy," and sentenced to death. He was thus not punished for his views as

---

35. Maître Reboul, *commissaire du gouvernement*, quoted by Jacques Isorni in *Le Procès Robert Brasillach* (Paris: Flammarion, 1946), pp. 137, 159. The reference, of course, was to Julien Benda's *La Trahison des clercs*.

such, even though these were much cited during the trial, notably his September 25, 1942, editorial in *Je suis partout* declaring, "We must put all the Jews away from us and not keep the little ones." And yet it was for his views that he was to die, since his whole public life consisted of the written word. With Brasillach, the court was proposing that for an influential writer to hold shocking opinions and advocate them to others was as serious as if he had followed through on those opinions himself.

A petition was circulated, largely by the efforts of François Mauriac, for clemency in Brasillach's case. Among the many who signed were Mauriac himself, Jean Paulhan, Georges Duhamel, Paul Valéry, Louis Madelin, Thierry Maulnier, Paul Claudel, and Albert Camus. Camus's support is instructive. He agreed to add his signature only after long reflection, and in an unpublished letter to Marcel Aymé, dated January 27, 1945, he explains his reasons. Quite simply, he opposed the death penalty. But as for Brasillach, he "despised him with all his strength." He placed no value on Brasillach the writer and, in his words, would "never shake his hand, for reasons that Brasillach himself would never understand."[36] Camus, then, was careful not to support a case for clemency on anything other than grounds of general principle—and indeed the petition itself referred only to the fact that Brasillach was the son of a dead hero of World War I, a link to his own life of which Camus can hardly have been unaware.

Camus's subsequent move, from the self-confident spokesman of the victorious resistance, through a reluctant petitioner for clemency in the case of one of Vichy's most notorious apologists, to a remorseful critic of the intolerant excesses and injustice of the postwar purges, can be traced through a series of public exchanges between himself and François Mauriac in the course of the postwar years. Divided by just about everything else— age, social class, religion, education, and status—Camus and Mauriac shared a common postwar role as the moral authorities within their respective post-Resistance communities. Each had a formidable perch from which to address the nation (Mauriac in his column for *Le Figaro*, Camus as director of *Combat*), and both men from the outset brought strikingly similar sensibilities (however differently expressed) to their writings.

Camus, like the masthead on his newspaper, saw his task as helping France to move "from resistance to revolution," and in the first flush of

36. Camus's letter is reprinted in Jacqueline Baldran and Claude Buchurberg, *Brasillach ou la celebration du mepris* (Paris: A. J. Presse, 1988), pp. 6–7.

Liberation missed few occasions to urge on the nation a radical renewal of its social and spiritual structures. Mauriac, in contrast, remained an essentially conservative man, brought to the Resistance through ethical considerations and separated from many in the Catholic community by this choice. His postwar political writings, rather like those of the later Camus, often have the feel of a man for whom this sort of polemic and partisan engagement is distasteful, who would rather be above the fray but who has been compelled to engage himself by the imperative of his own (ethical) commitments.

In late 1944, Mauriac and Camus disagreed publicly, and at times pointedly, over the conduct of the purges. For Camus, as we have seen, France was divided into "hommes de la Résistance" and "hommes de la trahison et de l'injustice." The urgent task of the former was to save France from the enemy that dwelt within her, "détruire une part encore vivante de ce pays pour sauver son âme elle-même." The purge of collaborators should be pitiless, swift, and all-embracing. Camus was replying to an article in which Mauriac had suggested that a rapid and arbitrary justice— the kind in which France was now engaged, with tribunals, special courts, and various professional commissions d'épuration—was not only inherently troubling (what if the innocent suffered along with the guilty?) but would pollute the new state and its institutions even before they had formed. For Mauriac, in turn, Camus's reply sounded like an apology for the Inquisition, saving the soul of France by burning the bodies of selected citizens. The distinction Camus was drawing between resisters and traitors was illusory, he argued; an immense number of the French had resisted "for themselves" and would form once again the natural "marais" of the political nation.

Mauriac returned to these matters in December 1944 and again in January 1945, at the time of the trials of Béraud and Brasillach. Of Henri Béraud he wrote that yes, the man was punishable for his writings; given the weight that his fanatical polemics had carried in those terrible days, he deserved ten years in prison and more. But to accuse him of friendship or collaboration with the Germans was absurd, a lie that could only bring discredit on his accusers. Camus did not directly address this last issue. But he did comment on Mauriac's increased tendency to invoke the spirit of charity in defense of the accused in these trials.

Whenever I speak of justice, he wrote, M. Mauriac speaks of charity. I am opposed to pardons, he insisted; the punishment we demand now is a necessary justice, and we must refuse a "divine charity" that, in making of us a "nation of traitors and mediocrities," will frustrate the public of its right to justice. This is a curious response, mixing realpolitik and moral fervor and hinting that there is something weak-kneed and unworthy about the exercise of charity or mercy in the case of condemned collaborators, a feebleness of the soul that threatens the fiber of the nation.

Up to this point, in early 1945, Camus was saying nothing exceptional, and others on the Left were echoing him. What distinguished Camus was that within a few months the experience of the purges, with their combination of verbal violence, selectivity, and bad faith, led him to change his mind in a quite remarkable way. Without ever conceding that the *épuration* (purge) had been unnecessary, he was able to allow, by the summer of 1945, that it had failed. In a much-quoted editorial in *Combat* in August 1945, he announced to his readers, "The word *épuration* is bad enough. The thing itself has become odious."

Camus had come to see just how very self-defeating the *épuration* had become. Far from uniting the nation around a clear understanding of guilt and innocence, crime and justice, it had encouraged just the sort of moral cynicism and personal self-interest he had sought to overcome. Precisely because the purges, especially of the intellectuals, had become so degraded in the public eye, the solution was now exacerbating the very problem it had been intended to resolve. The *épuration* in France, he concluded, had "not just failed but lost all credibility." If the way in which the French were atoning for past errors was any indication, then the country's longed-for spiritual renaissance lay far away.

Camus never came around wholly to Mauriac's point of view. Mauriac, for example, had from the very start taken the view that it would be better for the guilty to escape than for the innocent to be punished. He also— and in this he was unusual—rejected the suggestion that Vichy was somehow the work of a minority or an elite. The "double game" and "haggling" that marked the Vichy interlude was that of peoples and nations everywhere, he insisted, the French included. Why pretend otherwise? And his vision of a reunited France was closer to that of the Olympian de Gaulle than the partisan intellectuals of the domestic Resistance: "Should we try to remake the nation with former opponents, with those who committed no inexpiable crimes? Or should we eliminate them from public life, using methods inherited from the Jacobins and currently applied in totalitarian lands?"

But by 1945, the two men were moving toward the same conclusions.

Of all possible *épurations*, wrote Mauriac, we are experiencing the worst, which is corrupting the very idea of justice in the hearts and minds of the population. Later, as his polemics with the PCF grew bitter and the dividing line between them grew wider, Mauriac would claim that the purge had been merely a political card in the Communists' hand. But he was honest enough to concede that, at the time, he might have been premature in calling for forgiveness and amnesty; in a France torn by hatred and fear, some sort of score settling had perhaps been necessary, though not the one that took place. In other words, Camus might not have been as wrong as Mauriac had once thought.

By 1948, however, it was Camus, long since disabused of the prospects for revolution and already uncomfortable in the intellectual community of which he was still a leading member, who had the last word. In a lecture to the Dominican community at Latour-Maubourg, he reflected on the hopes and disappointments of the Liberation, on the rigors of justice and the requirement of charity. In the light of subsequent events, he declared, "Monsieur François Mauriac was right and I was wrong."[37]

In the debates over postwar retribution, caught between political justice and the claims of fairness and charity, Camus's transition from certainty to doubt had taken place over the course of time, albeit swiftly. In the tensions incurred by the divisions of the Cold War, he found himself in two minds almost from the start. The contrast here lay not across time but space—the space between Camus's official and public views and those he kept, for the most part, to himself. As a man of the Left, Camus took reasonably conventional public positions on the majority of issues that divided men and women in the decade after the defeat of Hitler. Like most other "progressives" he was initially reluctant to distance himself from the French Communists: in October 1944 he reiterated firmly the *Combat* group's Algiers statement in March of that year—anti-Communism is the beginning of dictatorship—even as he acknowledged that supporting and criticizing the Communists at the same time was not always easy.[38]

Even in later years, following the onset of the Cold War, and long after

37. For Camus, see, e.g., *Combat*, October 20, 1944, January 11, 1945, August 30, 1945, and *Actuelles: Chroniques 1944–1948* (Paris: Gallimard, 1950) (hereafter *Actuelles I*), pp. 212–13. For Mauriac see *Le Figaro*, October 19, 22–23, 26, 1944, January 4, 1945; also François Mauriac, *Journal IV* (Paris: Grasset, 1950), entry for May 30, 1945, and *Journal V* (Paris, 1953), entry for February 9–10, 1947.

38. *Combat*, October 7, 1944.

Camus's attitude toward Stalin and his crimes was on the public record, a shared desire for "peace" and a wish to find a "third way" brought Camus together for a few months in 1948 with Sartre and other non-Communist intellectuals of the Left in the Rassemblement Démocratique Révolutionnaire. He was even, like most of them, critical of Victor Kravchenko, the author of *I Chose Freedom* and plaintiff in a famous 1948 libel trial against the Communist journalist Pierre Daix, who had accused him of inventing the Gulag and writing his book at the behest of the U.S. intelligence services. Camus did not doubt Kravchenko's evidence, of course, but he found the man distasteful and even in 1953 could write that Kravchenko had "gone from being a beneficiary of the Soviet regime to profiting from the bourgeois regime,"[39] an unfortunate and probably unconscious echo of the Communists' own accusations.

Camus was no apologist for Communism. But for many years he could not fully disentangle himself from the desire to preserve his public legitimacy as a radical intellectual, while maintaining his intellectual independence and moral credibility. Hence, when discussing the crimes of left-wing dictatorships in the late forties and early fifties, he took some care to balance his remarks with allusions to similarly unappealing regimes favored by the Western allies; in a series of articles in *Combat* during November 1948 he insisted on the indivisibility of moral judgment: the deprivation of freedom of speech under Franco and Stalin was one and the same. This search for "balance" even led him on one occasion to exculpate intellectuals like himself from responsibility for the judicial murder then being carried out in Bulgaria, Hungary, and elsewhere: "We didn't hang Petkov. It was the signatories of pacts that divided the world in two who are responsible."[40]

This stance certainly distinguished Camus from many of his friends for whom the loss of freedom or judicial murder under a Communist regime was somehow qualitatively distinctive (and not always reprehensible). But the need to balance crimes on both sides, however just and fair, could become an act of bad faith. Camus knew this, and, as his notebooks suggest, he labored with some discomfort under his self-imposed burden of moral equity. Nevertheless, he continued to say, and to believe, that Western

---

39. See "Le Pain et la liberté" (1953), rpt. in *Actuelles II*, pp. 157–73. Note, though, that the occasion for Camus's remark was a talk given to the Bourse du Travail in Saint-Etienne.

40. Interview in *Défense de l'homme*, July 1949, in *Actuelles I*, p. 233.

freedom was a "mystification," however important it was to defend it; and
as late as 1955 he could condemn in the same breath "la société policière"
and "la société marchande."[41]

If the balance of Camus's attention began some time in 1948 to switch
toward the Communist problem, it was driven—like his second thoughts
on the *épuration*—by a concern with justice; that same concern which in
various guises intrudes upon most of his nonfiction and all his plays and
major novels. The very titles of his collected essays, articles, and prefaces in
the years between 1946 and 1951 are a guide to his obsessions: *Ni victimes ni
bourreaux* (essays on the moral underpinnings of a nondictatorial socialism)
and *Justice et haine* (articles on injustice and persecution under dictatorship). He had a gnawing sense that in his contributions to public discussion
of dictatorships, show trials, concentration camps, political terror, and the
rest, he had not been quite honest—to himself. He may have taken care
always to tell the truth as he understood it, but he had not always vouchsafed *all* of that truth, especially those parts likely to cause pain to his
friends, to his constituency, and to Camus himself.

For as Camus was already beginning to shape the arguments of what
would become *L'Homme révolté*, he was losing his attachment to the "progressive" party in French public life—not just the Stalinist faithful but
those who believed in progress and revolution (and the French Revolution
in particular); those for whom Stalin may have been a monster but to
whom Marx was still the guiding light; those who saw clearly the injustice
and racism in French colonial policy but were blind to the crimes and failings of its "progressive" opponents, in North Africa, the Middle East, or
Asia. This moral discomfort at his own compromises begins to surface in
his notebooks at the end of the forties; in an entry for March 1950 he notes,
"I seem to be emerging from a ten-year sleep—all wrapped up and entan-
gled in coils of unhappiness and false values."[42]

In one sense—and this is certainly how it seemed to Camus looking
back a decade later—Camus, like Clamence in *La Chute*, was punishing
himself to excess for his own cowardice. Clamence was haunted by the
voice of the woman he failed to save from drowning, Camus by all the
occasions when he had something to say but didn't say it, or else said it in

41. For "mystification" see "Le Pain et la liberté"; see also *L'Express*, October 8,
1955.
42. *Carnets, janvier 1942–mars 1951* (Paris: Gallimard, 1964), p. 315.

a muted and socially acceptable form for the sake of personal sensibilities and political loyalties. Few readers of Camus in those years would have thought of him in this light, though—which says something about the self-censorship of the rest of the French intellectual community in those post-war years. Camus was remarkably direct, open, and evenhanded in his feelings—castigating Gabriel Marcel in December 1948 for his failure to see in Franco's Spain the same crimes as in Stalin's Russia, just two months after he had spoken out against pressures brought to bear on intellectuals not to discuss the purge of artists in the Soviet Union for fear of giving "comfort" to the Right.

But in the France of those years, Camus's careful appearance of balance, his role as the detached voice of Justice, cost him something. He did not *feel* evenhanded. Whatever his criticisms of "materialism," however genuine his sympathies for a democratic socialism, he was not neutral between East and West, as so many of his contemporaries claimed to be. And in intellectual Paris, in 1950, to be "neutral" was to be quite distinctly on one side and not the other. Camus knew this, and knew, too, that his invocation of Franco's Spain, French colonialism, or American racism came close to bad faith; for he no longer believed, as he had perhaps once done, that the sins of the West were the equal of those of the East.

In suggesting such comparisons he was, in effect, buying the right to criticize Communism, to point to the Russian concentration camps and to make reference to the persecution of artists and democrats in Eastern Europe. But the cost in moral capital was high. What Camus really wished to do—or have the freedom to do if he so chose—was condemn the condemnable without resort to balance or counterreference, to invoke absolute standards and measures of morality, justice, and freedom whenever it was appropriate to do so, without casting fearful glances behind him to see if his line of moral retreat was covered. He had long known this, but as he confessed to his *Carnets* on March 4, 1950, "it is only belatedly that one has the courage of one's understanding."

But calling things by their name, speaking of what you wished to speak and in the way you needed to was no easy matter in the intellectual community of Paris at the height of the Cold War—especially if, like Camus (but unlike Aron) you retained a certain nostalgia for the sympathetic embrace of the Left and suffered from a measure of intellectual insecurity in addition. But in 1950, as in his earlier coming to terms with the moral dilemma of postwar retribution, Camus moved on; from the familiar soil of

`

conviction and "objectivity" to the lonely, rocky perch of an unpopular, untimely partisanship, that of the spokesman for the obvious. In his own words, again confided to his notebooks a year or so before the appearance of *L'Homme révolté:* "One of my regrets is to have sacrificed too much to objectivity. Objectivity, sometimes, is an accommodation. Today things are clear, and we must call totalitarian those things that are totalitarian, even socialism. In a manner of speaking, I shall never again be polite."[43]

The Algerian war that began in 1954 and did not end until two years after Camus's death, when de Gaulle opened negotiations leading to Algerian independence, had only a limited impact upon metropolitan Frenchmen. Of course, it provoked a military coup that indirectly overthrew the Fourth Republic; and the moral issues raised by French efforts to repress the Arab uprising divided the political and intellectual communities for years to come. But for most Frenchmen Algeria was foreign to their daily concerns (like Northern Ireland today for the mainland British), so long as they or their son were not being sent to fight there. Only when the civil war came to France itself, in the form of terrorist bombings by the far-right Organisation Armée Secrète during the early sixties, was the Algerian tragedy played out to any significant extent at home; but by then the war was all but over and Algerian independence inevitable, which accounts for the violent desperation of its extreme opponents.

For Camus, however, things were different. He was born in Algiers and grew up there, drawing on his experience of that time and place for much of his best work. The child of European immigrants, he could not imagine an Algeria without Europeans, nor conceive of indigenous Algerian Europeans of his milieu torn from their roots. The Algerian war, the moral and political issues it posed and the outcomes it suggested—all equally unsatisfactory to Camus—placed him in an impossible position. Already disposed to retreat from the sound and fury of Parisian public life and with little more to offer on the great intellectual debates of the hour, Camus found himself in growing disagreement with virtually all parties in the Algerian conflict. The intolerance of the opposing sides, the political errors and crimes of French and Arabs alike, the growing evidence of the impossibility of compromise, brought him from reason to emotion, and from emotion to silence. Torn between his moral commitments and his sentimental attachments, he had nothing to say and accordingly said nothing—a refusal to

43. Ibid., p. 267.

"engage" himself in the great moral issue of the hour that was held against him by many at the time and ever since.

It should not be inferred from this that Albert Camus was uncritical of the French stance in North Africa, or of colonialism in general. Like most intellectuals of his generation he had long been bitterly opposed to French policy in the Maghreb; not only did he condemn the use of torture and terror in the government's "dirty war" against the Arab nationalists, but he had been a vocal and well-informed critic of colonial discrimination against the Arab population ever since the thirties—at a time when many of the Parisian intellectuals who would later distinguish themselves in the anticolonial struggle knew little and cared less about the condition and needs of France's overseas subjects.

Camus was well informed about the Arab condition in Algeria. He undertook investigative journalism for the newspaper *Alger républicain* between the wars and in June 1939 published a series of eleven articles collectively titled "Misère de la Kabylie." He loathed the *colons*, to whom impoverished migrants like his parents were as alien as their Arab workers, and he undoubtedly meant it when, nearly twenty years later, he wrote, "Major and conspicuous amends have to be made . . . to the Arab people."[44] To be sure, Arabs figure more prominently in Camus's journalism and essays than in his fiction—and where, as in *Le Premier Homme*, there is an Arab presence it is offered to the reader in a rather more optimistic and even Panglossian key than circumstances (or Camus's own experience) might have suggested.

There was never any doubt about Camus's sympathies. In the issue of *Combat* dated May 10, 1947, he wrote a corruscating attack on French policing and military practices in North Africa. The fact is, he told his readers, we use torture: "The facts are there, hideous and clear: we are doing, in these cases, just what we condemned the Germans for doing." Camus knew that something had to change in North Africa, and he deeply regretted the lost opportunity of 1945, when the French could have proposed political reforms, a degree of self-government, and even eventual autonomy to an Algerian community that was not yet polarized and in which progressive Europeans and moderate Arabs might work together as he had proposed a decade earlier.

But therein lay Camus's difficulty. His vision of Algeria had been

44. "L'Algérie déchirée," in *Actuelles III*, p. 143.

formed in the thirties, at a time when Arab sentiment was being mobilized by men like Ferhat Abbas, whose vision of an (eventually) independent Algeria was at least in principle compatible with Camus's ideal of an integrated, cooperating community of Arabs and Europeans alike. By the mid-1950s Abbas had been discredited by the failure of a series of French governments to make timely concessions or promulgate serious economic or electoral reform. His place had been taken by a younger generation of uncompromising nationalists for whom Europeans (in France or Algeria) could never be partners, and who saw the indigenous European population of Algeria, the poor included, as their enemy—a sentiment that, by the late fifties, was warmly reciprocated.

The Algerian situation had thus changed a lot since Camus's departure at the outset of World War II. So had the broader international context. By the mid-fifties Algerian Arab nationalists could look to examples and models in Egypt, Iraq, and further afield, a perspective that further contributed to Camus's alienation from them. For him, Nasser or Mossadeq were mere echoes of the European revolutionary illusion, exploiting and confusing legitimate social discontent into a poisonous mix of nationalism and ideology that bore no relation to his own ideals or Algerian needs.

Here, as elsewhere, Camus's formation in the pedagogical crucible of Third Republican France is an important clue to his political outlook: he was not naive enough to suppose that either he or his former Arab neighbors shared "nos ancêtres les Gaullois," but he did believe, deeply, in the virtues of republican assimilation. France's failure to turn the population of Algeria into Frenchmen, with all the rights and privileges thereby entailed, needed to be addressed. But it remained a worthy objective—and whereas Camus dismissed that "divinized" History which saw in the coming of decolonization the inevitable unfolding of the project of Progress, he *was* rather disposed to see in the republican ideal of France something intrinsically superior. If the Arabs were susceptible to the appeals of nationalist demagogues, it was the French who were responsible, and thus it was up to the French to repair their own mistakes.

It was in this somehow innocent and increasingly poorly informed frame of mind that Albert Camus found himself asked to take a stand after the nationalist rebellion in Algeria finally broke out in 1954. His initial reaction was to seek once again the ground for compromise, supporting Pierre Mendès-France in the forlorn hope that he could achieve for Algeria what he had wrought in Indochina. But as he had confessed in an essay dating from 1947, "With Algeria I have a long link that will doubtless never break, and that prevents me from being fully clear-sighted about it." In 1955 he wrote to Charles Poncet: "I am so anguished over Algeria. That land is caught in my throat and it is all I can think about. The idea that . . . I might start writing articles again (and with some discomfort, since on this topic I find left and right equally annoying) is ruining my days."[45]

Camus's last written "intervention" on Algeria came in the form of an article in L'Express on January 10, 1956, calling for a civil truce in the Algerian war. But by then it was a hopeless cause and the audience for such an appeal hardly existed, neither in metropolitan France nor in Algeria, as he discovered when he spoke there two weeks later. Camus could never defend the position of the French government, which he had been criticizing in one form or another for two decades; military repression—and especially the use of torture to extract confessions from captured guerillas—was unforgivable in itself and led nowhere.

But the increasingly terrorist tactics of the FLN (Front de Libération Nationale) were equally to be condemned; one could no more be selective in one's condemnation of evil in this instance than in the Cold War debates over Soviet concentration camps. What was to be done? Camus had no idea, though he was nauseated by the confident and untroubled pro-FLN stance of his bien pensant Parisian colleagues—"finally convinced that the real source of our folly is to be found in the habits and workings of our political and intellectual society, I have decided not to take nay more part in these incessant polemics."[46]

Camus was not ashamed of his withdrawal into silence—"when speech can lead to the remorseless disposal of other people's lives, silence is not a negative attitude." But it was not an easy position to explain, and it exposed him to dismissive criticism even from otherwise well-disposed and fair-minded commentators. In La Tragédie algérienne Raymond Aron acknowledged that Camus was driven by a desire for justice and a wish to be generous and compassionate to all parties. But as a result, he suggested, he had not succeeded in rising beyond the attitude of mind of a well-intentioned colonizer. From Aron's realist perspective that was perhaps an appropriate observation, for the fact was that the conclusion to be drawn

45. Quoted in Todd, Albert Camus, p. 615. See also "Petit Guide pour des villes sans passé," first published in L'Eté (Paris: Gallimard, 1954), rpt. in Essais, pp. 845–51.
46. Preface to Actuelles III, p. 12.

from Camus's silence—maintenance of the status quo with the necessary reforms in addition—was by 1958 an empty wish. Either Algeria would be independent under the new nationalists or else it would be kept under French rule by the use of force, at growing human and social expense. There was no longer any third option.

But Camus did not understand his role as that of a provider of an-swers—"in these matters too much is expected of a writer." His attitude at the time of the Algerian crisis has to be understood in part as a sign of his inability to conceive of an alternative future for his country of origin, to accept that French Algeria had been destroyed for ever. Thus his view of Algeria's future prospects under independence was grim—at a time when many French intellectuals, however sincere their opposition to French co-lonial practices, were inspired by a glowing fantasy of life in postcolonial societies liberated from their imperial masters. Thirty-five years after gain-ing its independence Algeria is again in trouble today, divided and blood-ied by a fundamentalist movement temporarily held in check by a mili-tary dictatorship.

However naive Camus's appeal for a compromise between assimila-tionist colonialism and militant nationalism, his prognosis for a country born of terror and civil war was thus all too accurate: "[T]omorrow Algeria will be a land of ruins and corpses that no force, no worldly power will be able to restore in our century." What Camus understood perhaps better and sooner than his (metropolitan) peers was not the Arabs—though as early as 1945 he had predicted that they could not much longer be expected to tolerate the conditions under which they were governed—but the peculiar culture of Algeria's European population and the price that would be paid if it were to be shattered.[47]

But it was above all as a moralist that Camus exited the intellectual lists over Algeria. Where no one was wholly in the right and where writers and philosophers were invited to lend their support to partisan political positions, silence, in Camus's view, represented an extension of his earlier promise to himself to speak out for the truth, however unpopular. In the Algerian case there was no longer any truth, just feelings. From this per-spective Camus's deep personal involvement in Algeria contributed to his pain and shaped his decision to refuse to lend his support to either party; and so it should, since Camus, as we have seen, took seriously the impera-

47. See "Lettre à un militant Algérien" (October 1955), in *Actuelles III*, p. 128.

tives of experience and sentiment. But it was a conclusion that he might have reached in any case, or so he believed.

One of the things that he had come to dislike the most about Parisian intellectuals was their conviction that they had something to say about everything, and that everything could be reduced to the kind of thing they liked to say. He also remarked upon the characteristically inverse relationship between firsthand knowledge and the confident expression of intellectual opinion. On Algeria his knowledge, his memories, and his search for an evenhanded application of justice rendered Camus truly ambivalent. Once one had called down a plague upon both houses, there was nothing left to be said. Intellectual responsibility consisted not in taking a position but refusing one where it did not exist. In those circumstances, silence seemed the most appropriate expression of his deepest feelings.

I have so far presented Camus's relationship to his time and place in rather disjunctive terms. That he was not a philosopher, others had made clear. That he was not, in the established sense, a "public intellectual," was something he himself had come to know. To his unsuitability for any political camp, and to the hyperpoliticized atmosphere of postwar France, his writings bear copious witness. Of his longing for the familiar territory of Algiers and his enduring sense of misplacement in Paris, we have ample evidence.[48] These—philosopher, engaged intellectual, Parisian—are all the things Camus was not. But he was, despite his misgivings at the idea, quite assuredly a moralist.

This requires some explanation. There is a long history of *moralistes* in France, making of them something of a distinctive category in French public life and letters. The term, which has been applied through the past three centuries to theologians, philosophers, essayists, politicians, novelists, and occasionally professors, lacks the underlying pejorative and pedantic connotation normally present in its English usage, as in *to moralize*. A "moralist" in France has typically been a man whose distance from the world of influence or power allows him to reflect disinterestedly upon the human condition, its ironies and truths, in such a way as to confer upon him (usually posthumously) a very special authority of the sort commonly reserved in religious communities for outstanding men of the cloth. In another time and place the secular term employed was *soothsayer*, whose etymology captures part of the point: a moralist in France was someone who told the truth.

But there was more to it than simple truth-telling. Raymond Aron, after all, told the truth and was duly unpopular, but that hardly made him a moralist. It seems to have been an important feature of true moralists that they not only made others feel uneasy, but caused themselves at least equal disquiet too. The sort of self-regarding discomfort that is audible in the writings of Rousseau, for example, is that of a moralist. To be a moralist was to lead an unquiet life—which is precisely what distinguished a moralist from an intellectual, whose public anguish over affairs of ethics or state normally accompanied an easy and confident private conscience.

It is somehow fitting that France's leading intellectual, in the distinctive local use of the term, should also have grasped so clearly—albeit in retrospect—the character of his former friend. In his obituary for Camus, Jean-Paul Sartre said of him that "he represented in this century, and against History, the contemporary heir to that long line of moralists whose work perhaps constitutes whatever is most distinctive in French letters." Many years before, Jean Paulhan had written perceptively to François Mauriac about *L'Etranger*, of which it was then fashionable to say that it showed strong American influences: "The general construction of the tale and the arrangement of its episodes might be said to put you in mind of *Candide* or *Jacques le fataliste*. It is the very opposite of Hemingway."[49]

As a moralist, Camus thought and wrote against the grain of his times in distinctive ways, all of which help account for his difficulty in finding a home in his century. His suspicion of the overweening ambitions of modern man, released from the constraints of modesty imposed by faith, led him to think of human endeavors in terms not of possibilities but of limits. There is, in some of his essays from the late forties, a striking anticipation of the plea for modesty and humility later associated with the moral strictures of a man like Václav Havel. The age of scientific optimism, the great visions of the nineteenth century, were not, for Camus, a prelude to infinite prog-

49. Jean-Paul Sartre, "Albert Camus," in *France-observateur*, January 7, 1960, rpt. in *Situations IV*, pp. 126–29; Jean Paulhan to François Mauriac, April 21, 1943, in Paulhan, *Choix de lettres, 1937–1945*, p. 304.

ress, but a burdensome inheritance to be set aside for fear of the greater damage they could yet inflict on minds and bodies alike.

The lesson of the first half of the twentieth century was not the optimistic one of mankind's infinite capacities for collective advance and improvement, but evidence of the risks entailed in pursuing such Promethean ambition to further extremes. "These ideologies (socialism and capitalism), born a century ago in a time of steam engines and complacent scientific optimism, are outdated now; in their present form they are incapable of addressing the problems of an age of atoms and relativity."[50]

Camus did not mean by this that human beings should respond to their situation with resignation, circumspection, or even moderation. He continued to believe in the need (psychological and social) for *révolte* against evil in its manifold forms; but the contemporary passion for the idea of revolution, the collective mobilization of men around projects driven by *reason*, terrified him. What came to count for Camus was what the classical writers meant by *measure*, the preference for prudent wisdom over unleashed ratiocination. As a writer Camus thought in images and from direct experience, and tied all his understanding of human possibilities and limits to a sense of place—in contrast to the preference of his intellectual contemporaries for understanding humanity as constrained, if at all, only by time and History.

It is this, rather than any ideological or doctrinal predisposition that led Camus to rail against the politics of his day. In a culture so resolutely polarized between extremes of Right and Left, Camus was unassimilable. The consequences of this polarization for the moral condition of his countrymen were a source of enduring unease for Camus: "For the past twenty years, especially, we in this country have so much detested our local political opponents that we have ended up preferring anyone else, even foreign dictators." In this case the point is made against the philo-Soviet Left, though it would have been no less pertinent as a criticism of the intellectual Right between the wars.

Camus's real target was not of course the Left, but political extremism itself. In *La Peste* the enduring image is of men of moderation and moral measure revolting not for an ideal but against intolerance and intransigence. In his writings during the Cold War he strove to warn of the moral

50. "Réponse à Emmanuel d'Astier de la Vigerie," in *Caliban*, 16, 1948, rpt. in *Actuelles I*, pp. 183–98.

and political costs of ideological rhetoric—"Starting with a wise healthy mistrust of bourgeois society's abuse of freedom, we have ended by becoming suspicious of freedom itself." Finally, despairing at the intellectual and political polarization over Algeria, Camus concluded thus: "The Right has given the Left exclusive rights to morality and received in return a monopoly of patriotism. France has lost twice over. It could have used some moralists less cheerfully resigned to their country's troubles."[51]

Central to Camus's politics, and to his pleas for measure in all things, was his growing awareness of the sheer complexity of the world, or rather the worlds in which humans must live. His arguments in *L'Homme révolté* drew on an intuition already present in his first major novel, and spelt out in *Sisyphe*: there is not one truth but many, and not all of them are accessible to us. Like Meurseault in *L'Etranger*, we are living and narrating a story that we can never fully understand. It was as much this as Camus's postwar calls for justice and retribution that led Mauriac to see in him a fundamentally religious (Christian?) sensibility. But for Mauriac, perfect understanding existed in principle; it was simply not vouchsafed to mere men. Camus, adrift in a world without God, believed no such thing. There were, as we might now say, no "metanarratives." We must decide what is right as we proceed.

It was this thought, worked out in his early writings, that caused many to see in Camus an "existentialist" like Sartre, seeking moral positions in a world shorn of absolute knowledge. But as *L'Homme révolté* would show, Camus had for a long time been moving to opposite conclusions from those of the circle at *Les Temps modernes*. Conceding to Necessity, aligning one's choices with those of History, in the sense used by Carl Schmitt (or by Hegel as interpreted by Alexandre Kojève) was a reactionary, not a radical solution, and made no more appealing by the invocation of reason. In an early postwar essay Camus was to remark that what distinguished an ancien régime reactionary from a modern one (of Right and Left alike) was that the former claimed that reason determined nothing, whereas the latter thought that reason determined everything.

In place of reason Camus invoked responsibility. Indeed, his writings bear witness to an ethic of responsibility deliberately set against the ethic of conviction that marked and marred his contemporaries—though Camus's

51. *Actuelles II*, p. 163; *Actuelles III*, preface, p. 19.

concept of responsibility differed sharply from that conceived by Weber or deployed by Aron. In retrospect we can see that he was struggling toward a wholly alien notion, and one for which in the French political and moral philosophy of that time there was no easy means of expression: the idea, made familiar to English readers through the writings of Isaiah Berlin, that life and thought consist of many sorts of truths and that these might be incommensurate. It was this idea that Roland Barthes almost stumbled across in *La Peste*, and which he found so troubling and politically incorrect.

Characteristically, Camus's thoughts were presented most effectively when he set them in an unconventional and unphilosophical key. In the 1938 essay "L'Eté à Alger," he observed, "I am coming to see that there is no transcendent happiness, no eternity beyond the curve of the days. The only truths that move me now are relative ones; only paltry and essential goods have true value. For other, 'ideal' ones I lack the necessary soul." The same half-ironic tone can be heard in "Entre oui et non," an essay originally published in Algiers in 1937 as part of the collection *L'Envers et l'endroit*, but which was no less the voice of the mature Camus who republished it in 1958 to a deafening silence: "Thus, every time I thought I had grasped the deeper meaning of the world, it was its very simplicity that overwhelmed me." He was thus right to conclude, in 1959, that French critics of his work had missed his "hidden side, the blind, instinctive one. French critics are interested primarily in ideas."[52]

The paradoxal consequence of Camus's insistence upon the multiplicity of truths was that he became an isolated defender of absolute values and nonnegotiable public ethics in an age of moral and political relativism. He was scornful of historical relativism as he understood it—if no one can ever be sure that they are right, he asked Merleau-Ponty, how can you say, as you do, that Hitler was a criminal?—and set himself against the error of deducing from the inadequacy of modern "bourgeois morality" the fraudulence of any and all moral measure.[53] As a result, he found himself in the increasingly uncomfortable role of public ethical assessor.

52. Quoted by Todd, *Albert Camus*, p. 12. For "Entre oui et non" and "L'Eté à Alger," see *Essais*, pp. 23–31, 67–79.

53. For the comment on Merleau-Ponty, see *Carnets, janvier 1942–mars 1951*, p. 212; note, too, this observation from *L'Homme révolté*, reprinted in *Essais*, p. 653: "In order to be creative, revolution needs moral or metaphysical rules, to balance the delir-

This situation was made all the more difficult in that Camus, who made a point of rejecting any hierarchical system of values or authority, ideological or religious, was in effect trying to impose a "view from no-where"—"I continue to believe that there is no higher meaning to life. But something does have a meaning—man, because he alone strives for one."[54] This stance, so out of step with the mood of the hour, was clearly articu-lated by Tarrou in *La Peste*: there is and can be only *one* unambiguous moral injunction, the duty to fight evil. Establishing just what evil consists in is not the problem, *pace* Camus's many critics—the "plague" itself is at once obscure and obvious. The real problem and greatest risk is that one may become a plague-carrier oneself. Or as Camus expressed it in his various discussions of show trials, "political" justice, and capital punishment: in an absurd world only an approximation of justice is possible—and no one kills for an approximation.

To many readers, Camus's pronouncements rang more than a little sanctimonious. In 1949 Lionel Abel, writing in *Partisan Review*, noted that "Camus's political writings, from what I have seen, have become windy, soft and vaguely noble. . . . Of late he has taken to identifying the morally desirable and the politically effective. . . . Camus will only raise his voice for what is clearly good."[55] Abel was right, though he was also hearing what Olivier Todd has called Camus's Spanish part, a self-conscious air of honor and rectitude that could shade into a tone of superiority that others grew to resent. Camus was aware of this and protective of the side of himself that it revealed.

This accounts for his vulnerability to a certain sort of criticism, against which he was for many years shielded in France by his almost iconic public standing. With the publication of *L'Homme révolté*, and the exchanges it provoked with his opponents, that protection fell away. Hence the force of Sartre's sallies. Who do you think you are, he wrote in *Les Temps modernes* in August 1952, to express such haughty disdain for your critics? "*Who* are you, to elevate yourself thus?" By what right do you proclaim yourself prose-cutor in chief on behalf of the good and the right—"Who appointed you

ium of history. Its distrust of the formal and mystificatory morality of bourgeois society is certainly justified; but the mistake has been to extend that distrust to moral claims of any kind."

54. *Lettres à un ami allemand* (Paris: Gallimard, 1948), fourth letter (July 1944), p. 74.
55. Qtd. in Lottman, *Albert Camus*, p. 452.

Public Accuser? The Republic of Superior Persons?" Catching Camus at his weakest point—his gnawing sense that he was speaking into a void and that his arguments and public pronouncements were empty of impact—Sartre concluded to devastating effect: "You pronounce sentence and the world remains unmoved. Your condemnations disintegrate upon contact with reality and you are obliged to begin again. If you stopped you would see yourself as you are: you are thus condemned to condemn, Sisyphus."[56]

Camus would have been a little less exposed to this sort of attack had he showed a greater disposition toward political realism. But for a man who spent many years writing about politics, and who for a time commanded a degree of public authority, he was peculiarly uncomfortable with the very idea of power. It was his suspicion of power in all its forms that led him to his critique of revolution as an abuse of the healthy human impulse to rebel. As early as December 1944 he had been sarcastically critical of the Provisional Government's demand that former resisters and armed *maquis* hand in their weapons, mourning the "ruin" of a revolution—and revealing a romantic inability to recognize not just the political realities of the hour but the very principles of stable government.[57] His later criticisms of Sartre and company for their own inability to reason politically and their obsession with the "material base" of everything might have had greater force had Camus himself not been at least as open to the charge of political (and economic) illiteracy.

As it was, Camus's own view of "man in revolt," and indeed of political man *tout court*, depended rather too much on the rejection of disagreeable undertakings and outcomes of any kind. Raymond Aron, in his polemics with the progressive intelligentsia, could charge his opponents not only with epistemological confusion but also with the no less telling defect of political incoherence. Camus was constrained to operate in a single key, that of ethical insufficiency, since his own writings, when it came to practical politics, often verged on incoherence themselves. In his final foray into the public argument over Algeria, the *Express* article of January 1956 noted earlier, his willfully unworldly (and from the Aronian perspective irresponsible) outlook is laid bare: "I firmly believe in the possibility of a free association between Arabs and French in Algeria. I also believe that such an

56. "Réponse à Albert Camus."
57. See *Combat*, December 17, 1944.

association of free and equal persons is the most equitable solution. But how to get there? After thinking long and hard about the different arguments, honesty compels me to admit doubts about all of them."

Naturally, Camus himself did not accept that his refusal to acknowledge the requirements of political decision-making rendered him powerless. In Olivier Todd's words, "Aron thinks about rulers, Camus addresses his readers." A year after his appeal for an Algerian truce Camus contributed a moving preface to a *livre blanc* on Imre Nagy and the Hungarian Revolution of 1956, and the following passage from it can perhaps stand as his definitive account of the purposes and limits of a moral stand in hopeless situations: "In the face of the Hungarian tragedy we were and are somehow powerless. But not completely. The refusal to accept a fait accompli, a vigilance of heart and mind, the denial of public space to lies and liars, the desire not to abandon innocence even after it has been done to death; these are the rules of a possible action. Inadequate, undoubtedly, but needed—in order to face down that other necessity, the so-called 'historical' one, to respond to it, to stand up to it, occasionally to neutralize it, and in the long run to overcome it and thereby advance, however little, the true history of humankind."[58]

The Hungarian Revolution of 1956, and Albert Camus's engagement in defense of its victims, is a useful reminder that Camus moved in another community as well; that of the displaced intelligentsia of the twentieth century. It is a striking thought that some of the most influential European writers and thinkers of the twentieth century came from the geographical peripheries of their own cultures—from Vilna and Königsberg, from Danzig, Trieste, Alexandria, and Dublin. Before World War I, and in a few cases after, these cities on the outer margins of German, Polish, Italian, Greek, and British cultural influence produced some of the most important figures within those cultures: Milosz, Grass, Joyce, Yeats, Wilde, Svevo, Cavafy, and Arendt, to name just the best known. Algiers could never aspire to a similar fame—no Kant ever flourished there, and few chose to think or write there—but it, too, sat uncomfortably on the periphery of a great cen-

58. Cited at length in Pierre Grémion, *Intelligence de l'anticommunisme. Le Congrès pour la Liberté de la Culture à Paris, 1950–1975* (Paris: Fayard, 1995), p. 268; Todd, *Albert Camus*, p. 386.

ter and passed that sense of vulnerable cosmopolitanism along to its more sensitive children.

What Camus also had in common with Milosz, Grass, Arendt, as well as with Konrad Jelenski, Arthur Koestler, Manès Sperber, and many others whom he met in Paris, was that they, too, were exiles—voluntary or otherwise; heirs to the vanished cosmopolitan communities of eastern and southern Europe in which Germans, Jews, Greeks, Italians, Poles, French, and others had lived for years in productive disharmony. Torn from their roots in World War I and obliterated in World War II and its aftermath, these men and women constituted a very special, transient community, that modern republic of letters formed against their will by the "chance survivors of the deluge," as Arendt put it in a 1947 dedication to Karl Jaspers.

Paris was the natural gathering place for these people—the only safe haven between 1933 and 1940, and the only interesting one for most of them after 1945. Britain was safe, but inhospitable in more senses than one, and New York was still a semialien world even for those, mostly Jewish, who had reached it and made a home there. It was in Paris that Camus met the German and East European exiles as well as Ignazio Silone, Nicola Chiaromonte, or Denis de Rougemont, men for whom voluntary or occasional exile in Paris made their political or cultural marginality back home in Italy or Switzerland more tolerable.

The mutual sympathy between Camus and the "foreign" intellectual community in 1950s Paris is very clear, and in striking contrast to the distance that often separated him from his fellow Frenchmen. It was Witold Gombrowicz (in distant Argentina) who asked Czeslaw Milosz to send Camus his own works as an act of solidarity after the publication of L'Homme révolté, and Hannah Arendt who wrote him in April 1952 a warm and admiring letter of praise for the book. He was well acquainted with the circle of writers around Preuves, even if he did not always share their politics, and was warmly received in Italian journals like Il Mondo and Tempo Presente.

Camus was one of the rare French intellectuals to welcome the "Polish October" of 1956, and Central Europeans, especially, returned the compliment, appreciating and understanding the drift of his work. Jeffrey Isaacs has perceptively noted the influence of Kafka on Camus's thought: in State of Siege the secretary at one point remarks, "We start with the premise that you are guilty. But that is not enough. You must learn to feel yourself that you are guilty." Milosz summed up the affinity in his obituary: "I now see what it was that allowed Camus the writer to take up the challenge of an age of gas ovens and concentration camps: he had the courage to make the elementary points."[59]

It has to be said that whereas Camus stands out from his French contemporaries in his grasp of the truth and the dilemmas of his age, his qualities of honesty and percipience seem less unusual in the company of Koestler, Arendt, Sperber, Silone, Milosz, Boris Souvarine (the biographer of Stalin), or Orwell, who should perhaps be counted in spiritual solidarity with this group. What all these writers had in common was an awareness, even an obsession, with the *crimes* of the twentieth century. In Arendt's words, "the problem of evil will be the fundamental question of postwar intellectual life in Europe—as death became the fundamental question after the last war."[60]

Camus did not make a notably distinctive contribution to the discussion of this question, but that is beside the point. He was part of that discussion, and much of his written work, published and unpublished, fictional and nonfictional, should be seen in that light. In contrast with most other French writers who, even if they raised similar themes, almost always did so with half an eye to a social, political, or historical constituency, Camus (like Koestler and Orwell) spoke only for, and often to, himself. In a time when many writers in France especially strove to be part of a larger process (the Revolution, Progress, the struggles of various oppressed communities at home and abroad), to be or to identify with Gramsci's organic intellectuals, Camus was one of the outsiders, the incarnation of the "inorganic" intellectual.

There is another foreign writer with whom it is instructive to compare Albert Camus. Like him, the English novelist and essayist E. M. Forster also made a point of emphasizing personal and private values over those prized by the community. The aesthetic sensibilities of the two men were of course vastly at odds, as were their literary concerns and material, but Camus admired Forster's work greatly—in October 1945 he quoted with

59. Milosz, "L'Interlocuteur fraternel"; Isaacs, *Arendt, Camus*, pp. 33, 57. But note, too, that Molière got there first: "Ils commencent ici par faire pendre un homme et puis ils lui font un procès" [Here they hang a man first and then they try him], *Monsieur de Pourceaugnac*, act 3, scene 2.

60. Hannah Arendt, "Nightmare and Flight," *Partisan Review* 12, no. 2 (1945), rpt. in *Essays in Understanding*, ed. Jerome Kohn (New York: Harcourt, Brace, 1994), p. 133.

approval Forster's assertion that only a work of art can be truly harmonic; society promises harmony but always in vain.

And it is curious to note an apparent similarity. In *What I Believe*, Forster wrote, "I hate the idea of causes, and if I had to choose between betraying my country and betraying my friend, I hope I should have the guts to betray my country." On the occasion of a famous exchange with a heckler at the time of his Nobel Prize, Camus defended his silence on Algeria and his refusal to take sides thus: "I have always condemned terror. Therefore I must condemn a terrorism operating blindly on the streets of Algiers, for example, and which one day might strike at my mother or my family. I believe in defending justice, but first I will defend my mother."[61]

Both men appear to be saying that in any system of values one must place loyalty, love, friendship above public duty or an abstraction. And in the context of their times (Forster was writing in the charged political atmosphere of the thirties, Camus's speech was made at the height of the Algerian war) their assertions were both unusual and controversial. But the similarity is only an apparent one, and the differences are a guide to what was truly distinctive about Camus. Camus was not stating a general preference for one form of loyalty over another, a distinction he would have been hard put to recognize (he saw his work during and after the Resistance, for example, as an indivisible instance of both friendship and patriotism).

He was quite simply, and angrily, reminding himself and his listeners of his distaste for abstractions—and revealing to a surprised audience one of the fundamental reference points in his life and work, his defensive relationship to his mother and his home. Moreover, and in this Camus is unmistakably French and Forster no less typically English, Camus juxtaposed an utterly concrete and solipsistic unit (mother) to a universal ethical abstraction (justice); whereas for Forster the alternatives were both less precise (country, friend) and more circumstantial (betray, causes).

For Camus, the larger problem was not how to choose between morality and politics, but how to forge a politics of moral engagement, in the absence of which only silence would do. In this way, and perhaps despite himself, he was constrained by his circumstances and even by certain very French habits of mind. One of these was the great difficulty he had in breaking with the "Left," in contrast with his friends among the Parisian

61. As reported in *Le Monde*, December 14, 1957, and reprinted in Todd, *Albert Camus*, p. 700.

foreigners. In his 1952 letter to *Temps modernes* he assured his readers, "If truth, in the end, seemed to me to be on the Right, I would join it there." But in practice he managed to avoid the choice.

Throughout the fifties he remained close to *Révolution prolétarienne*, the journal and group of unattached syndicalists, "pure socialists," and disillusioned but still idealistic ex-Leninists that represented, in France, the last outpost of the nineteenth-century anarcho-syndicalist movement. He probably continued to believe what he had written in *Combat* in October 1944, that any politics that took its distance from the working class was doomed; and he informed a syndicalist correspondent (in private) that whatever his silence over public affairs, this did not mean he had ceased to have a position or retreated to a "monastery."[62]

Clinging to the remnants of a defensible radical tradition, Camus imposed upon himself a considerable degree of discomfort. On the one hand he condemned Marxism, the "philosophical materialism" that he insisted on distinguishing from the otherwise healthy heritage of libertarian collectivism; like Simone Weil, he placed great faith in the unalienated capacity of real workers—"Bakunin lives in me." On the other hand he prefaced a 1953 edition of Alfred Rosmer's *Moscou sous Lénine* with the thought, "The difficult thing is to watch a revolution go wrong and still not lose one's faith in the need for it. That is precisely our dilemma." Camus thus endorsed Rosmer's view—widely accepted at the time and until quite recently, though long since dismissed by Aron, Souvarine, and others—that there had been a "good" Russian Revolution (that of Lenin) followed by a "bad" Soviet dictatorship, Stalin's.[63]

Albert Camus understood his situation all too well. He nearly always found himself stretched between the form his sentiments took in public and the rather different and inchoate intimations he had of them in private. This was as true of his political outlook as it was of his ethical and literary opinions and even his personal relations. "I tried for years to live according to everyone else's morality. I tried to live like everyone else, to be like everyone else. I said the right things even when I felt and thought quite differently. And the result is a catastrophe. Now I wander in the ruins,

62. See his editorial in *Combat*, October 1, 1944; letter to *Les Temps modernes*, June 30, 1952, rpt. in *Actuelles II*, pp. 85–124. See also Todd, *Albert Camus*, p. 677.

63. See Camus's May 1952 letter to the journal *Libertaire*, reprinted as "Révolte et romantisme," in *Actuelles II*, pp. 77–85; preface to *Moscou sous Lénine*, 1953, reprinted in *Actuelles II*, pp. 147–57.

cut off, alone and accepting my fate, resigned to my peculiarities and my weaknesses. I shall have to rebuild a truth—having lived my whole life in a sort of lie."[64]

In politics at least, Camus's dilemma, like that of so many other Frenchmen in postwar France, was that he was instinctively a social democrat. But in France, then and until recently, social democracy was the politics that dared not speak its name. For many of his contemporaries, in the Socialist Party and outside it, to abandon Marxism and the promise of a revolutionary *grand soir* was not only to give up a seductive myth but also to abandon to the Communists the well-tilled terrain of radical politics in France; they remained trapped in this dilemma until the disillusionment that followed François Mitterrand's 1981 presidential victory. In Camus's case, his tragic worldview and his instinctive adhesion to the romantic nostrums of rebellion and proletarian purity barred the road to social democratic language and politics, even though much of what Camus wrote and virtually everything he did after 1946 suggests he would have been much more *politically* at home in a northern European social-democratic milieu than ever he was in France.

Despite his rare lucidity, then (at a time when so many dwelt on lyrical clouds of willful ignorance), Albert Camus was in some ways a true mirror of France. It is conventional among students of Camus to see in him a man who could not reconcile his personal needs, his ethical imperatives, and his political engagement. He thus moved, so the story goes, from a passionate radical to a moderate reformer before becoming the voice of "reason" and detachment, a position barely distinguishable from withdrawal into private disappointment and silence. But there is more to it than this, and Sartre, despite his malicious intent, came closer. "Your personality, real and alive when nourished by events, has become a mirage; in 1944 you were the future, in 1952 you are the past, and what seems to you most intolerably unjust is that all this has happened to you from the outside while you have remained the same."[65]

For what Sartre said of Camus was actually true, perhaps more true, of France itself, a country that had passed from the self-confident morning of Liberation to the sullen resentment of the middle years of the Fourth Republic, aware that the world was changing around it and indignant at that

64. *Carnets III*, April 1959, p. 266.
65. "Réponse à Albert Camus," p. 121.

fact. Sure of themselves and their country at first, the Resistance generation had grown uncertain and cynical by the mid-fifties. Camus's silence
over Algeria was matched by the collective silence of his intellectual contemporaries in the face of the unprecedented social and economic transformation their country was about to undergo. They either did not notice
what was happening around them or else turned their face resolutely
against it, attending first to the promise of revolution in the East and
thence to its echo in the South and further afield. The thought would
hardly have pleased any of the parties concerned, but Camus's own trajectory—from confidence through uncertainty to silence—is all too sugges-
tive a metaphor for twentieth-century French intellectuals as a whole.

Today things are very different. With the disappearance of the Marxist mirage, and after two decades of painful and incomplete inquiry into
France's recent past, with Vichy a still festering sore and the intellectual
giants of the recent past reduced to a rubble of embarrassing citations, Camus
the Just remains, in the prescient words of one critic, "the most noble witness of a rather ignoble age." In an era of self-promoting media intellectuals,
vacantly preening before the admiring mirror of their electronic audience,
Camus's patent honesty, what his former schoolmaster called "ta pudeur
instinctive," has the appeal of the genuine article, a handcrafted master-
work in a world of plastic reproductions. That was already how he seemed
to Julien Green in February 1948: "I was struck by his face, so human and
sensitive. There is in this man such an obvious integrity that it imposes
respect almost immediately; quite simply, he is not like other men."[66]

In La Chute, Camus writes of being a "prophète vide pour temps médi-
ocres." There is little doubt that he had by then long since come to see
himself, in his gloomier moments, as an empty prophet, preaching to a deaf
and unconcerned audience. In Arendt's phrase, though not used to describe
him, Camus was indeed a "man in dark times," at odds with his time and
his place. But Camus's tragedy, perhaps, was that he lived and wrote in a
time when France, more than ever before or since, was the France of Jean-
Jacques Rousseau; heir to the codifications of thought and allegiance that
we now associate with the late French Enlightenment.

---

66. See Pierre de Boisdeffre, "Camus et son destin," in Camus (Paris: Hachette,
1964), pp. 265–79; Louis Germain to Albert Camus, April 30, 1959, published as an
annex to Le Premier Homme (Paris: Gallimard, 1994), pp. 328–31; Julien Green, Journal,
February 20, 1948, quoted in Todd, Albert Camus, pp. 419–20.

In *this* France Camus, for all his concern with the modern condition and the illusions of History, was an alien. He was assuredly French in certain fundamental ways, but his Frenchness came from another, earlier age. Camus did not speak for the France of Malraux, or even that of Zola. He has little in common with the great French thinkers of the nineteenth century—unlike Aron he was not interested in Tocqueville, for example. He lacked both the skepticism of Voltaire and the analytical detachment of Montesquieu.

Instead, he harked back to an earlier century and a different French tradition. In his self-interrogating earnestness, his *pudeur*, his Jansenist seriousness, he recalls and recaptures—more than anyone else in our time—something of the passion of Blaise Pascal—the Pascal who, writing three hundred years earlier, noted, "And thus we never live but only hope to live; forever setting out to be happy, it is inevitable that we never are." The distinctive combination of optimism and doubt that tortured Camus was of course familiar to Pascal—though there was open to him the option of resolving it by an appeal to faith in a way that his modern successor could never fully endorse, for all his religious turn of mind.

But on his own terms Camus, too, threw out a challenge, a twentieth-century coda to Pascal's more famous wager. In a discussion with Sartre, Malraux, Koestler, and Manès Sperber that took place on the evening of October 29, 1946, Camus suddenly addressed to his four companions the following question: "Don't you agree," he asked, "that we are all responsible for the absence of values? What if we, who all come out of Nietzscheanism, nihilism, and historical realism, what if we announced publicly that we were wrong; that there are moral values and that henceforth we shall do what has to be done to establish and illustrate them. Don't you think that this might be the beginning of hope?"[67]

Fifty years later much has changed. But in France as elsewhere, Camus's wager is still on the table—now more than ever. In all his uncertainty and his ambivalence, with his limitations and his reticence, Camus got it right where so many others went astray for so long. Perhaps Hannah Arendt was correct all those years ago—Albert Camus, the lifelong outsider, was indeed the best man in France.

67. *Carnets, janvier 1942–mars 1951*, p. 186.

THREE

The Peripheral Insider

RAYMOND ARON AND
THE WAGES OF REASON

*W*hen Raymond Aron died, in 1983, he had achieved a unique status in French public life. He was almost universally admired and respected; his writings and opinions had been elevated to near-canonical standing across a broad swathe of academic, intellectual, and public opinion. As the only prominent French thinker of his generation who had taken a consistent liberal stand against all the totalitarian temptations of the age, Aron represented not just a symbol of continuity with the great traditions of French thought but also a beacon of light pointing to the future at a time of confusion and doubt within the intellectual community. Where a few years earlier Aron had been, for the '68 generation, the vile and vilified incarnation of all that was wrong with the French mandarin elite, so by 1983 he was—in the opinion of some of the same people, now shorn of their illusions and ideals—the best hope for a revival of liberal thought. Institutes and journals sprang up to continue his work and pursue his objectives. Upon the funeral pyre of Sartrean radicalism a new generation of French intellectuals began to erect a monument to Aronian reason.

To anyone who recalls the hostility that Aron encountered in the French academic and intellectual establishment over the course of nearly three decades following the end of World War II, this was a striking reversal of fate. Raymond Aron lived just long enough to experience this transformation—hastened by the publication of his *Mémoires* in the year of his death—which gave him some pleasure and much cause for ironic reflection. Having knowingly chosen the discomforts of honesty and clarity in a political and intellectual culture marked by confusion and bad faith, Aron never complained at his exclusion from the mainstream intellectual community. But despite his widely acknowledged impact upon generations of students, his respectful audience among the readers of his column in *Le Figaro*, and his admirers in the fellowship of scholars across four continents,

Aron was largely excluded from the company of his peers in France. He lived much of his adult life on the periphery of his natural home.

There is, of course, something mildly counterintuitive about describing Raymond Aron as peripheral. He was, in one sense, a consummate insider, an exemplary Frenchmen of his generation and pedigree. Born in 1905 (the same year as Sartre), he followed the career path of an outstandingly successful scholar, surpassing his peers at every stage. He attended the elite classes of the Lycée Condorcet, was admitted to the Ecole Normale Supérieure at a time when it was still the leading *grande école* of the country, took the national *agrégation* in philosophy in 1928 and was awarded first place. He prepared and defended a doctoral thesis in philosophy and was universally regarded as the most promising philosopher of his generation when World War II put a temporary end to his academic career.

After the war he postponed his return to the university for a while, turning his attentions instead to journalism—he would write some four thousand editorial articles for *Le Figaro* and other papers in the course of the postwar decades—but in 1954 he was appointed to the Sorbonne chair (albeit in sociology) for which he had long seemed destined. From then until his belated election to a chair at the Collège de France in 1971 Aron's progress was consistently blocked by a de facto alliance of opponents from Left and Right, but he was nonetheless elected to membership of the Académie des Sciences Morales et Politiques in 1963 and taught a regular seminar at the Ecole des Hautes Etudes en Sciences Sociales. By the time of his death he was widely regarded, in the words of François Furet, as "not just a great professor, but the greatest professor in the French university."[1]

There is little doubt that of all the accolades awarded him, this is the one that best fits both Aron's talents and his deepest aspirations. His natural disposition to think and write as a scholar, together with his often-attested qualities as a teacher, were complemented by the pleasure he took throughout his life in the company of ideas and men of ideas. In his memoirs, composed shortly before his death, he reflected back on his feelings upon entering the Ecole Normale for the first time, sixty years earlier : "My first impression, on entering the rue d'Ulm, was, I confess at the risk of appearing ridiculous, one of wonder. Even today, if I were asked: why? I

1. François Furet, "Raymond Aron 1905–1983: Histoire et Politique," *Commentaire* 28–29 (1985): 52.

would reply in all sincerity and innocence that I have never met so many intelligent men gathered in such a small space."[2]

Moreover, and alongside his scholarly writings and teaching, Aron was a characteristically French "insider" in another sense. His contacts at the Ecole, his years with the Free French in London where he spent the war, his decades of political journalism had provided him with a broad range of contacts and friends throughout the upper reaches of French public life. It was his unusually good connections in government, public administration, and parts of the business world, for example, that gave Aron's editorial writings their special authority.

In addition to the moral authority and rigorous argument conventionally associated with the upper reaches of French intellectual journalism, Aron's articles had the air of credibility that derived from the author's evident command of his subject. Aron always seemed to know what he was talking about, and his authority in this respect derived in large measure from his close acquaintance with the men who were making the decisions he was analyzing. Without ever being a man "in" the French establishment—Raymond Aron served only once in government, as *chef de cabinet* in a short-lived Ministry of Information in 1946, and that was under André Malraux—Aron was very close to the political elites of France for many years (as he was to those of the United States, Germany, and Britain at various times). He thus wrote from the outside, but with an insider's sense of realities and limits.

There is another dimension to Aron's qualities as a man very much at home in and part of the French public world of his day. For in addition to being an academic mandarin, a confidant of men of power and a prominent journalist, Raymond Aron was also an intellectual. This does not necessarily follow from his scholarly ambitions or attainments—many French intellectuals of his time were not scholars or teachers, and relatively few of his fellow academics were intellectuals in the sense usually understood. But Raymond Aron unquestionably was. He took an active lifelong interest in public matters beyond his sphere of professional expertise (though, as we shall see, he made a point of knowing more than most of his fellow intellectuals before intervening in public debate), and he took very seriously the responsibility of intellectuals to be involved in important public debates.

2. Raymond Aron, *Mémoires: 50 ans de réflexion politique* (Paris: Julliard, 1983), p. 31.

But most of all, he came to the role of the public intellectual from the same starting point as that of many other well-known French intellectual activists—that of the philosopher.

For his contemporaries this was no surprise. To Claude Lévi-Strauss as to many others, Aron was and remained above all the author of *Introduction à la philosophie de l'histoire,* his doctoral thesis on the nature and limits of historical knowledge, first defended in front of a disapproving audience of Sorbonne philosophers and sociologists in March 1938. The striking originality of Aron's argument, and the impact of his philosophical rigor, is muted for us today. He was building a case against the historical positivism then dominant in the French university but now long defunct. His argument was that historical understanding cannot be separated from the position and limits of the person seeking that understanding and that a consciousness of one's own place in the process one is seeking to describe and explain both deepens and restricts the scope of all such explanation. Shorn of its epistemological rigor and empirical illustration, this claim now forms the core of much of what passes for relativism in modern academic cant, and we have some difficulty seeing just how original and even courageous it was at the time.

That Aron was courageous, even provocative, in his reasoning is made very clear if we recall the context. Academic philosophy in France in the 1930s was a long way behind that of Germany or Austria. History and the social sciences were practiced on unself-consciously realist principles, to the extent that they recognized any methodological concerns at all. What Aron called the "dialectic" had hardly made its presence felt within the university, and the new philosophical thinking of Husserl and Heidegger or the sociological revolution of Max Weber, with their implications for all forms of social investigation and political action, were virtually ignored. Even Hegel was a largely unknown quantity, and those young radicals who did study him, at the feet of Alexander Kojève, did so with more than half an eye to his contribution to the thought of Marx. To claim, as Aron did in his thesis, that history was something we construct as we live ("Everyone, according to his idea of himself, chooses his past"), was a radical departure from all that his teachers held most dear.[3]

---

3. Raymond Aron, *Introduction à la philosophie de l'histoire. Essai sur les limites de l'objectivité historique* (1938; rpt. Paris: Gallimard, 1986), p. 70.

Of course there were others in France at the time who were also breaking out from the straitjacket of French academic positivism—Marc Bloch
and Lucien Febvre, the founders and editors of *Annales;* or Marcel Mauss,
Maurice Halbwachs, and others who were beginning to shape the distinctively French school of cultural anthropology. But Aron was different, precisely because he was not abandoning old schools of thought but engaging
and dismantling them on their own ground. He was not ignoring the objectives of any good social science, the need "above all to establish necessary
connections through the observation of regularities." Nor was he suggesting for a moment, in contrast to his contemporary *normalien* Paul Ni-
zan, that facts and truths were somehow class- or context-dependent.

Aron merely wished to argue, in an exercise whose analytical rigor was
itself something unusual for its scholarly era, that there are limits, epistemological limits, to historical objectivity; that we come closer to the latter,
paradoxically, by recognizing these limits; that these limits arise from the
situated position of the historical actor; and that this dilemma cannot be
overcome by some sort of philosophical sleight of hand but by the uncomfortable recognition of the necessary duality of the past: "Thus a dual
knowledge of the past would be possible, one dealing directly with the
mind as inscribed in the material world, the other with the consciousness
of a person or group accessible through such objectifications; an alternative
deriving not only from the situation of the historian, but also from the
essential structure of reality."[4]

Here Aron was leading his audience toward the delicate balance that
would shape his thinking for the rest of his life. There *is* reason in history,
just as there is knowledge about the past. But whether or not there are
ultimate reason and *absolute* knowledge is beside the point since we cannot
have access to them—our own place within the story deprives us of that
Archimedean point from which to see the whole. A quarter of a century
later he would make essentially the same point: "Theoretical elaboration,
in our view, should serve to sharpen awareness of the plurality of goals and
aims, rather than favoring the tendency to monoconceptual interpretations, always arbitrary and partisan."[5]

4. Aron, *Introduction,* p. 91.
5. Aron, "A propos de la théorie politique," in *Revue française de science politique* 12,
no. 1 (1962), rpt. in *Etudes politiques* (Paris: Gallimard, 1972), p. 168.

For Aron's admiring contemporaries, his thesis and his energetic de-fense of it before an audience of skeptical senior professors, taught three important lessons. First, that there is a plurality of possible interpretations of men and women and their works, and the decision to privilege one inter-pretation above the others is and must be an act of choice. Second, which follows from this, nothing is determined—the past and the present are composed of choices, and while these choices have consequences, they rep-resent directions that might under other circumstances not have been taken. Third, though human beings are free to choose how to make their world (and how to interpret it, which also counts), the actions they take have real outcomes, for which they must accordingly take responsibility.

Taken together, these conclusions justified the response to Aron by his contemporaries and peers: that he had elaborated, for his generation, the outline of a properly *existential* philosophy of history. Sartre himself was in no doubt. When, a little later, he presented his college friend with a copy of his own new work, *Being and Nothingness*, he described it as merely an "ontological introduction" to Aron's work. And he was not mistaken. Aron had presented his thesis as an attempt to get beyond morality and ideology and determine the "true content of possible choices, limited by reality it-self"; the Sartrean existentialist project, if one can write thus, would con-sist in accounting for the situation Aron had laid bare, and behaving ac-cordingly.

Aron's immersion in the philosophical concerns of his generation—and the crucial role he played in introducing phenomenology and existen-tialist reasoning to his French contemporaries, hitherto ignorant of such matters—have been largely forgotten. After 1945, as Aron became ac-tively engaged in political journalism and the academic social sciences, and he and Sartre took opposite sides in the Cold War, their common critique of philosophical idealism and historical positivism was obscured by their disagreements. And yet it was Aron, even more than Sartre and his fellow intellectuals, who remained loyal to the demands of his own reasoning. In recognizing that human beings are always *in* history and make it them-selves, he wrote, we do not have to give in to relativism or nihilism, aban-doning any hope of understanding our world. "On the contrary, we affirm thereby the power of the man who makes himself by assessing his place in the world and in making choices. Only thus can the individual overcome relativity through the absoluteness of decision, and only thus can he take possession of the history that he carries within him and that becomes his own."[6]

There is another sense in which Aron was absolutely at one with the French intellectual world of his day. He was obsessed, for much of his adult life, with Marxism. In contrast with most French intellectuals, including most French Marxists, Aron was a careful reader of Marx—and his obsession with Marxism derived in some measure from his frustration at the ignorance and inconsistencies of what passed for Marxist thought in French hands. Moreover, some of Aron's interest in the writings of Marx has to be understood through the vector of his concern with the Soviet Union—again, something he shared with his political opponents. But it remains a striking fact about Aron that he returned again and again to the subject of Karl Marx, so much so that in his memoirs he pauses at one point to wonder whether he didn't perhaps spend too much time on debating that "secular religion." Some of his best analytical writings and all his most powerful polemical essays deal with Marxism and Marxists, and it is tempting to agree with Aron that his interest in combating the error of his era amounted to a form of transposed "anticlericalism."[7]

Nonetheless, Aron's interest in Marx and his followers was consistent with his earlier philosophical concerns. His best-known and most influential critique of *marxisant* delusions among the left intelligentsia, *L'Opium des intellectuels*, is in certain respects a companion volume and successor to his *Introduction à la philosophie de l'histoire*. And Marx himself interested Aron in part for his place in the story of modern social thought, in part for his trenchant observations on nineteenth-century capitalism, but above all for his *own* unsuccessful efforts to construct a philosophy of history at once "objective" and open to decisive human intervention. Aron could not help but admire this Promethean project, all the more so since it had informed his own initial writings, and his empathy for Marx's ambitions provided him with greater insight into the strengths and failings of the Marxist undertaking than was the case for most would-be Marxists among his fellow intellectuals. The irony of this was not lost on Aron himself.

6. *Introduction*, pp. 420–21.

7. See "Un philosophe libéral dans l'histoire" (1973), in Aron, *Essais sur la condition juive contemporaine* (Paris: Editions de Fallois, 1989), p. 222.

If Aron shared so many of the salient characteristics of the French intellectual of his day and was in most respects a leader in his generation and recognized as such, in what ways was he not "one of them"? The simple answer, of course, was that after 1947 he took a firm stand in support of the Western Alliance at a time when most French intellectuals either favored the Soviet bloc or else dreamed of a neutral "third way." But while it is true that the Cold War did indeed shape for thirty years the configuration of public intellectual life in France as elsewhere, it is not enough to note that Aron took an unpopular position and paid the price for it within his natural community.

The question is, why did he choose thus? He was by his own account a socialist; in 1945 he had joined the editorial board of *Les Temps modernes* with Sartre, de Beauvoir, and others; his philosophical inclinations and intellectual tastes were not strikingly at variance from those of his contemporaries on the intellectual left, and the lifelong polemics he exchanged with them suggest that in spite of being the best-known liberal commentator in France (which in practice defined him for most of his audience as a conservative) he remained at heart a member of the left-leaning community. The reasons for his choices, the ways in which he became the Raymond Aron known to a later generation, must be sought not in his political choices but in the ways in which he came to them. And it is here that he distinguishes himself, in every sense and in a variety of keys.

To begin with, Aron was the most cosmopolitan French intellectual of his time. I have already noted his interest in German thought, first acquired during his extended period of study in Germany during the dying years of the Weimar Republic, 1930–33. Indeed, until he became interested in Tocqueville and Montesquieu in the fifties, most of Aron's intellectual debts were to German thinkers. From reading Husserl in particular he derived the shape of his philosophy of history. From Max Weber, about whom he wrote in a number of essays, he developed his complex vision of the relation between understanding and action. At odds with the dominant (Durkheimian) strain of French social theory, with its prejudice in favor of the identification of "scientific" laws and processes, Aron was attracted to Weber's careful interrogation of the relationship between consciousness and choice, his appreciation of the *responsibilities* of the social scientist toward both his subject matter and his own epoch. In *La Sociologie allemande contemporaine*, first published in 1936, he introduced French readers to a tradition of social reasoning and criticism radically different from that inherited from Comte and Durkheim and far better attuned, as it seemed to Aron, to the needs and predicaments of the hour.

The crucial difference lay in Weber's famous distinction between conviction and responsibility. The task of the social scientist (or intellectual) could not be restricted to the business of understanding social processes, in the past or in the present. For the reasons Weber gave, which were not so different from those Aron himself offers in his philosophical writings, the intellectual must always face the decision of how to act in a given situation—understanding is not sufficient. But it was at least in principle possible to choose between acting either *in* history or else in the *light* of history—to engage in the debates and conflicts of one's time from a feeling of conviction or from a sense of responsibility.

In later years Raymond Aron would come to question Weber's own presentation of this option: the temptation to find necessity or even inevitability in a given historical moment, something to which Max Weber, like Carl Schmitt, was always prone, could lead persons of conviction and responsibility alike to abdicate to History choices that should have been left to human beings.[8] But the Weberian calculus, the sense that we can behave coherently and responsibly without making partisan commitments—or else that a partisan engagement may under certain circumstances be the responsible option—lay behind many of Aron's own public utterances, as he explicitly recognized when approving the title of a book of interviews with him late in life—*Le Spectateur engagé.*

After the war, the center of gravity of Aron's interests shifted steadily away from German thought toward the great social commentators of an earlier French tradition. But here, too, Aron was at odds with his contemporaries, who were as unconcerned with Montesquieu or Tocqueville as they had been with the great Germans (Marx always excepted).[9] What seems to have brought Aron to the writers of what he called, following Elie Halévy, the "English school of French political thought," was his frustration with the grand scale of analysis characteristic of German thought—as

8. See Aron, "Max Weber et la politique de puissance" (1964), in *Machiavel et les tyrannies modernes* (Paris: Editions de Fallois, 1993), p. 226.

9. Aron claimed never to have come across the name Tocqueville during his studies, neither at the Ecole Normale nor the Sorbonne! See Aron, *Le Spectateur engagé* (Paris: Julliard, 1981), p. 27.

early as 1936 he would remark that the value of even Weber's "bird's-eye view" of history was uncertain, however seductive. What distinguished Montesquieu and his heirs, by contrast, was their understanding of the *political*, and their willingness to accord politics an autonomous and important place in social and historical explanation.[10]

Montesquieu, however, posed a difficulty. His approach, which assigned governments and institutions to different social and geographical and historical milieus, seemed to run the risk of abdicating (moral) judgment. If each society has, and can only have, one appropriate form of government or leadership, from what perspective may the observer or analyst ever hope to criticize or condemn such "natural" institutions? Aron understood why the question in that form would not have troubled Montesquieu, but it troubled *him*. Nevertheless, in his two-volume study of Clausewitz, a work of which he was particularly proud, Aron made the point that what he most admired in the nineteenth-century German strategist—his capacity to treat each historical problem or choice in its singular context—was distinctively Montesquieu-like in its clarity and honesty. "Clausewitz's thinking resembles that of Montesquieu more than anyone has ever suggested, much more than it does that of Kant or Hegel." The challenge was to combine an appreciation of historical particularity—whether in military strategy or sociological description—with the call for conceptual explanation. The modern world sorely missed Montesquieu's grasp of the place of "les lois et les moeurs" in the human condition; the contemporary disposition to simplify, to attribute "the misfortunes of some to the advantages of others" served only, in Aron's view, to give nationalism a clean conscience.[11]

In Tocqueville, Aron found a kindred spirit, a man whose grasp of both social *and* political explanations gave him a platform from which to see further into the historical and contemporary sources of the problems of his time than any of his peers. Of the three social theorists of the nineteenth

10. See Aron, *German Sociology*, trans. Mary Bottomore and Thomas Bottomore (Free Press, New York, 1964), p. 51; originally published in 1936 as *La Sociologie allemande contemporaine*. Commenting elsewhere on the airy reflections by André Malraux and others about postindustrial society, the end of a civilization, etc., Aron remarked, "These vast bird's-eye perspectives terrify me. I plead ignorance." See Aron, *La Révolution introuvable* (Paris: Fayard, 1968), p. 46.

11. See Aron, *Penser la guerre: Clausewitz*, 2 vols. (Paris: Gallimard, 1976), 1:98. See also Aron, "Réveil du Nationalisme?" *Le Figaro*, February 24, 1964.

century who interested Aron most, it was Tocqueville whose vision "most resembles West European societies in the 1960s."[12] Tocqueville's account of French instability since the ancien régime, in which elites proved consistently unable to agree on the forms of political life, and his insights into the "querulous satisfaction" of modern societies helped shape Aron's understanding of his own age. But perhaps more important, Aron could not help seeing, in Tocqueville's isolation amid the ideological currents of the nineteenth century, a foretaste of the difficulties of the liberal thinker in a later age: "Too liberal for the side from which he came, not enthusiastic enough about new ideas for the republicans, he was taken up neither by the Right nor the Left, but remained suspect to them all. Such is the fate reserved in France to the English or Anglo-American school."[13]

It was from his reading in French and German social thought alike that Aron would thus forge his distinctive critique of historicized interpretations in general, and Marxism in particular. It did not follow, he would argue, that because a particular political system, or even a system of reasoning, could be located in a given social context or historical moment, one could derive from this knowledge any judgment as to its suitability or value in general terms. But, conversely, it was equally mistaken to attempt to assess the value of different political systems or ideologies without reference to their truth or falsity (an error he attributed to Karl Mannheim). If one wished to understand politics and political ideas, it was necessary *both* to situate these in their proper context *and* to measure them against criteria of good and evil, true and false, which could not be derived from those contexts alone. Immune, thanks in part to his Weberian sympathies, to the appeal of abstract neo-Kantian evaluations of political choice, Aron was unusual in his equally rigorous dismissal of the genetic fallacy.

Accordingly, Aron's polemical engagements with the Marxism of his contemporaries reflected the complexity and range of his concerns. Since he saw the Soviet ideological project as a device for saving Reason-in-History at the price of reason itself, the latter was his chief weapon. Why, he asked, even supposing that human history possesses a purpose and a goal, would the crucial test of that goal take place in the mid-twentieth century,

---

12. Aron, *Les Etapes de la pensée sociologique* (Paris: Gallimard, 1967), p. 229. Note, though, that Aron hastened to add that in the 1930s it was Marx's account of the human condition that rang most true.

13. Ibid., p. 18.

in a country curiously unsuited for such a "sublime role"? And who authorized us to draw such definitive conclusions anyway? "Either History is the ultimate tribunal, and it will not pronounce sentence until the day of judgement; or conscience (or God) is the judge of History, and the future has no more authority than the present." No observer—historian, sociologist, or whoever—can hope to know the *meanings* of actions, institutions, and laws. History is not absurd, but no living being can grasp its final meaning.[14]

The danger of holistic historical reasoning, in Aron's view, lay less in the damage it does to people's minds than in the threat it poses to their bodies—"Ministers, commissars, theorists and interrogators . . . will try to make men what they would spontaneously be if the official philosophy were true."[15] Where the cunning of History fails, men will intervene on its behalf. For the same reasons, the simple category error of confusing economic competition ("class struggle") with political conflict—the mistake of identifying the struggle over the instruments of power with the struggle for power itself—substitutes for power (which is a human relationship) arbitrarily chosen determinants of that relationship.

This conflation of the social (or the economic) with the political permits a confusion of political language that not only defeats its own purpose—to reveal the world to itself—but contributes fatally to the very political outcomes it purports to oppose. Political argument of this kind is at once arrogantly overambitious—since it fails to grasp the partial and historically determined quality of all understanding, its own included— and dangerously foreshortened, in its unwillingness to engage the world not as it should be but as it is.

In later years Aron would come to wonder whether he had not squandered his energies in such polemics, bringing a powerful epistemological and empirical artillery to bear on debates "whose scientific value seems to me thin. . . . Men, and especially intellectuals, believe what they want to believe—me as well, perhaps—and are, in the final analysis, impervious

---

14. Aron, *D'Une Sainte Famille à l'autre. Essais sur les marxismes imaginaires* (Paris: Gallimard, 1969), p. 20; *The Opium of the Intellectuals,* trans. Terence Kilmartin (Lanham, Md.: University Press of America, 1957), pp. 133, 137, originally published as *L'Opium des intellectuels* in 1955.

15. Aron, "Macht, Power, Puissance: prose démocratique ou poésie démoniaque?" (1964), in *Etudes politiques,* p. 179.

to arguments."[16] But it is significant that for at least twenty years, from 1947 to 1968, the debate over Marxism—or rather the exchange of polemics, since no debate ever took place—seemed to Raymond Aron to merit his full attention. Were it not for his sense that the errors of Marxism were part of a larger, and more interesting, set of problems in social analysis and historical explanation, it is unlikely that he would have attended to them quite so fully, or written about them with such moral and analytical intensity.

The difference between Aron and many of his contemporaries, on both sides of the political divide, was that for Aron these matters of high theory spoke directly to real, and in his view urgent, political worries. Ever since his student years in Germany, Aron was absorbed with, perhaps even obsessed by, the fragility of liberal polities and the threat of anarchy and despotism. This marked his writings in a way that nothing about his comfortable childhood and youth could have predicted, and it sets him apart from almost every other French intellectual of his generation. It accounts for his remarkable prescience during the thirties, when most French politicians and intellectuals alike were tragically slow to grasp the meaning of Hitler's revolution, and for his response to almost every major crisis in postwar French life, from the turmoil of the Liberation to the events of May 1968.

Writing from Cologne in 1931, Aron described to Jean Guéhenno a Germany "on the edge of the abyss" and expressed his sense of despair at French insouciance and at the hopelessness of trying to arouse the public to awareness of the crisis. "If you read both French and German newspapers, if you live in both countries, it is awful. Where are we heading?" By 1933 he had given up the effort to convince his correspondents or readers of the danger of a Nazi revolution already on the verge of consummation, and focused instead upon the (equally forlorn) task of arousing a degree of political realism in French policymaking.

In an article published that year in *Esprit*, Aron called for an end to "idealist aspirations" in French foreign policy and for a recognition that with the defeat of Weimar the Versailles era had come to an end. Disarmament and negotiation could no longer substitute for defense: "Left-wing Frenchmen use a sentimental language (justice, respect) that shields them

16. *La Révolution introuvable*, p. 132.

from harsh realities. In their desire to make amends for our mistakes they forget that our policies must take into account not the past, but Germany today. And it is no reparation of past faults to commit new ones in the opposite direction. . . . A good policy is measured by its effectiveness, not its virtue."[17] A typically Aronian sentiment.

No one was listening, of course, and even anti-Fascist intellectuals in France as elsewhere preferred to speculate about revolution at home (or in Spain) than to recognize the inevitability of a coming war with Germany. Raymond Aron thus lived the 1930s in anxious frustration, watching the slow unraveling of civil society and the political system in France as he had first observed it in Germany. His second experience of civic disorder and collapse, in the spring of 1940, confirmed his growing understanding of the workings—and vulnerability—of democracies and accounts for his (strictly conditional) support for de Gaulle in the early years of the Fourth Republic. Thereafter he interpreted events and decided his own stance with constant reference to these formative experiences of his own early adult life—even his attitude to the Vichy regime was shaped by them: until November 1942 he was willing to allow that it had at least contributed to preventing civil conflict between the French.[18]

Thus, in the postwar years, Aron was a vigorous critic of those who sought a "catastrophic" solution to the social woes of postwar France (or anywhere else). As he recognized, this taste for violent, "definitive" solutions, as though the road to utopia *necessarily* lay through destruction, was in part born of the experience of war. But he opposed it energetically, and when France came as near as it ever has in this century to a real peacetime civil conflict, at the time of the Communist-led strikes of 1948, Aron took a hard line: "The inevitable struggle will be muted only to the extent that the state has strengthened its means of action. It is just not acceptable that in the mines and electrical plants of France people are

17. Aron in *Esprit*, February 1933, pp. 735–43. See also Marie-Christine Granjon, "L'Allemagne de Raymond Aron et de Jean-Paul Sartre," in *Entre Locarno et Vichy: Les relations culturelles franco-allemandes dans les années 1930*, ed. H-M. Bock, R. Mayer-Kalkus, and M. Trebitsch, 2 vols. (Paris: CNRS, 1993), notably 2:468–77; and Nicole Racine, "La Revue *Europe* et l'Allemagne, 1929–1936," in Bock, Mayer-Kalkus, and Trebitsch, pp. 631–58.

18. See, e.g., *Le Spectateur engagé*, p. 88.

more afraid of the Communists than of engineers, directors, and ministers combined."[19]

His argument in favor of Algerian independence, as we shall see, was similarly driven by a concern for French civil stability and order. But it is in Aron's reaction to the events of 1968 that the salience of this theme is most obvious. Despite his general sympathy with the students' criticism of French higher education, and his growing dislike of the authoritarian Gaullist state and its policies (domestic and foreign alike), he took an absolutely uncompromising line against the student movement, its intellectual supporters, and the public disruption it brought about. Like Edgar Morin and other professorial enthusiasts for student radicalism, Aron saw that the order of modern societies is inherently fragile.

Unlike them, he found this to be a source of anxiety. Once a carnival turns into anarchy, he wrote, it rapidly becomes less tolerable than almost any form of order. Analogies with revolutions past were misconceived, he noted: "To expel a president elected by universal suffrage is not the same thing as expelling a king." Even the university, whatever its well-recognized defects, depended upon a degree of order: "The University, any university, requires a spontaneous consensus around respect for evidence and for unforced discipline. To break up this social unit without knowing what to replace it with, or in order to break up society itself, is aesthetic nihilism; or rather, it is the eruption of barbarians, unaware of their barbarism."[20]

Aron's criticism of French intellectuals, and their student followers, was thus driven as much by what he came to see as their political irresponsibility as by their philosophical or moral errors. Writing in 1969, he assimilated the French "existentialists" to the "Marxists and para-Marxists of the Weimar Republic" and held them implicitly responsible for any political crisis they helped bring about—a point he had made explicitly thirty years earlier, in an article that accused the German and Italian socialists of having contributed in different ways to their own nemesis. In the introduction to Les Désillusions du progrès, also written in 1969, he makes the link quite explicit: "Violence, even in the name of ideas diametrically opposed to those of interwar fascism, risks dragging liberal societies toward the same

19. "La Cité déchirée: L'Etat et les Communistes," Le Figaro, April 11, 1948.
20. See La Révolution introuvable, pp. 13, 35.

tragedy as that of thirty years ago. . . . Self-proclaimed non-Communist
Marxists actively helped bring down the Weimar Republic: some of them
speak and act as though they dream of repeating that achievement."[21]

The link in Aron's thought between political stability, civil order, and
public liberties is thus clear—and as with Tocqueville, it was in essence a
product of experience and observation rather than theory. This helps us
understand his way of thinking about liberty in general, and the totalitarian
threat to it. Unlike social commentators in the United States, for example,
Aron was not an especially enthusiastic advocate of the term *totalitarian* as
a general category covering various modern threats to the open society. His
distaste for grand theory extended to anti-Communist rhetoric as well, and
his thoughts about totalitarianism derived in the first instance from his
concern for its opposite—the partial, always imperfect reality of liberty,
constrained and threatened by necessity and history. If the United States
was to be preferred in the global conflicts of the day, it was not because it
represented some higher or more logically satisfying order of life, but because it stood as the guarantor, however defective, of public liberties.

The Soviet Union, on the other hand, was marked by the very extremism of its system—the way in which all its particular defects were integral
to its general project. This distinguished it from the authoritarianism of
Franco, for example: the prison camps of Spain were a weapon of repression, but not part of the very workings of a slave economy in the manner
of the camps of the KGB or the SS. It was this same integrated quality
that paradoxically made truly totalitarian systems so appealing to utopian
intellectuals, as Aron understood : the dialectic of a "violence that over-
comes violence itself" was what appealed to someone like Maurice
Merleau-Ponty in the early postwar years. And just because imperfect, in-
termediary, partial institutions were the main bulwark of political freedom,
so they were most vulnerable to the revolt against "alienation," the search
for final, logical solutions to what was in practice the human condition.[22]

In Aron's thinking, then, there was an intimate link between the
French revolutionary myth—that desire to "bridge the gap between moral
intransigence and intelligence" as he put it—and the distinctively *total*

21. Aron, *Les Désillusions du progrès* (Paris: Calmann-Lévy, 1969), pp. xviii–xix. See
also *D'Une Sainte Famille à l'autre*, p. 43, and "Le Socialisme et la guerre" (1939), in
Machiavel et les tyrannies modernes, pp. 309–31.

22. See Aron, "Messianisme et Sagesse," *Liberté de l'Esprit*, December 1949, pp.
159–62.

threat to freedom represented by a certain kind of repressive society. Hence the remarkable capacity of highly intelligent men and women to deny the evidence of their eyes; writing in 1950, at a time when the appeal of Stalin extended well beyond the boundaries of those parties and countries under his direct control, Aron commented, "The ludicrous surprise is that the European Left has taken a pyramid-builder for its God." The fault lay in the disposition of intellectuals to take words for things—"It requires the naïveté and remoteness of the Christians of *Esprit* or the humanists around Saint Germain des Près to be taken in by the phraseology of Stalinist Marxism."[23]

But it was not enough to lay bare the unpalatable facts about totalitarianism. There were some uncomfortable truths about free societies, too, that intellectuals were equally disposed to ignore. For Aron's generation in the twenties and thirties, the widespread appeal of the writings of the philosopher Alain (Emile Chartier) had lain in his treatment of *all* political authority as incipiently, potentially tyrannical. Aron vigorously rejected Alain's innocent nostrums: "Alain's doctrine can only be applied just where it does more harm than good. Where it is really needed, against the ravages of fanaticism, there is no one left who can put it to work."[24] All the same, he recognized a central truth in Alain's thought: that the adoration of all powers—any powers—and their wish to *be* adored lay at the root of modern tyranny.

But Aron reasoned that it is absurd to propose that the sole task of the theorist of freedom *in a free society* lies in opposing and restricting authority wherever it may touch him. For resisting and denying the moderate claims and capacities of government in a free society is precisely the way to clear the path for the immoderate variety (Weimar, again). The lesson of totalitarianism, in short, was the importance of order and authority under law— not as a compromise with freedom, nor as the condition of higher freedoms to come; but simply as the best way to protect those already secured.

In the years following World War II it was axiomatic for Aron that the totalitarian threat came from the Soviet Union and not from some hypothetical future revival of Fascism. In his own words, "Every action, in

---

23. See "Fidélité des apostats" (1950), in Aron, *Polémiques* (Gallimard, Paris: 1955), p. 81; "Les Deux Allemagnes," *Le Figaro*, August 25, 1948.

24. "Remarques sur la pensée politique d'Alain," *Revue de métaphysique et morale*, April–June 1952, rpt. in *Commentaire* 28–29 (1985): 411.

the middle of the twentieth century, presupposes and involves the adoption of an attitude with regard to the Soviet enterprise. To evade this is to evade the implications and constraints of historical existence, however much one may invoke History." But he was always perfectly aware—again, in contrast to some of his friends and admirers across the Atlantic—that even though *totalitarian* might be a necessary description of Stalin's state, it was hardly sufficient. There were real differences between Communism and Fascism/ Nazism: "For those who wish to 'save the concepts,' there remains a difference between a philosophy whose logic *is* monstrous, and one that lends itself to a monstrous interpretation."[25]

Aron's preoccupation with liberty—its sources, its fragility, the threats to it and the ways in which these might be understood and thwarted—colored all his other concerns, just as his philosophical turn of thought and his sympathy for a certain style of social explanation shaped his responses to those concerns. His own sense of responsibility—and his lifelong prejudice against posing questions for which he was unqualified to offer an answer—led him to the study of a number of topics to which other French thinkers of his day paid little attention. As early as 1937 he spelled out his reasons: "It isn't every day that a Dreyfus affair allows you to invoke truth against error. If intellectuals want to offer their opinions on a daily basis, they will need knowledge of economics, diplomacy, politics, etc. Whether it concerns deflation and inflation, Russian alliance or entente cordiale, collective contracts or wage rates, the point at issue is less about justice than about effectiveness."[26]

One outcome of this desire to engage the real was a preoccupation with the idea of "industrial society." For most other French thinkers, of left or right, society was either capitalist or socialist, the forms of production and property ownership determining all other features. The Soviet Union and the West were categorically different systems, and there was widespread agreement across the political spectrum that it was a serious *political* mistake, as well as an analytical error, to suggest that the two antagonistic political systems shared certain fundamental modern elements in common.

25. *Opium of the Intellectuals*, p. 55; *Clausewitz*, 2:218.

26. Aron, "Réflexions sur les problèmes économiques français," *Revue de métaphysique et morale*, November 1937, pp. 793–822, quotation from p. 794.

Aron took a rather different position. He regretted the neglect of a question that had preoccupied early-nineteenth-century writers: "What is the meaning, what is the nature of a society shaped by science and by industry?" Unlike a number of "industrial society" theorists in the United States, he did not want to claim that the East and the West were somehow converging, their distinctive ideological disagreements being cast in the shade by a common drive toward the social, managerial, and rationalist goals of an industrial economy. He was too conscious of politics—of the contrast between societies where state and society were collapsed into one and those where they were distinct—and too well informed about the place of ideology in Soviet thinking to make this elementary mistake.

That error merely reflected the Marxist one of concluding from a similarity of forces of production to an identity of political institutions and beliefs. But from as early as 1936 Aron had already observed an aspect of the Soviet "experiment": while freedom and private enterprise had been essential to the *origins* of industrial production, the latter might *now* thrive under Soviet-style conditions of planning and public ownership (though he also noted that to the extent that East and West *were* converging in certain respects, this undermined Communist claims based on the necessary incommensurability of the two economic systems).[27]

In later years Aron would modify this position, concluding that technical developments could at best attenuate certain formal differences between political regimes. Nevertheless, those technical changes were a fact of the modern world, and Aron was caustically dismissive of those French critics who fondly imagined that the rationalist and economistic traits of all modern (Western) societies were something gratuitously foisted upon Europeans by the United States for its own purposes. In his view the problems of modernity could not be cast in the simple old ways: private property versus public ownership, capitalist exploitation versus social equality, market anarchy versus planned distribution. Accordingly these themes of socialist doctrine and left-right polemic had largely lost their meaning. The paralysis of the French state—what Aron in 1954 called the "French disease"—lay at the heart of French political and economic stagnation and could neither be understood nor addressed in the terms of an outdated

27. See, e.g., "Marxisme et contre-Marxisme," *Le Figaro*, October 5, 1959. See also *German Sociology*, p. 127.

partisan debate over the impropriety or otherwise of industrial modernia-tion.[28]

In order to enter the discussion on the nature of and prospects for in-dustrial society, Aron taught himself economics. For the purpose of becom-ing an influential commentator on foreign affairs, he familiarized himself with the language and arguments of nuclear strategy and international rela-tions. He almost certainly had very little respect for "international rela-tions" as a discipline, and his own forays into it—notably *Paix et guerre entre les nations*—were not a source of great satisfaction to him. But a com-bination of cool realism and copious information stood him in good stead—for thirty years Aron commented regularly on almost every aspect of French foreign policy and international affairs, and his opinions and pro-jections stand up better today than those of almost anyone else, in France or abroad.

Raymond Aron was among the first in his generation to grasp the truth about post–World War II politics: that domestic and foreign conflicts were now intertwined and the traditional distinction between foreign policy and domestic policy had thus disappeared: "The truth is that in our times, for individuals as for nations, the choice that determines all else is a global one, in effect a geographical choice. One is in the universe of free countries or else in that of lands placed under harsh Soviet rule. From now on every-one in France will have to state his choice."[29] In the late forties Aron laid out a "two-track" explanation of Soviet international strategy that would become conventional wisdom by the seventies but was original and provoc-ative in its time. According to his analysis there was a fundamental conti-nuity of Soviet goals, but these might be sought either by the tactic of alli-ances—as in the era of the Popular Front, or for a brief moment after Hitler's defeat—or else by confrontational attitudes at appropriate times and in vulnerable places.

The implication, that Stalin's state was run by men who thought in terms of cynical statecraft as well as ideological objectives, was not in fact offensive to Communists themselves—though they could hardly admit it. But it was deeply wounding to the illusions of fellow-traveling intellectuals

28. Aron, "La société industrielle et les dialogues politiques de l'Occident," in *Col-loques de Rheinfelden* (Paris: Calmann-Lévy, 1960), p. 13; also "1788 ou le malade imagi-naire?" *Le Figaro*, October 19, 1954.
29. "La Fin des illusions," *Le Figaro*, July 5, 1947.

of the neutralist Left, like Claude Bourdet or Jean-Marie Domenach; the ease with which Aron burst the bubbles of their own internationalist fantasies, and his ability to relate the French Communists' domestic practices to a broader Soviet strategy, deeply offended the sensibilities of such men and contributed mightily to their lifelong enmity toward him.[30]

It is hard to recall, today, the Manichaean mood of those early Cold War years. For the *bien pensant* left-wing intelligentsia, anyone who wasn't sympathetic to the French Communists and the Soviet Union, who was unwilling to give them the benefit of every doubt, to ascribe to them every good intention, must be a conscious agent of the United States, an active advocate of confrontation and even war. In fact Aron was strikingly moderate, not unlike George Kennan in later years. He held the opinion that the Soviet Union would never deliberately push the world to the brink of war, preferring to attain its objectives by subtle pressure—hence the alternating styles of compromise and confrontation.

For this reason Aron, like postwar British foreign secretary Ernest Bevin, saw the construction of the Western Alliance as a political, even a psychological move rather than a military one—designed to reassure Western Europe and in so doing render it less vulnerable to Communist pressure at home and abroad. In these circumstances, as Aron famously put it in an article in September 1947, peace might be impossible, but war was improbable.[31]

Aron's cool realism in these matters allowed him to see beyond the illusions and switchback hopes and disappointments of the post-Stalin decade, as Western politicians and commentators scrutinized every gesture of Soviet leaders in the search for some evidence of détente or a new approach. In Aron's eyes the inscrutable Mr. Molotov was a useful prophylactic against a return to the interwar illusions of "Geneva"—the idea that "peace depends on words rather than on the courage of men and the balance of forces." Writing in 1956, after the upheavals in Poland but before the repression of the Hungarian revolution, Aron reminded his readers that "if the Soviets felt truly threatened, they would return to the rigidity of earlier years. . . . Let us not mistake our dreams for near reality." And when Khrushchev did indeed return for a while to the style and methods of Sta-

30. See "La Fin des illusions," and "Les alternances de la paix belliqueuse," *Le Figaro*, February 26, 1948.

31. "Stupide Résignation," *Le Figaro*, September 21–22, 1947.

linist foreign policy, Aron used the occasion to point out how little influence Western actions really had on Soviet behavior: when it suited the
Soviet leadership to end the Korean War, sign the Austrian Peace Treaty,
or make up with Tito, they just went ahead and did so; but only then and
not before.[32]

Aron's insights derived in part from his grasp of the ideological and
political nature of Communism, but at least as much from his more old-
fashioned understanding of interstate relations. In his words, "The division
of humanity into sovereign states preceded capitalism and will outlive it."
There were limits to what even the great powers could do, but there were
equally limits on what could be done to prevent them doing as they
wished—hence his mildly skeptical attitude toward the United Nations
and other international agencies. This fundamentally tragic vision—the
belief that there can be no end to the conflicts among states and the best
that could be hoped for was constant vigilance to limit the risks and damage of confrontations—placed Aron at odds with the dominant sensibility
of his era: the view, held by many on both sides, that the object of international relations was somehow to put an end to all wars; whether through
nuclear stalemate, the negotiation of a definitive "peace settlement," or
else a final victory by one side or the other. Aron was too conscious of the
unusual situation and history of Europe to be drawn into such illusory
hopes: "Europeans would like to escape from their history, a 'great' history
written in letters of blood. But others, by the hundreds of millions, are taking it up for the first time, or coming back to it."[33]

Despite sharing some of de Gaulle's criticism of American foreign and
economic policy, and reacting with the wounded sensibilities of a Frenchman to attacks on his country at the United Nations, Aron was reluctant
to support the broader Gaullist objectives of nuclear autonomy and independence. This was partly because he regarded any weakening of the Western Alliance as a gift to the Soviet Union; but his chief objection to Gaullist dreams of nuclear grandeur lay elsewhere. Raymond Aron saw very early
on, at least two decades before most professional military strategists, the

32. "Conférence sans surprise," Le Figaro, July 27, 1955; "Après Poznan détente sans
reniement," Le Figaro, July 3, 1956; "Reprise de la guerre froide," Le Figaro, June 28,
1958.

33. D'Une Sainte Famille à l'autre, p. 13; Clausewitz, 2:283. A little later Aron ruefully observes that "what honorable professors lack is a sense of history and of the tragic"
(Clausewitz, 2:285).

limits to the diplomatic and military uses of nuclear weaponry. In 1957, ten years before the British retreat from east of Suez, he pointed out that the British military's growing reliance on atomic weapons and its reduced expenditure on the conventional variety would undercut its freedom of military and therefore diplomatic maneuver without doing anything to improve its security. Two years later he made the identical point about the French *force de frappe*—French nuclear weapons only made sense in the hypothetical context of a conflict between NATO and the USSR, whereas for France's real problems in Africa or the Middle East they would be of absolutely no use whatsoever.[34]

Despite his emphasis upon the main conflict—with the USSR—Aron was thus alert to the changes already taking place in the postwar world from the late fifties. Even in 1954 he had warned against betting all one's military budget and calculations on a single weapon; the wars of the future were likely to be quite different and require a very different sort of arsenal. Moreover, such local wars need not lead to international conflicts on a nuclear scale—on the contrary, since if the nuclear "umbrella" secured anything, it was the space for greater and lesser powers to engage in local or partial conflicts without putting "peace" at risk. The logic of power politics remained in force, and with it the need to think militarily in a variety of keys and not just that of nuclear devastation. "One does not increase the risk of total war by accepting the obligations of local wars."[35]

Aron's sense of the limits and realities of international politics contributed to his attitude toward the question of a new "Europe." Unlike Jean Monnet and his acolytes in the French planning ministries, Aron was not at first a wholehearted enthusiast for continental European political unity. The future of postwar Western Europe, in his view, depended upon economic reconstruction and collective defense, neither of which could be achieved except in close association with the United States and Great Britain. He was even initially sympathetic to British desires to keep a healthy distance from European political projects—"the example of French and Italian parliaments hardly inspires unconditional confidence"—though by the sixties the altered situation led him to chastise the British for their

<hr/>

34. "Après Eden, Lord Salisbury: La crise du Parti Conservateur," *Le Figaro*, April 4, 1957; "L'accession au club atomique," *Le Figaro*, August 14, 1959.

35. "Neutralité ou engagement," presentation to Congress for Cultural Freedom in Berlin, July 1950, rpt. in *Polémiques*, pp. 199–217.

failure to adapt to a changed world: "Don't be half a century behind. Accept that the Old Continent is seeking its future beyond nationalisms."[36]

But although his instincts preserved him from the illusion of a single European economy—Aron always understood that the *economic* community represented a happy arrangement of fortuitously compatible national economic strategies—the same grasp of postwar realities led Aron to the conclusion that the age of independent European nation-states was gone for good: "Without denying the hurdles to be overcome, the idea of a united Europe represents, in our century, the last hope of old nations lacking the immense spaces of Eurasia and America."[37] He thus navigated steadily between the twin dangers of Gaullist national illusion and leftist disdain for a "capitalist" Europe.

But the "ever-closer union" of the founding fathers of the European community held little appeal to Aron, and not just because he was skeptical of their chances of forging a single European economic entity. He also appreciated from an early stage something that has only just now begun to dawn upon the political and administrative leadership of the western half of the continent: that without a European foreign policy, and a European army to enforce it, the continent lacked the fundamental building blocks of any sovereign entity and would remain at the mercy of its separate interests. Until this situation changed, international political and military crises would continue to be addressed not by some present or future "European Assembly" but by the powers directly involved—an observation as pertinent today as when Aron first made it in the context of an early crisis in NATO's leadership in 1959.[38]

But Aron's chief interest in the project of Europe was indeed one shared with at least some French and other European policymakers: the need to address and resolve the "German question." Writing in *Combat* in February 1947, at a time when intellectuals and politicians in France were still advocating a variety of solutions to the German dilemma, from multiple partition to unified neutrality, Aron argued that the only hope for a secure European future lay in reconstituting a stable German state *within* a

36. "L'Echec des négotiations Franco-Brittaniques sur l'Assemblée Européenne," *Le Figaro*, January 26, 1949; "Lettre à un ami Anglais," *Le Figaro*, April 7, 1960.

37. "Peut-on gouverner sans les Communistes?" *Le Figaro*, June 29–30, 1947;

38. "Peut-on gouverner sans les Communistes?"; "Force de frappe européenne?" *Le Figaro*, December 10, 1959. See also "Universalité de l'idée de nation et contestation" (1976), in *Essais sur la condition juive contemporaine*, pp. 231–51.

West European setting. He would return again and again to this theme: never again would Germany be so *disponible*, so open to an international solution and too weak to oppose it. Now, he wrote in January 1949, is the time to act—"never have circumstances been so propitious for putting an end to a century-long conflict."[39]

For the same reasons, Aron was a committed advocate of West German rearmament, when the question arose in the early fifties. Like so much else in Aron's style of reasoning, this conclusion was reached not on principle but as the recognition of a reality, albeit unwelcome: "It is unfortunate that circumstances oblige us to arm Germany. It would be even more unfortunate if those arms were to come from the 'pacifists' in the Kremlin."[40]

The overwhelming strategic goal was first to invent a democratic German state, then to tie it and its citizenry to the Western Alliance, and then to give it the means to play its role in the defense of that alliance. This outcome was by no means guaranteed, or even likely, in the immediate postwar years and was fought at each stage in France by an unholy alliance of Communists, pacifists, nationalists, and Gaullists. Aron himself recognized the irony and unpopularity of a remilitarized German state a mere decade after the defeat of Hitler—just as he warned as early as 1956, in an essay coauthored with Daniel Lerner, about the risks of talking pompously of "European unity" as though the other half of Europe (and Germany) simply didn't exist. But in neither case did he make the mistake of confusing his desires (or emotions) with harsh reality.

Throughout Raymond Aron's writings, whether philosophical, "social scientific," or political, there is one constant: that of realism. The task of the commentator is to address the world as it is and to offer credible answers to the problems it poses. As he wrote of Max Weber, "He was prepared at any moment to answer the question that disconcerts all our amateur politicians: 'What would you do if you were a Cabinet minister?'" Intellectuals who confined themselves to describing—or admonishing—the world stood condemned: "If one has nothing to say about politics except to explain what other people are doing, it would be better not to write about it at all." This distinctive understanding of the duties of the intellectual set

---

39. "L'Echec des négociations."
40. "Quelques faits et quelques mots," *Le Figaro*, December 27, 1954.

Aron quite apart from his fellow writers, for whom the idea of the public intellectual was inseparable from irresponsible grandstanding. Even when he agreed with their goals, Aron preferred not to put his name to collective intellectual utterances—he refused to join the Committee of Anti-Fascist Intellectuals in the thirties because of what he regarded as their pacifist illusions, and he took his distance from advocates of neutrality in the following decade, not because he thought that neutrality was in itself an undesirable objective but because to advocate it for France in 1949 was to deny the facts of international political life: "The formula of neutrality, even armed neutrality, is typical of the refusal to face reality, of the desire for escape which characterise a large fraction of the western intelligentsia."[41] Men like Claude Bourdet or Maurice Duverger were irresponsible, unable to transcend in their imagination the difference between writing an article and governing a country.

It was in large measure to combat such illusions, to lay bare the unreality of intellectual political engagement, that Aron resorted to a rigorous logic in his arguments. This could be disconcerting even to his friends. Despite his unambiguous commitment to the Free French (he spent the war years in London writing for their newspaper), Aron took great care in his analyses to present Vichy as preeminently an error of political judgment. The Pétainist mistake had been to suppose that Vichy might benefit from its place in Hitler's Europe—a dangerous and ultimately tragic misjudgment, but one that needed to be understood in the context of the events of 1940. The point was to acknowledge the facts, however uncomfortable or inconvenient—"the analyst doesn't create the history that he interprets."[42]

This awareness of the troubling and confusing quality of reality was shaped in part by Aron's sense of the distance that lay between his own world and that of the great social observers of an earlier time. Auguste Comte, he noted, could arrange the world according to the tidy rules of a universally applicable positivism. Tocqueville could bring to bear upon his social observations a theory of the virtues and defects of democracy in what

---

41. *German Sociology*, p. 86; see also *Commentaire* 28–29 (1985): 394, 402. Note, too, the observation in Aron's memoirs: "For a half-century I have restricted my own criticisms by posing this question—'what would I do in their place?'" (*Mémoires*, p. 632).

42. For an example of the bemusement of his wartime colleagues at Aron's cool dispassion, see Daniel Cordier's remarks in *Commentaire* 28–29 (1985): 24–27; *Clausewitz*, 1:53.

he understood to be its universal (American) incarnation. Marx could apply the universal panacea of socialism as a future solution and thus prospective explanation for the contradictions of his own world. But the mid-twentieth-century commentator has no such certainties. The modern world is too complex to be reduced to a formula, a condemnation or a solution: "Modern society . . . is a democratic society to be observed without transports of enthusiasm or indignation."[43]

Nevertheless, at no point did Aron ever conclude from this observation that the commentator is left with little choice but to accept the verdict of history. Indeed, it was implicit in his critique of Karl Mannheim, his later thoughts about Max Weber, and his polemical engagement with the whole Marxist project that fatalism—whether it consisted of "taking the long view," ascribing to History some transcendental meaning, or assigning to a class or nation a privileged role in the unfolding of that meaning—was an epistemological error that could only bring political disaster. The danger of justifying false realists (or idealists) was ever present in all such forms of historicism.

Nor was Aron a "realist" in the sense people mean when they speak of "realpolitik"—the practice of making political judgments derived exclusively from a calculation of possibilities and outcomes based on past experience. He had no time for that sort of "theoretical realism" which led in practice to unrealistic decisions like that of Chamberlain at Munich. His objection to this style of thinking lay partly in its frequently misguided conclusions, but above all in its rigidity, with the result that what begins as empirical calculation nearly always ends up as rule-bound dogma: "In my opinion pseudocertainty, based on the relationship between the stakes and the risks, on some rational calculation ascribed to a likely aggressor, is of no more value than the dogmatism of the Maginot Line."[44]

What does it mean, then, to speak of Raymond Aron as a realist? In properly philosophical terms he most certainly was one. But that was not what he himself meant when he described himself as a realist. He meant, rather, that he took in to account, in his efforts to understand the world, all that he took to be real about it—and only what he took to be real. As he had explained in 1938, in the defense of his philosophical dissertation: "My book proposes that we renounce the abstractions of moralism and ide-

43. *Etapes de la pensée sociologique*, p. 296.
44. *Clausewitz*, 2:179.

ology and look instead for the true content of possible choices, limited as they are by reality itself."

But, and this is the important point, Aron's reality encompassed not only interests and power but also ideas. Like Clausewitz, he took it for granted that *Glaubensache*—beliefs of all kinds—constitute a fact about society. Human beings have beliefs and are moved by them in various ways, and this is as much a part of reality as the disposition of armaments or the forms of production. "Realism," in Aron's view, was simply unrealistic if it ignored the moral judgments that citizens pass on governments, or the real and imagined moral interests of all actors in a society. It is for this reason that Raymond Aron's realism was so much better at explaining and predicting events in his time than the disabused and "realist" commentaries and prognostications of Sovietologists and others who shared his concerns but not his breadth of understanding.

But the same sensitivity to the varieties of human motivation that made Aron's realism so different from the knowing skepticism of some of his colleagues also set him firmly against any inclination to what he contemptuously dismissed as "moralizing." In one of his earliest pieces of writing, the January 1934 article arguing against conscientious objection that first brought him to the attention of Elie Halévy, among others, Aron spelt out the distinction that would inform his political analyses throughout his life: "The minister who condemns war and prepares for it cannot be accused of hypocrisy. It is simply a question of the distinction between personal ethics and real politics." The point is repeated in a long-unpublished manuscript from the later thirties, where Aron quotes Pareto: "Whoever looks at the facts objectively and who does not deliberately close his eyes to the light, is all the same forced to recognize that it is not by playing the nervous moralists that rulers bring prosperity to their peoples."[45]

This careful extrusion of the moralizing dimension from all his analytical writings has given Aron the reputation of a cold writer, unmoved by feelings (his own or others) and confined in the grip of what François Mauriac once called his "icy clarity." There is no doubt that Aron made a point of being clear and rational above all else—"ce vertige de lucidité,"

45. Aron, "De l'objection de conscience" (January 1934), rpt. in *Commentaire* 28–29 (1985): 292; Elie Halévy, *Correspondance 1891–1937* (Paris: Editions de Fallois, 1996), p. 775; Aron, "La Comparaison de Machiavel et Pareto," in *Machiavel et les tyrannies modernes*, p. 101.

as Alfred Fabre-Luce described it—and saw no virtue in appealing to a reader's or an audience's sentiments or sensibilities. This did not mean that he lacked feelings. Far from it—but the private tragedies of his life (one child died of leukemia when she was six, another was born handicapped) had taught him to isolate his emotions from his reason, the better to preserve the latter. As he described himself when he was admitted to the Académie des Sciences Morales et Politiques, he was a "man without a party, whose opinions offend first one side and then another, who is all the more unbearable because he takes his moderation to excess and *hides his passions under his arguments.*"[46]

Such men have always been at a disadvantage in France. "Representatives of the critical spirit in France are discredited through the accusation of coldness. They are presumed to lack imagination, hope, and generosity, as though intelligence can only thrive at the cost of atrophied sensibilities."[47] In Aron's case, the consequences can be seen perhaps most clearly in his contribution to the agonized French debate over Algeria.

Raymond Aron was not against French colonies on principle. He resented the American and British failure to assist the embattled French forces in Vietnam and shared the view, widespread in the political class of his time, that France's identity was intimately bound up with her worldwide possessions and influence; France has a duty, he wrote in *Le Figaro* in October 1955, to try and keep North Africa "in the sphere of modern civilization." But lacking any personal experience of North Africa in general, and Algeria in particular, he felt no particular emotional attachment to the Maghreb and came to see his country's embroilment there as costly and pointless. The rebellion in Algeria made it depressingly clear that France could retain control of the country only by the application of considerable force.

Accordingly, as Aron argued in two trenchant pamphlets published in 1957 and 1958, the time had come to give the Algerians their independence. He based this conclusion on three characteristically Aronian grounds. To improve the condition of the indigenous population of Algeria to a level compatible with equal membership of the French nation, and to

46. Quoted in Nicolas Baverez, *Raymond Aron* (Paris: Flammarion, 1993), p. 338; emphasis added.
47. See the introduction by Bernard de Fallois to Emmanuel Berl, *Essais* (Paris: Julliard, 1985), p. 13.

provide them with equal political rights and representation, as proposed by liberal-minded defenders of the status quo, would be unsustainably expensive (and therefore unpopular with the taxpaying citizenry). It would also entail a degree of Algerian presence in French political life—projecting ahead the far higher growth rates of the Arab population—that was likely to be unacceptable to the metropolitan French themselves. In short, the French were deluding themselves, not to speak of misleading the Arabs, when they promised equality and equal representation in the future—having steadfastly refused it in the past.

Second, while it was true that the Arab Algerians would be vastly better off if they stayed under French rule, this was not a factor that they could be expected to take into account. "It is a denial of the experience of our century to suppose that men will sacrifice their passions to their interests." While he had no interest in the nationalist case as such, Aron was capable of understanding its power to move millions, and the foolhardiness of opposing it. And he saw no point in debating whether or not there truly *was* an "Algerian nation" with claims to self-government and the like, as though the assertion by some that "Algerianness" was a modern invention would somehow undermine the case for independence. "It hardly matters whether this nationalism is the expression of a real or an imaginary nation. Nationalism is a passion, resolved to create the entity it invokes."

Third, once it was clear that the only mutually acceptable solution to the Algerian imbroglio was a parting of the ways—and to Aron this was obvious by 1957—it made absolutely no sense to wait. "The multiplication of would-be sovereign states, lacking the intellectual, economic, and administrative resources necessary for the exercise of sovereignty, is not inherently desirable. I am not a fanatic for the 'abandonment of sovereignty.' But I am more opposed to colonial wars than to the abandonment of sovereignty, because the former anyway produces the latter—under the worst possible conditions."

Note that Aron is not invoking historical inevitability here, much less a theory of necessary progress. The Algerian war need not have happened. The interests of its participants were not best served by the outcomes they sought. And even if the outcome was in one sense foreordained, if only by French colonial malpractice, that did not make it "right." But the French had failed to hold on to North Africa, and the time had come to recognize this and draw the only possible conclusion. Reasonable men might disagree on this—as Aron wrote in a different context, "Faced with this tragic dilemma men of equal patriotism might make utterly opposed choices."[48] But for just that reason, patriotism could not be invoked on either side—though France's practical interest might be, as Aron sought to demonstrate.

Raymond Aron thus came down in favor of Algerian independence, like the overwhelming majority of other French intellectuals. But his arguments were utterly unlike theirs. He did not seek to show the legitimacy of the Arab claim to independence. He was not interested, for these purposes, in the moral debt the French had inherited from their colonial past and which could only be liquidated by the abandonment of colonial power. He never invoked the course of history or the "natural" move to a postcolonial world. And, above all, he did not refer to the emotive issue of French military and police practices in Algeria itself, the use of torture to extract confessions from suspected terrorists, and the price that was being paid for these crimes in the soul of the French Republic. The Algerian tragedy, for Aron, lay not in the moral dilemma posed to individuals caught in the "dirty war," but in the absence of a satisfactory third alternative to a continuing conflict or a "catastrophic" independence. "Political action is a response to circumstances, not a theoretical disquisition or the expression of feelings."

Aron was accused at the time of having precisely neglected the "moral" dimension of the France's Algerian crisis, of failing to grasp the true heart of the tragedy in his frozen concern with logic. His reply, when this charge was put to him again many years later, is revealing. Why did he not add his voice to those who were speaking out against the use of torture? "But what would I have achieved by proclaiming my opposition to torture? I have never met anyone who is in favor of torture." And, more generally, why did he not invoke moral criteria in his case for Algerian independence? Others were doing that already, and anyone who was open to that sort of argument was probably already convinced. "The important thing was to convince those who were arguing the opposite position."[49]

There can be no doubt that those were Aron's motives, and they are as consistent and as rational as always. But the care Aron took to avoid *any* appearance of passion or feeling at a time of highly emotive public debate

48. See "L'unité française en péril," *Le Figaro*, October 15, 1955. The reference is to June 1940. For Aron's views on Algeria see *La Tragédie algérienne* (Paris: Plon, 1957), and especially *L'Algérie et la République* (Paris: Plon, 1958).

49. *Le Spectateur engagé*, pp. 193, 210.

raises the suspicion that, in addition to the rewards of influence and respect that came his way as a result of such carefully disengaged reasoning, he took perhaps excessive satisfaction in icy dispassion for its own sake. As he noted admiringly of Clausewitz: "*Sine ire et studio:* he neither approves nor condemns, he merely records." But that is not a stance entirely compatible with political responsibility, and as Aron noted in his memoirs à propos his own support for U.S. policy in Vietnam, one cannot restrict oneself to the role of "the observer of the follies and disasters of mankind." There was thus a self-inflicted discomfort in Aron's ultrarational approach to especially heated debates: he deprived himself of the pleasure of indulging his own human feelings. As he said, again in the context of his study of Clausewitz, "Whoever reflects today upon wars and strategy must erect a barrier between his intelligence and his compassion." But Aron forced his readers to admire him, despite themselves, for the sheer power of his reasoning: "Democrats and liberals, if they understand him properly, can at least learn from him conceptual rigor."[50]

Whatever its costs, this conceptual rigor made Aron, for his admirers at least, the "ethical and logical anchor in contemporary French thought."[51] His singular ability to see clearly the developments of his time, and to interpret them accurately, marks him out from his fellow intellectuals. On almost every issue of importance to his former colleagues on the Left, Aron understood the stakes sooner, and better. He was remarkably prescient not only about the rise of Fascism but also its likely outcome: in 1939 he noted that whereas Mussolini's regime might well give way to a legal or conservative political restoration, the Nazi revolution could not.

By the beginning of the sixties Aron was correctly predicting that French support for Israel, then quite marked, would be replaced by an inevitable effort at reconciliation with former colonies across the Mediterranean. By 1956 he had already anticipated, thirty years ahead of most other commentators, the problems that the Soviet Union would face in its "colonial" holdings in Central Asia, paying the price for its encouragement of anticolonialism elsewhere; and in 1969 he foresaw the coming explosions

---

50. See *Clausewitz*, 2:12, 267–68.
51. Serge-Cristophe Kolm, *Commentaire* 28–29 (1985): 101.

in Poland, remarking upon the alienation of people and institutions from the regime, at a time when Communism's grip on that country seemed unshakable for decades to come.[52]

Even Aron's "reactionary" stance of 1968, in horrified recoil at the disproportionate civic turmoil brought on by the "psychodrama" of the student revolt, was accompanied by his dissent from the conventional, conservative response. He had no patience for those who condemned "consumer society" while poverty still stalked much of the globe; "but those who are obsessed with rates of growth or levels of prosperity are no less irritating." The Gaullist regime was now paying the price for its smug authoritarianism, he concluded: it needed the shock brought on by "a reservoir of violence and mass indignation." Aron combined understanding for French frustration at inefficiency and the abuse of power in educational institutions and the workplace with a skeptical dismissal of the delusionary "revolutionary" mood of the hour.[53] In retrospect, this seems a reasonable, and on the whole fair, assessment of events, though it won him few friends at the time.

What he perhaps did not fully grasp was the characteristic mood of the "generation of '68," with the result that his dismissal of their self-indulgent imitation of revolutionary style led him to underestimate the longer-term impact on French public life and culture of the events of that year. But here, too, his response seems if not all-comprehending, then at least somehow fitting. There was something embarrassing and occasionally grotesque about the enthusiasm with which many other senior professors grew their hair, renewed their opinions, spiced their language, and strove demagogically to outdo their own students in iconoclastic fervor. What Aron lost in support he gained in respect and dignity; this, too, is a way of being right.

Aron was not, of course, always correct or consistent, even by his own lights. During the 1950s he occasionally struck an inappropriately alarmist

---

52. See "Machiavélisme et tyrannies," in *Machiavel et les tyrannies modernes,* p. 139; "1955, année de la clarification," *Le Figaro,* January 7–8, 1956; "Les juifs et l'Etat d'Israel," *Figaro littéraire,* February 24, 1962, rpt. in *Essais sur la condition juive contemporaine; Les Désillusions du Progrès,* p. 178.

53. See *Les Désillusions du Progrès,* p. 340, and *La Révolution introuvable,* p. 106. Aron had anticipated the coming demand for *autogestion* (self-management) in the preface to his *La Lutte de Classes: nouvelles leçons sur les sociétés industrielles* (Paris: Gallimard, 1964).

note, usually in his journalism. In February 1955 he seems to have been unnecessarily worried that Adenauer might be unable to keep, not just the Federal Republic, but even his own Christian Democrats free from the temptations of neutralism. His angry dislike for Nasser ("the Egyptian Füh- rer") led him at the time of the Suez crisis to make implausible and mis- leading analogies with Munich, and utterly to misread American interests and intentions ("Forced to choose, Washington will not opt for Nasser's Egypt against Great Britain and France"—which is, of course, just what Eisenhower did). He even ventured wild and unsupported predictions of disaster in the event of Nasser's victory: "If pan-Islamism pushes the British out of the Near East and the French out of North Africa, it will not be long before the Americans are chased out of Europe."[54]

As that last remark suggests, such mistakes as Aron made in his assess- ment of the political situation in the postwar years usually derived from his overwhelming concern with the Soviet Union and the threat it posed. Having been one of the first to grasp, in 1945, the part that would be played by the USSR after Hitler's defeat, Aron fell occasionally victim to the So- viet Union's own assessment of its prospects. In 1975 he could write that "the superiority of the American republic over the Soviet Union belongs to the past." But he also understood the risk of distortion that he ran in this unswerving attention to the Soviet threat—at the end of the sixties, in a mildly self-critical passage, he acknowledged how easy it was to forget that the United States, in its fear of global Communism, also sustains inde- fensible regimes. It may be, as André Maurois once remarked and Aron half admitted, that he might have come a lot closer to being the Montesquieu of our times had he taken a little more distance from the course of events.[55]

Whether or not he aspired to emulate Montesquieu (or Tocqueville), there is no doubt that Aron, especially in his later years, was moved by the sense that he had not fulfilled his promise. The clue to this lies in his an- swer to a journalist who asked him, a few years before his death, which of his own books he liked the best. He passed over all his occasional pieces, his postwar journalism, his polemical essays, and his many forays into socio- logical theory, political science, and international relations. What he most

54. See "L'europe en péril: Les responsabilités de la France," *Le Figaro,* February 3, 1955; "L'unité Atlantique: Enjeu de la crise de Suez," *Le Figaro,* August 8, 1956; "La démonstration nécessaire," *Le Figaro,* September 13, 1956; "La Force n'est qu'un moyen," *Le Figaro,* November 2, 1956.

55. See *Clausewitz,* 2:284; *Les Désillusions du Progrès,* p. 304.

admired in his own writing, he thought, were three books: the *Introduction à la philosophie de l'histoire; Histoire et dialectique de la violence* (his lengthy analysis and response to Sartre's *Critique de la raison dialectique*); and *Penser la guerre: Clausewitz.* Perhaps also his *Essai sur les libertés.*

This is a very revealing list. It shows that even at the end of his career Aron saw himself as what he had been at the outset—a philosopher. And he clearly regretted not having written the great work of philosophy that had been expected of him. Instead, history had intervened. As he wrote to Guéhenno from Cologne, in May 1931, "I believe that in another time I would have been tempted to wander among the dilemmas of metaphysics; but like all my generation I feel a sense of instability and anxiety that allow little space for leisurely pursuits." Instead, Aron expended his time and energy on a dozen different fields, none of them fully worthy of his talents. It is not clear whether the book he would have written would have been a sequel to his dissertation or a full-length commentary on Marxism, "the book . . . I have been thinking about for nearly forty years." In either case it would have completed a whole. As for the works he *had* written, "All that forms no unity, it is imperfect and unfinished; but whoever wants to learn everything can pursue to the full none of the subjects he engages."[56]

The two-volume study of Clausewitz, whatever its virtues as a revisionist account of the nineteenth-century German military theorist, is interesting (and perhaps found favor with its author) because it is so revealing an account of Aron's own sensibilities. He identified closely with Clausewitz's loneliness and independence of mind: "Of conservative opinions, he was taken for a killjoy, a wet blanket, such was his insistence upon sticking to an opinion if he thought it right." And Clausewitz, too, was consumed at the end with a sense of having not quite met his own demanding standards—"As to my innermost feelings: if I have not recorded a great body of exploits I am at least free of any burden of guilt."[57]

But of all Aron's self-criticisms, the most revealing is the one that may prove most perplexing to posterity. And that is his lifelong complex of inadequacy vis-à-vis Jean-Paul Sartre. It is not that Raymond Aron felt him-

56. See *Le Spectateur engagé*, pp. 10–11, 300. On his lifelong engagement with Marx, Aron had this to say: "Like the friends of my youth I never separated philosophy from politics, nor thought from commitment; but I devoted rather more time than them to the study of economic and social mechanisms. In this sense I believe I was more faithful to Marx than they were" (*D'Une Sainte Famille à l'autre*, 11).

57. *Clausewitz*, 1:71; quoted by Aron in *Clausewitz*, 1:44.

self in any way Sartre's inferior as a philosopher—indeed, he was one of the few men of his generation who could match Sartre in this field and engage him on his own terms (as Sartre well knew and had acknowledged in earlier, friendlier days). Nor did Aron have much respect for Sartre's forays into political or social argument over the course of the postwar decades, as he showed in his devastating polemical destruction of his old friend's various convoluted efforts to marry "existentialist" reasoning with Marxist analysis.

But that is just the point. Aron spent an inordinate amount of time reading and replying to Sartre's publications, treating them with utter seriousness. He remained, from their break in 1947 until their formal reconciliation shortly before Sartre's death, the latter's best and most sympathetic reader and critic. Sartre, in contrast, royally ignored Aron's own writings after 1947, distorted their content and meaning on the rare occasions when he did refer to them, and refused any exchange or discussion.

Aron's behavior is readily explained. He admired and thought he found in Sartre just what, by his own account, was lacking in his own work. Sartre was ambitious, a maker of systems, an "original" thinker who could write plays and novels with the same ease that he turned out multivolume tomes of applied epistemology. Aron, in contrast, was driven by fear of error, saying and writing only what he knew to be true and could support with logic and evidence. He lacked—or thought he lacked—the spark of creative, risk-taking originality that would have freed him to write his great book. He was well aware that Sartre's philosophical output was a failure (typically, he did not feel competent to judge his fiction and drama); but it was a *grand* failure.

Aron's own writing was, in his eyes, on the whole a success. But it was a *partial* success, and he envied Sartre the *grandeur* of his capacities and his ambitions. This lifelong sense of inadequacy—the full extent of which was not revealed until the publication of his memoirs just before he died, and even then only in a muted key—was, like so much about Aron, to his credit. He was too honest and too self-critical to withhold admiration from a political opponent or deny an earlier intellectual companionship. But far from making him friends, this distinctively *moral* stance, in an intellectual community characterized by personal rivalry and bad faith, simply isolated him further from those to whom he was instinctively drawn.

That Aron was a lonely figure in French intellectual life for most of his adult life, until he became at the very end an object of uncritical adulation and respect, is beyond question. But one should not exaggerate his isolation. According to Branko Lazitch, "It is an understatement to say that he was not welcome in the Parisian intellectual establishment. He was banished from the community";[58] and it is true that his uncompromising anti-Communism made Aron unwelcome in *bien pensant* intellectual and academic circles from 1947 until the early seventies. But there were other worlds, and in these he was well received and greatly respected. He was a founding member of the Congress for Cultural Freedom in 1950, a frequent contributor to *Preuves* and other respected periodicals, and a regular and highly regarded participant in scholarly and intellectual gatherings abroad, where he gathered many honors and accolades.

Moreover, Aron probably took some pleasure in provoking the animosity and resentment of his erstwhile companions among the left-leaning French intelligentsia. Like Clausewitz, he had little but "scorn" for the "higher idiocies of philosophers and public opinion." His haughty dismissal of the demagogic populism of his fellow professors in 1968 catches something of this: "Intellectuals—real ones, great ones, and even the not so great and the not very real—will continue to despise me for not playing the game, for not chasing after popularity by flattering the young and by making concessions to fashionable ideas." If Aron was alone—in December 1967 he described a book he had just written as "this testimony of a solitary man"—the condition was not wholly unpleasing to him.[59]

There were other benefits to intellectual isolation. As François Furet has noted, Aron's avoidance of engagements of all kinds served as a "system of mental protection," allowing him to pick and choose among his affinities and styles of argument without being in thrall to any. He was a political liberal writing in a conservative daily paper; an economic liberal who abhorred Hayekian system-building (while admiring the Austrian's nonconformist courage); a critic of the establishment who evinced deep distaste for all forms of disorder and confusion, mental and social alike; an anti-Communist who found little to admire or emulate in the American "model"—"the U.S. economy seems to me a model neither for humanity nor for the West"—and so on.

From this uncomfortable but unimpeachable perch atop a variety of

58. Branko Lazitch in *Commentaire* 28–29 (1985): 48.
59. See *La Révolution introuvable*, p. 135, and *Essais sur la condition juive contemporaine*, p. 42.

fences he denied himself the easy pleasure of submitting either to history or principle. When it came to deciding about first-order public institutions such as forms of suffrage or levels of taxation, Aron found fault with *all* forms of dogmatism and came close to a version of pragmatic reason—"It is not some general principle that decides such matters, but rather the agreed values of the community."[60]

Nonetheless, isolation is isolation, and Aron paid a price. He was regularly vilified by his former friends and their followers for over a quarter of a century. His intellectual and scholarly instincts drew him to seek engagement with a community that refused to listen or respond. It took considerable moral courage—and physical courage too, on various occasions—to stand up against intellectual fashions and political currents and deny himself the pleasures of communion with his natural peers. Like Machiavelli, he had the courage to pursue the logic of his ideas—with some similar consequences in the degree to which they became distorted at the hands of his enemies.

His friend Manès Sperber noted Aron's unusual independence of mind and his ability to stand his ground in the face of "the provocations of the powerful," and it was Sperber, too, who offered a general observation about intellectual independence that applies with special force to Aron: "Every person determines on his own authority the price that he can pay, or refuse to pay, for his life, and in the same way everyone decides what *sacrificium intellectus* he can make for the preservation of the valuable concord with his friends." Aron determined quite early in his life that in his case the intellectual sacrifice would not be paid. In the revealing phrase that he employed in 1950 to describe David Rousset's public stand against Stalin's concentration camps, Aron "came out" against intellectual confusion and compromise, and he stayed out.[61]

There is, however, one dimension of Aron's life and thought where some degree of confusion did indeed reign and where, by his own admission, he made compromises he would later regret. Raymond Aron was a Jew. Like most French Jews of his generation and background (his family came originally from Lorraine) he was thoroughly assimilated; in his own eyes he was a Frenchman of Jewish origin with none of the objective or

---

60. *Essai sur les Libertés* (Paris: Calmann-Lévy, 1965), p. 128.

61. See Manès Sperber, *Until My Eyes Are Closed with Shards* (New York: Holmes and Meier, 1994), pp. 137, 234.

subjective traits of membership in a distinctive Jewish community. But this did not mean that Aron was unconscious of his Jewishness, or that it played no part in his public actions.

On the contrary: in his efforts to arouse public awareness of the German threat in the thirties he quite deliberately played down the anti-Semitic aspect of Nazism. In an article published in September 1933 Aron even "acknowledged" the German Jews' own share of responsibility for their current plight—"To be sure, the Jews were imprudent. They were too visible." Here, as on other occasions, Aron was conscious of his situation, writing as a Jew at a time when anti-Semitism was on the rise in French public life. Many years later he would attribute to this his limited involvement in French public affairs before the war: "I was a Jew, I was suspect."[62]

During the war years in London, Aron's equally cautious criticism of the Vichy regime, which never took up the question of its treatment of Jews, is striking to present-day sensibilities. Some of this can be attributed to his generation, for whom the crimes of Vichy were always in the first instance political rather than moral. But there is no doubt that Aron experienced 1940, as he later wrote, "both as Frenchman and as Jew" (though at the time it was probably his sensibilities as a Frenchman that suffered the greater injury). In exile, however, he took the "emotional precaution" of thinking as little as possible about what Frenchmen were doing to Jews, and his writings in the Free French press revealed no interest in the subject (though in this he was no different from his fellow Gaullists and other resisters). Even after the war he showed only an occasional interest in the subject of Jews, addressing B'nai B'rith in 1951 in the first-person plural— "we Jews"—but writing very rarely about Israel and never about the Shoah.[63]

This "repression," as Aron would later come to see it, was of course characteristic of assimilated Jews everywhere in the aftermath of Auschwitz. But for Aron, as for many French Jews, everything changed on November 27, 1967. On that day President de Gaulle held a press conference on the subject of the Middle East, designed in part to recover France's audience and friends in the Arab states, alienated by what they saw as France's

62. See Aron, "La Révolution Nationale en Allemagne," in *Europe*, September 15, 1933; *Le Spectateur engagé*, p. 49.

63. See *Clausewitz*, 2:227 (where Aron's own divided identity gets a footnote); *Le Spectateur engagé*, pp. 85, 101; *Essais sur la condition juive contemporaine*, p. 29.

military contribution to Israeli success in the Six Day War earlier that year. In the course of a prepared statement de Gaulle described the Jews as "an elite people, self-assured and domineering [*sûr de lui et dominateur*]." From that moment on, and until the end of his life, Aron was to grapple unhappily with his Jewishness, unwilling to suppress it in the face of prejudice, unable to assume it fully. This private struggle was largely masked from public view, partly because Aron always kept his private troubles to himself, partly because it was overlain with more visible public disputes—over the events of May 1968, over the Common Program of the Left in the 1973 elections, and so forth. But its salience in Aron's own thinking is beyond question.

Aron's anger at de Gaulle's language has been described by one biographer as a compensation for the frustration—and perhaps guilt—of his London years, his long silence about Vichy. Perhaps. But there can be little doubt that, in Aron's own words, "a burst of Jewishness exploded within my French consciousness." And it began to invade Aron's political thinking, retroactively as it were. He became ever more preoccupied with the war years—"In a way, the events of the war have burrowed ever deeper inside me. They mean more for me now [1981] than in 1945 or '46. It is a paradox, but there it is." He started to use Jewish examples in his theoretical writing—in a 1969 article he illustrated the concept of "negative freedom" by reference to the right to attend or not attend temple. He contemplated calling his planned memoirs "Souvenirs d'un Français juif." And he began to reflect critically upon his earlier intolerance of Jews who claimed to be fully Jewish while rejecting both religion and Zionism.[64]

On Israel itself he had always shown a degree of ambivalence, even before de Gaulle's speech. In 1955 he confessed to a natural sympathy for the Israeli "case": "My feelings are not neutral and I will willingly defend them." But, utterly in character, he pointed out that he could for just that reason understand the Arab position as well: "I see no reason why an Arab would not be irresistibly drawn to the opposite position." The following

64. See Baverez, *Raymond Aron*, p. 185; *Mémoires*, p. 500; *Le Spectateur engagé*, p. 106; "Liberté, Libérale ou Libertaire?" (1969), rpt. in *Etudes Politiques*, p. 235–74, quotation from p. 237; "De Gaulle, Israel et les Juifs" (1968), rpt. in *Essais sur la condition juive contemporaine*, pp. 35–183, quotation from p. 171.

year, after his first visit to Israel, Aron expressed warm admiration for the army and its "fighting pioneers" and declared himself convinced that a self-confident Israel would grow and thrive.[65]

But it is curious to note that in the aftermath of 1967 Aron's analytical grip on the whole complex of issues entailed in his Jewish identity grew less firm, and not only, as he admitted after the Six Day War, because his judgment of Israel's military prospects in that war had been clouded by his fears for its future. Thus the essays in the 1968 collection *De Gaulle, Israel et les juifs* are uncharacteristically loose and inconclusive, as though the author had not been able to bring his arguments to a sharp resolution. In the course of the 1970s the issue of his relation to Israel as a French Jew comes up in unlikely places—in the conclusion to his study of Clausewitz, where he wanders uncertainly across the terrain of Israeli-Palestinian claims, or earlier in that same book where Clausewitz's own odyssey, from Jena to Waterloo, is implausibly compared to that of the Jews of the ship *Exodus*, driven from port to port "in search of a soil where they might exercise the rights of men by becoming once again citizens." In various essays and lectures he engages the problem of Jewish identity—is it ethnic, religious, historical, cultural, national?—and the reader is surprised and disappointed to discover that Raymond Aron has nothing more interesting or clearheaded to say on these vexed topics than any other commentator.

Finally, in 1983, Aron gave an interview to the French-Jewish journal *L'Arche*, in which at one point he was asked why he, a nonpracticing, assimilated French Jew, felt unable to break his links with Judaism and Israel, particularly in view of his criticisms of Israeli politics in recent years. His answer may stand as a marker, a guide to the outer limits of Aronian rationalism: "In the final analysis I don't know. I know I don't wish to make that break. Maybe out of loyalty to my roots and to my forefathers. Maybe from what I would call the fear of tearing those roots from their soil. *But that is all abstract: it is merely the justification for an existential choice. I cannot say more.*"[66]

---

65. See, e.g., "Millénarisme ou Sagesse?" in *Polémiques*, p. 63 n. 1, and "Visite en Israel," *Le Figaro*, June 12, 1956.

66. "Un Interrogateur permanent," *L'Arche*, September–October 1983, rpt. in *Essais sur la condition juive contemporaine*, pp. 267–80, quotation from p. 272; emphasis added.

Raymond Aron wrote and acted against the grain of the France of his time in so many ways that it takes an effort of the imagination to see in him the man he truly was: a patriot for France and an utterly French thinker. His patriotism is palpable—he once described his two passions in politics as France and freedom, and it is clear that in important ways the two were for him but one. On more than one occasion in the fifties his feelings as a Frenchman were audibly hurt by international criticism of his country—in one angry commentary on "Third World" attacks at the United Nations he wrote, "We have had enough of being lectured by governments who do not apply and have no intention of applying the ideas they got from us and in whose name they condemn us."[67] This wounded national sentiment occasionally colored his judgments, as we have seen at the time of Suez.

It was Aron's identification with France and her interests that brought him close to General de Gaulle, though he was never a Gaullist (Jean-Louis Crémieux-Brilhac describes him as the "only nonpassionate anti-Gaullist in wartime London"). In the immediate postwar years he supported the general, recognizing in him a man who had, in Aron's words, all the qualities and all the defects of Machiavelli's Prince, and he offered his guarded support again when de Gaulle returned as a result of the Algerian crisis of 1958. During the fifties he even shared de Gaulle's own views on the hypocrisy of American policy toward the Third World: "The Americans don't have a bad conscience when oil companies pay feudal rulers millions of dollars to support sordid regimes; but they would feel bad if their influence or their money helped the North Africans (French and Moslem) to build together a community shaped by the spirit of Western civilization."[68]

But their relationship was always a difficult one. Aron regarded the Gaullist approach to foreign policy, nuclear arms, and the Atlantic alliance as cavalier, contradictory, and at times irresponsible. His reading of de Gaulle's belligerence, which did nothing to enhance France's security but everything to isolate her from her friends, is interesting: the general, he thought, didn't take half of what he himself said very seriously, deriving

67. "Le scandale de l'O.N.U," *Le Figaro*, October 4, 1955.
68. "L'unité française en péril." See also Jean-Louis Crémieux-Brilhac, *La France Libre* (Paris: Gallimard, 1996), pp. 192, 389.

instead some pleasure from the confusion that he sowed. He watched from an Olympian height while his followers and his critics dredged his rhetoric and his writings for clues to his deepest convictions, while they were in practice nothing more than the "temporary instruments of his acts." Aron found such behavior irresponsible, the worst possible combination of autocracy and self-indulgence and boding no good for the country.

De Gaulle, who wrote regularly to Aron to commend him on his publications, was no less caustic in return. His response to the publication of *Le Grand Débat*, Aron's 1963 essay on the problems of the Western Alliance, is typically Gaullist but perceptive nonetheless: "I have read *Le Grand Débat*, as I often read you, here and there, on the same subject. It seems to me that if you return to it incessantly and with such verve it may be because the line you have adopted does not fully satisfy even you. In the end everything: 'Europe,' 'Atlantic Community,' 'NATO,' 'Armaments,' etc, comes down to one single dispute: should France be France, yes or no? It was already the question in the days of the Resistance. You know how I chose, and I know that theologians can never be at rest."[69]

Aron remained a firm critic of Gaullist international illusions long after the general's departure—in April 1981 he reminded readers of *L'Express* that the French attitude toward the USSR, born of fantasies about playing a role between and independent of the "two hegemonies," was the work of de Gaulle. It was he who must take responsibility for bequeathing to his successors the illusion that France had some special place in the hearts and policies of Soviet leaders. The issue here was not so much France's impact on international affairs—which Aron rightly took to be negligible—but rather the widespread French failure to look clear-sightedly at the true condition and capacities of their country.

Indeed, from his very first postwar article, in *Les Temps modernes* in October 1945 and titled "The Disillusions of Freedom," through his daily journalism of the fifties and sixties and on to his final years, Aron insisted that the first duty of the French was to understand what had befallen their country and what had now to be done. France, he explained, was a second-order country—on the world scale in 1949 it was what Belgium had been in Europe in earlier decades. What it needed above all was to set aside the self-serving myths—about France's wartime role, about its postwar pros-

69. Charles de Gaulle, *Lettres, Notes et Carnets janvier 1961–décembre 1963* (Paris: Plon, 1986), letter to Raymond Aron, December 9, 1963, p. 400.

pects—and address practical and glaring deficiencies: in its governing apparatus, its economic infrastructure, its political culture. It was absurd to the point of tragedy, he wrote in 1947, that "in Year Three of the Atomic Age" the country's political debates were still focused upon a nineteenth-century squabble over the place of religion in education.[70] The anachronistic flavor of French political language was a theme that would preoccupy him for the next three decades.

It was Aron's close attention to the practical problems of his country—and his frustration at the failure of intellectuals and politicians alike to see them and take them seriously—that contributed to the acerbic tone of his engagements with his contemporaries. It was their ignorance and *irresponsibility* that he found so annoying, and in such contrast (in the case of intellectuals) with the claims they made on their own behalf. More than anything else, they were utterly provincial—and their uninterest in the reality of France, their preference for engaging with universal problems and foreign utopias, paradoxically confirmed this.

French thinkers, Aron observed in 1955, subscribe enthusiastically to the great ideas of yesterday—Sartre especially being "always one turning-point behind." The loyalty of French writers, thinkers, and professors to their ideas was only matched by their utter indifference to reality. And outsiders were right to be suspicious of French intellectual life—the self-regarding isolation of French thinkers was such that they never considered anything important or essential unless the debate in question was being conducted on *their* terms and regarding matters of interest to *them*.

Yet this critique conceals a paradox. There is a distinctively *French* tone to Aron's condemnation of his fellow Frenchmen, and it is not without an elitist edge. Aron knew that he was not only better informed and more engaged with the real world than most French intellectuals, but also more talented and cleverer. He writes on a number of occasions of "nos agrégés-théologiens" (much as Camus writes of the same people as "nos juges-pénitents") and had an abiding scorn for the superficiality of many intellectuals, notably those of the structuralist and poststructuralist era: "Our Parisian philosophers prefer a rough sketch to a finished work, they appreciate mere drafts if they are sufficiently obscurantist. . . . Only the hidden is truly scientific, burbles the tribe of Parisian philosophizers—none of whom has ever practiced any science at all."

70. *Les Temps Modernes* 1, no. 1, August 1945; "Stupide résignation."

In France, Aron concluded, a certain "general culture" is prized largely because it allows one to disquisition agreeably on things about which one knows nothing. Despite his own criticism of the sclerotic effect of the French system of selection and examination, Aron, who was one of the most brilliant products of that very system, could not help but be suspicious of the compromised objectives of mass higher education. In 1968 he drew the typically Aronian conclusion that if the "university is to prepare people for nothing, then let it be reserved for a minority. Open to the mass, it will have to do more than train people to read Virgil, *with the help of a dictionary, moreover*."[71]

In view of Raymond Aron's broad appeal to the non-French scholarly world, and the ease and familiarity with which he moved in Anglo-American and German intellectual circles, it is worth emphasizing that his polemical relationship with his fellow French intellectuals, as well as his properly scholarly writings, reveal him to be a distinctively *French* thinker. His close familiarity with the German philosophical tradition that so dominated recent French thought did not disarm his very French skepticism: "The German language is exceptionally supple in philosophy, as a result of which we tend to think German philosophers more profound than they really are." Nor would he have situated himself in the British or American traditions. Logical positivism he dismissed as "just as provincial, perhaps more provincial, than [the philosophy of] Saint German des Près and the French intelligentsia of the Left."

Aron was decidedly not an empiricist, for all his concern with facts, and he was instinctively averse to the skeptical minimalism of modern English-language analytical philosophy. As he argued in 1938, "History is always made and studied in relation to a philosophy, without which we would be faced with an incoherent plurality," a position from which he never moved very far. Thirty years later the same epistemological a priori led him to conclude, "It is mere wordplay and an abuse of false analogies to present all human aspirations in the language of rights and liberties."[72]

It is worth pausing to reflect upon that last remark. A third of a century later a new generation of French political thinkers is only now beginning

71. *La Révolution introuvable*, p. 77; emphasis added. See also ibid., p. 122 and *D'Une Sainte Famille à l'autre*, pp. 172–75.

72. See *Le Spectateur engagé*, p. 38; *Opium of the Intellectuals*, p. xiv; *Introduction*, p. 452 and annexes; *Etudes sur la Liberté*, p. 224.

to grapple with modern American liberal political philosophy and to recognize its limits, the reduction of so much of human aspiration and experience to a laudable but constricting debate about rights. When Aron made his comment in 1965, he was acknowledging the central failing of modern French political thought, its persistent failure to engage the issue of rights as an ethical and political problem, while warning against the mirage of an easy, all-encompassing imported solution. Aron was assuredly a liberal, but in a distinctively French, eighteenth-century sense; in certain important ways the British liberal tradition and its contemporary descendants remained quite alien to him.

This inheritance from an earlier, lost tradition of French political reasoning is above all what distinguishes Aron and establishes his claim upon the attention of posterity. The radical romanticism of Sartre and his followers was paradoxically conservative. Posing no threat to the habits of mind of its audience, and showing no concern to investigate the space between changing "everything" and doing nothing, it was in its essence conventional. It was thus *irresponsible* in just the way that Sartre himself had once warned against, whereas Aron took utterly seriously the original meaning of engagement, to which he added a distinctive concern with coherence and consistency.

French intellectuals, he once observed, seek neither to understand the world nor to change it, but to *denounce* it. In so doing they not only abdicate responsibility for their own circumstances but misunderstand the nature of the human condition. Ours "is never a struggle between good and evil, but between the preferable and the detestable." This assertion, which has become a commonplace truism among a new generation of French writers but risks being quickly forgotten, was both courageous and truly "countercultural" in the time and place that Aron made it. Like the Owl of Minerva, Aron brought wisdom to the French intellectual community in its twilight years; but the belated appreciation of his work and his long isolation have obscured the heroic scale of his contribution to French public life. Aron was no moralist. But his whole career constituted a bet on Reason against History, and to the extent that he has won he will in time be recognized as the greatest intellectual dissenter of his age and the man who laid the foundations for a fresh departure in French public debate.

$\mathcal{F}$or anyone interested in learning more about the three men discussed in this book, these essays are no substitute for a full-length biography. There have been a number of studies devoted to Léon Blum, though most of them are now rather dated. The best work in English has long been that of Joel Colton, *Léon Blum: A Humanist in Politics*, first published in 1966 and reissued in 1987. Colton's life of Blum is still an important book. But it places a perhaps disproportionate emphasis upon the Popular Front years, which, however important, represented only a small part of Blum's public career. Colton also underplays the importance of Blum's Jewishness and pays little attention to the torrent of anti-Semitic hatred to which he was subjected for many years.

Jean Lacouture's *Léon Blum*, published in Paris in 1977, is better balanced in these respects, though it is less sympathetic than Colton to some of Blum's political dilemmas and the choices he made. Unfortunately, it is not available in an English translation. Ilan Greilsammer's recent book, *Blum*, also available only in French, is by far the most informative on Blum's private life and on his personality and sensibilities; but the result is an imbalance that conveys the quite misleading image of a bohemian aesthete accidentally and somewhat uncomfortably deposited in the political limelight. In the words of James Joll, whose 1960 essay on him is still invaluable, Blum was above all an intellectual *in politics* (James Joll, *Intellectuals in Politics: Three Biographical Essays: Blum, Marinetti, Rathenau* [London, 1960]).

Albert Camus has been well and widely served by students of his life and writing. Until recently the best introductions to him in English were by Patrick McCarthy (*Camus: A Critical Study of His Life and Work* [London, 1982]) and Herbert R. Lottman (*Albert Camus: A Biography* [New York, 1979]). Where McCarthy engages critically with Camus's fiction and plays, Lottman's book is a straightforward narrative account of Camus's life. Like his other studies of France in this period (*The Purge*, *The Left Bank*), it is readable and very well informed. But Olivier Todd's recent massive biography (*Albert Camus. Une vie* [Paris, 1996]) supercedes these and all other general studies of Camus, though it makes no claim to be a work of literary criticism. Unfortunately the English version (New York, 1997) is too abbreviated and foreshortened to be of comparable interest.

Raymond Aron died in 1983, and he has not yet been the subject of a fully satisfactory biography, though Nicolas Baverez's *Raymond Aron* (Paris, 1993—not available in English) is an intelligent and sensitive introduction to the man and his work. Part of the difficulty lies in the range of disciplines and interests covered by Aron's huge oeuvre, though when Ariane Chebel d'Appollonia publishes her study of Aron's thought this dimension of Aron's career will have been well served. But a further problem arises from the difficulty of penetrating Aron's carefully constructed intellectual carapace in order to see the man within. His private life was much less romantically exotic than that of Camus and underwent fewer dramatic changes than Blum's, though he suffered greater human losses than either of them. But it would be a daunting challenge to try and write a fully rounded biography of the man. He took great care in his *Mémoires* (1983) to arrange the narrative of his life tightly and exclusively around his intellectual output and his public engagements, and that is likely to be the way in which we shall continue to see him.

I have done my best in the course of these essays, when translating passages from the work of Blum, Camus, or Aron, to remain faithful to their style; but there is no substitute for reading them in their own language. All three were master stylists, each in his own way and each, too, in a distinctive French tradition. Blum and Aron both wrote exquisite analytical and expository prose, though Blum's was inflected with a measure of moral and emotional engagement, while Aron had the cool, formal precision of classical French philosophy before its unfortunate and lasting flirtation with postromantic German thought. Of Camus's literary qualities my own assessment would be presumptuous and redundant. But it is perhaps worth recording that as an essayist and diarist Camus was caustic, witty, and frequently funny, especially when he avoided the temptation to philosophize. To be sure, he could not match Aron for intellectual firepower, nor could he challenge Sartre's merciless polemical ascendancy. But then neither Aron nor Sartre shared Camus's comprehensive sensitivity to his time and its troubles.

A broad selection of Blum's writings is collected in his eight-volume *Oeuvres*. These contain his early literary and theatre criticism, his political and social essays, some of his major speeches in and out of the Chambre, and a representative assortment of his newspaper editorials, as well as the published and unpublished works of the war years. They do not, however, include all Blum's unpublished notes and manuscripts, and the selections from his daily journalism are very incomplete.

Camus's published nonfiction writings are most accessible in the Pléiade edition of his *Essais*. To these should be added the three volumes of his notebooks, the *Carnets*. But the line between fiction and nonfiction in Camus's work is at best a convenience; the short stories, the famous early novels (*L'Etranger, La Peste*), the didactic plays, and the last full-length work published in his lifetime (*La Chute*) were intimately related to the themes of his journalism, essays, and books and should be read in juxtaposition to the latter. In some cases, like *La Chute*, they represented the pursuit of a polemical engagement by fictional means. And with *Le premier homme*, published long after his death, Camus brought fiction and autobiography together in a way that represented for him a new departure and one that might have signaled a very different Camus, in literary style and concerns, had he lived to complete it.

There is no single collection of Aron's writings, which are scattered through nearly four dozen published books. However, the *Mémoires* themselves represent a useful, if occasionally overdiscriminating guide to the writings of their author. There, and on one or two other occasions, Aron makes clear just how he ranks his own output, and readers may find it helpful to follow his guidance in the first instance. In any case, the *Mémoires* should be treated as an indispensable primary source in their own right. The studies of sociological thought (*Étapes de la pensée sociologique*); the two-volume discussion of Clausewitz (*Penser la guerre, Clausewitz*); the peerless polemical essay on fellow-traveling intellectuals (*L'Opium des intellectuels*); the icy analytical demolition of Sartre's magnum opus (*Histoire et dialectique de la violence*); and his doctoral dissertation on the philosophy of history (*Introduction à la philosophie de l'histoire. Essai sur les limites de l'objectivité historique*) illustrate Aron's extraordinary range and depth, as do the numerous essays gathered into various collections and the editorial articles published in *Le Figaro* over the years 1947–77 (of which those for 1947–65 have been gathered together in two published volumes).

INDEX

Abbas, Ferhat, 118
Abel, Lionel, 126
Action française: anti-Semitic attacks on
   Blum in, 74–75; Benda's criticism of,
   10–11
Actuelles III (Camus), 102
Adenauer, Konrad, 170
Alain (Emile Chartier), 42, 153
"A l'échelle humaine" (Blum), 61, 67,
   69, 82
Algeria: Aron on independence for,
   151, 165–68; Camus on crisis in,
   21, 93, 105, 116–21, 127–28, 131;
   Camus's Algerian background, 19,
   116
anarcho-syndicalist movement, 132
Annales (journal), 141
antifascism, 14, 162
anti-Semitism, 19, 43–44, 73–80, 175
Aragon, Louis, 80
Arendt, Hannah: on awkward figures, 26;
   on Camus, 87; Camus anticipating
   "banality of evil," 106; and Camus
   on terror, 95; crimes of twentieth
   century as obsession of, 130; as displaced intellectual, 128; as exile,
   129; on *L'Homme révolté*, 129; on political involvement of Camus's generation, 105
Aron, Raymond, 137–82; on Algerian independence, 151, 165–68; as anti-
   Communist, 22, 25–26, 173; and
   anti-Semitism, 175; as awkward figure, 26–27; on Blum's attitude to-

ward Communism, 23; on Camus's
   Algerian position, 119; on Camus's
   arguments, 100; on Camus's *Combat*
   essays, 88; Camus's education compared with that of, 99; on Camus's
   philosophy in *L'Homme révolté*, 90;
   Camus's public criticism compared
   with that of, 127, 128; on catastrophic solutions to social woes,
   150; clarity of, 164–65; on
   Clausewitz, 146, 177; on
   Communist-led strikes of 1948,
   150–51; as cosmopolitan, 144; as cultural insider and outsider, 18–19,
   138–39; *De Gaulle, Israel, et les juifs,*
   177; *Les Désillusions du progrès*
   (Aron), 151–52; on Ecole Normale
   Supérieure, 138–39; education of,
   138; *Essai sur les libertés,* 171; on European unity, 159–60; exclusion
   from mainstream intellectual life,
   137–38, 144, 172–73; on the French
   disease, 155; as French thinker, 181;
   German influences on, 144–45; on
   German unification, 160–61; *Le
   Grand Débat,* 179; *Histoire et dialectique de la violence,* 171; on holistic
   historical reasoning, 148; inadequacy felt regarding Sartre, 171–72;
   independence of mind of, 174; on industrial society, 154–56; as an intellectual, 139–40; on international relations, 156–61; *Introduction à la
   philosophie de l'histoire,* 140–42, 143,

187

29, 79–80; as cultural insider and
outsider, 18–19; decency of, 59; devaluation decision, 60; as Dreyfusard, 19, 31–32; at Ecole Normale
Supérieure, 31; economic policy of,
48–49; exercise and conquest of
power distinguished by, 53–54; feminism supported by, 83; on French
Jews, 43; on the French Revolution,
37–38; on governmental reform,
68–71; as half-forgotten man, 29; as
hostage to his party, 56–57; international field of vision of, 65–66; as in-
toxicated with his own rhetoric,
57–58; Jewishness of, 19, 41–44, 73–
74, 84; as jurist, 31–32; leaving office with sigh of relief, 60; as literary
critic, 31, 36; loneliness of, 61–62;
on Marxism, 52–53; as moralist not
ideologist, 39–40, 83–84; move to
the right opposed by, 41, 51; national government called for in
1940, 71; as not interested in power,
45; "Nouvelles Conversations de
Goethe avec Eckermann," 39–40,
85; On Marriage, 40, 75, 83–84; optimism of, 58; as outsider, 85; Pétain
opposed by, 22, 34, 79; Popular
Front's downfall distorting contribution of, 21, 29–30; in postwar transitional government, 80; as prime minister, 19, 33–34, 45–49, 69; on
proletarian dictatorship, 55; as republican, 37–38, 82; return to
France in 1945, 35; as seductive presence, 35–36; sexuality of, 75; as Socialist, 32, 38–41, 52, 82; as Socialist
leader, 23–24, 33, 49–62; Socialist
party as his family, 59; "Souvenirs
sur l'Affaire," 43, 73; Spanish Civil
War policy, 47, 61; as speaker, 35–
36, 62–65; "Stendhal et le beylisme," 32; surrounding himself with
intellectual inferiors, 57; as wanting
to be liked, 62; as Zionist, 43–44
Bourdet, Claude, 88, 157, 162

Brasillach, Robert, 102, 108–9
Breton, André, 103
Briand, Aristide, 43
Buber-Neumann, Margarete, 16

Caillaux, Joseph, 76
Caligula (Camus), 89
Camus, Albert, 87–135; on abstraction,
131; on the absurd, 90–91, 91n.7;
Actuelles III, 102; Algerian background of, 19, 116; on Algerian crisis, 21, 93, 105, 116–21, 127–28,
131; Algiers as home for, 97–98; on
anti-anti-Communism, 24; as anti-
Communist, 22, 24–25; as artist, 92;
as awkward figure, 26–27; balance as
goal of, 24, 113–15; Brasillach petition signed by, 109; Caligula, 89; in
the Cold War, 112–13; Combat essays, 88; contrasting personalities of,
103–4; as cosmopolitan, 104; the
critics on, 100; as cultural insider
and outsider, 18–19; current French
opinion of, 20; as displaced intellectual, 128–29; educational credentials
of, 19, 98–99; "Entre oui et non,"
125; L'Envers et l'endroit, 97, 101,
102, 125; "L'Eté à Alger," 97, 125; as
exile, 97, 101–3, 129; L'Exil et le royaume, 97, 102; as existentialist, 89–
91, 103, 124; Forster compared with,
130–31; as the French intellectual,
87, 88; Frenchness of, 135; Justice et
haine, 114; Kafka as influence on,
129–30; Lettres à un ami allemand,
107; and Mauriac, 109–12; measure
in, 123; as moraliste, 121–22; Ni victimes ni bourreaux, 114; Nobel Prize,
20, 87, 102; "Noces à Tipasa," 98; as
not a philosopher, 90; on objectivity,
116; parents of, 104; Pascal compared with, 135; on polarization of
Left and Right, 123; Les Possédés,
100–101; on power, 127; as public
ethical assessor, 125–27; public versus private views of, 132–33; in Ras-

Soviet Union (*continued*)
mus on criticizing, 115; French Com-
munists as controlled by, 66; as indus-
trial society, 154–55; Khrushchev,
157; Leninism, 22–23, 33, 51, 68;
Stalin, 113, 114, 132, 153. *See also*
Molotov-Ribbentrop Pact
Spanish Civil War, 29, 47, 61
Sperber, Manès, 82, 129, 130, 135, 174
Stalin, Joseph, 113, 114, 132, 153
Stendhal, 36, 59
"Stendhal et le beylisme" (Blum), 32
syndicalism, 132

Talmon, Jacob, 95
Temps modernes, Les (journal): Aron on
editorial board of, 144; Camus on
the Savonarolas of, 94; Jeanson's review of Camus's *L'Homme révolté* in,
94, 95
terror, 67, 95–96
Third Republic: Blum on reform of,
68–71; Camus as product of schools
of, 99; constitutional revision es-
chewed by, 9; failings of, 68; leadership of, 12
"third way," 113, 144
Thorez, Maurice, 66, 81
Tocqueville, Alexis de, 135, 144, 145,
146–47, 162–63
Todd, Olivier, 91n.7, 126, 128
totalitarianism, 152–54

Tragédie algérienne, La (Aron), 119
Trahison des clercs, La (Benda), 10–11

United Nations, 158

Vaillant-Couturier, Paul, 80
Valéry, Paul, 109
Vallat, Xavier, 76
Vergniaud, Pierre Victurnien, 38, 55
Versailles treaty, 71
Vichy regime: administrative change under, 8; anti-Semitic aspects of, 44,
73; archaism and distaste for modernization in rise of, 8; Aron on, 150,
162, 175; Blum as most important
political enemy of, 19; Blum on seizure of power by, 78–79; Camus on
punishment for collaborators,
107–12; and French disunity, 6; the
National Revolution, 7, 8; political
irresponsibility of, 13; unrestricted
presidential authority in, 9

Waldeck-Rousseau, René, 50
Weber, Eugen, 52
Weber, Max, 140, 144–45, 146, 161, 163
Weil, Simone, 132
Weizmann, Chaim, 44

Zay, Jean, 79
Zionism, 43–44, 176
Zola, Emile, 31, 74

Printed and bound by CPI Group (UK) Ltd, Croydon, CR0 4YY

09/06/2025

14685683-0001